KENYA

PROFILES · NATIONS OF CONTEMPORARY AFRICA
Larry W. Bowman, Series Editor

Also of Interest

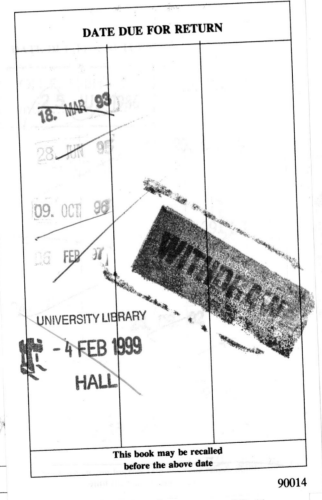

KENYA

The Quest for Prosperity

Norman N. Miller

Westview Press • Boulder, Colorado

Gower • London, England

For Judy

Profiles/Nations of Contemporary Africa

Jacket/paperback cover photo: Vendors with vegetables from the wholesale market in Haile Selassie Avenue, Nairobi (photo by David Keith Jones).

Copyright © 1984 by Westview Press, Inc.

Published in 1984 in the United States of America by Westview Press, Inc., 5500 Central Avenue, Boulder, Colorado 80301; Frederick A. Praeger, Publisher

Published in 1984 in Great Britain by Gower Publishing Company Limited, Gower House, Croft Road, Aldershot, Hampshire GU11 3HR, England

Library of Congress Cataloging in Publication Data
Miller, Norman N., 1933–
  Kenya: the quest for prosperity.
  (Profiles. Nations of contemporary Africa)
  Bibliography: p.
  Includes index.
  1. Kenya—Politics and government—1963–1978.
2. Kenya—Politics and government—1978–   . 3. Kenya—
Economic conditions—1963–   . 4. Kenya—Social con-
ditions—1963–   . 5. Kenya—Foreign relations.
I. Title. II. Series.
DT433.58.M55 1984   967.6'2   84-5164
ISBN 0-86531-095-5
ISBN 0-86531-096-3 (pbk.)

British Library Cataloguing in Publication Data
Miller, Norman N.
Kenya
 1. Kenya—Social Conditions—1963
I. Title
967.6'204 HN793.A8
ISBN 0-566-00547-6

304525

0566005476

Printed and bound in the United States of America

10   9   8   7   6   5   4   3   2   1

Contents

Illustrations

Preface

Kenya has had a pervasive influence on my life since I came ashore in Mombasa from a cargo vessel in the spring of 1960, three years before independence. I had sailed from India, as part of a two-year "walkabout," and with a knapsack I struck out on foot from Mombasa across Kenya's magnificent landscape, stopping to work on a highland farm and then in Nairobi on the newly established *Daily Nation*. My travels, which had begun in the Far East, later took me to the Congo, then down the Nile through the Sudan and Egypt, and finally home through Europe. No part of the world I saw during those two years could compare to Kenya, in terms of either hospitality or natural beauty. Above all, I was intrigued by Kenya's potential and the difficulties it would face in the transition from colony to independent state. Although I did not realize it then, Kenya was to become my second home. In the next two decades I would spend more than eight years there in the course of a dozen research and teaching assignments.

For helping me evolve from a dusty traveler to an Africanist, I shall always be indebted to my graduate mentor and friend at Indiana University, J. Gus Liebenow. Because of him and my colleagues at Michigan State University, where I held my first teaching post, I was able to take advantage of the new American interest in Africa. Africans and American Africanists were to become my professional reference group and my main social network.

Paramount among these individuals is my lifelong friend, Rodger Yeager, author of the Tanzania volume in this series. Frank Holmquist and John Spencer are other close friends who have read and commented on my writings for many years. By reading the draft of this book all three saved me from more foolish mistakes than I care to admit. In Nairobi, David Court and Goran Hyden, both astute observers of East African affairs, have been invaluable commentators on my writing. Three of my age-mates, Gerald Hartwig, James Hooker, and Francis Okediji, are with the ancestors now. The memory of each and the good works they left behind are a part of this endeavor.

My involvement in various Kenyan institutions led me to other colleagues who became in effect my instructors on Kenyan affairs. At the University of Nairobi these include Wanjiku Mwangiru, Cyrus Mutiso, James Shiroya Okete, and John Okumu. Others in Nairobi are Penelope and Peter Fleming, Alan Fowler, Edward Greeley, Allison Herrick, Richard Hook, Esmond Bradley Martin, Hilary Ngweno, Kenneth Prewitt, Philip Ransley, Parmeet Singh, Peter Thacher, and Peter Walker. I am also indebted to Kenya's Ministry of Environment and Natural Resources and the United Nations Environment Programme in Nairobi.

During the last five years I have divided my time between teaching at Dartmouth College and serving as the East African correspondent for the Universities Field Staff International (formerly the American Universities Field Staff). I am particularly grateful for the support of James Hornig, Nelson Kasfir, James Strickler, Dean Seibert, and Michael Zubkoff at Dartmouth and of Peter Martin, Manon Spitzer, and John Thompson at the Field Staff. Patricia Carter of the Baker Library at Dartmouth and Marie Furnary, my research assistant, were exceptionally helpful in numerous ways during the final drafting of the manuscript. David Keith Jones and the editors of the *Daily Nation* (Nairobi) have generously provided photographs for the text. Series editor Larry Bowman made important editorial contributions to the manuscript in its final stages and helped me to sharpen several basic arguments. Lynne Rienner, associate publisher of Westview Press, and Deborah Lynes, senior editor, are gratefully acknowledged for their patience and encouragement.

As I have learned repeatedly in East Africa, sustaining energies come from family as well as from age-mates and friends. My elders, Ruth Miller Brown and the late William Earl Brown, not only applauded my African work, but themselves traveled to Kenya to study and learn about the country, becoming its advocates in the American circles they touch. To my wife, Judy, editor, safari-mate, mother *par excellence*, and life's companion, this book is dedicated.

Norman Nees Miller
Norwich, Vermont
Nairobi, Kenya

KENYA

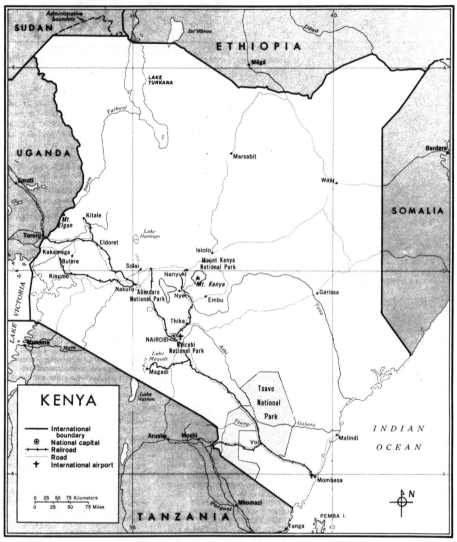

FIGURE 1. Map of Kenya

Introduction

The central theme of this book is the evolution of the entrepreneurial, innovative, aggressive way of life that characterizes modern Kenya. Nairobi has been called the "Hong Kong of Africa," a free-wheeling, materialistic place where the search for individual profit is the commanding ethic. Such a way of life is unique in eastern Africa. It has been simultaneously heralded as one of achievement and economic success and condemned as one of exploitation and elitism.

My view of Kenya is positive, although I believe one can support a system and still criticize it. The inequities in Kenyan society are great but not necessarily permanent; the economy is in difficult straits but untapped potential does exist. The political system has been periodically repressive but far less so than that in any other state in the region. My concern is to describe the characteristics of modern Kenya, to pinpoint key issues, and to offer a brief analysis.

To answer the question, "How did Kenya come to be what it is today?" the first two chapters lay out some historical influences behind the nation's quest for prosperity, including early trade patterns and colonial influences, important private property agreements at independence, and the policies of the Kenyatta and Moi governments. The last four chapters focus on the contemporary period, demarcated by the beginning of the Moi era in August 1978, and assess it in terms of current social, political, economic, and international dimensions.

Socially, the people of Kenya form a disjointed society, a human mosaic of forty African ethnic groups plus Asian, Arab, and European subcultures. The society is overwhelmingly rural in nature and agricultural in life-style. In 1984 Kenya's population passed 18 million, growing at an estimated rate of 4 percent per year. This growth rate and the limited arable land are one of Kenya's most compelling problems. Over 85 percent of the population live on less than 20 percent of the land, a maldistribution of people that is beginning to have destructive effects on the environment, particularly on the carrying capacity of the soil. High population density in the fertile areas has also led to rural-urban migration, resulting in an unprecedented urban growth of over 20 percent per year in several of Kenya's secondary cities.

Politically, Kenya is a hierarchically organized, patron-client system with brokers and go-betweens as important elements. Power flows from the top, from the Office of the President, through both formal and informal institutions. Kenyan politics has a rough and tumble aspect, seen in the brokerage process and in the open contests for favors, contracts, and jobs. A "Horatio Alger approach" characterizes young Kenyan politicians. With up-by-the-bootstraps, free-wheeling attitudes, they eagerly compete for influence in the political party, labor unions, the parastatal bodies, and numerous informal societies. Within the bureaucracy the civil service is a governing elite, and although there is talent and dedication here, a sizable number of bureaucrats, especially administrators and teachers, carry on moonlighting activity. Conflict-of-interest rules are not a major concern. The practice leads to slowdowns in daily operations and to inefficiency and ill-defined policies. The system has been described as "disjointed incrementalism," a piecemeal approach to solving problems. The positive side to such free-enterprise politics is that local profits are often plowed back into the society; the negative side involves political opportunism, waste, and bureaucratic inefficiency.

Economically, Kenya has been the center of capitalism in eastern Africa, a diversified agricultural state that until the 1982 attempted coup had been considered a paragon of stability. The 1982 uprising by junior air force personnel was blamed on social issues, food and transport shortages, income inequities, and alleged government mismanagement. In the aftermath of the coup and in the period before Daniel Moi's reelection in the fall of 1983, economic stability became the key concern for both the government and international investors in the country. Some 350 multinational corporations working throughout Africa are based in Nairobi, as are 15 United Nations and multilateral donor offices. Over half the 40,000 Europeans resident in Kenya are part of the international economic community, working in corporations as development officers, in UN or foreign missions, or as advisors in nongovernmental organizations.

ENVIRONMENT AND HUMAN ECOLOGY

Kenya has an astonishing environment. Located astride the equator on the Indian Ocean, it has a total area of 224,960 square miles, roughly the size of France, or slightly larger than Texas. Most of the land is arid, some 75 percent classified as desert, semi-desert, or arid bush. Another 18 percent of the land is highland steppe, and although dissected by the equator, these highland areas of central and western Kenya have a temperate climate. Only the narrow coastal strip is considered tropical.

Kenya's all-important rainfall is dependent on climatic patterns that begin with dry winds that flow south from the Sahara Desert and meet moist air masses blowing in from the Indian Ocean. During April and May the monsoon winds from the sea reverse their northeast pattern,

Zebras with Mt. Kenya in background (photo by David Keith Jones)

and the prevailing southwest trade winds begin, reversing again in November and December. The most abundant rainfall occurs in the April-May season, the moisture coming from the southern Indian Ocean. Coupled with variations in the dry air masses coming into western Kenya, these airstreams give Kenya its basic annual climatic cycle.[1]

Mt. Kenya is roughly in the center of the nation (Figure 1). From a high-altitude aerial view looking down on the mountain, Kenya would look like an upside-down saucer rising gradually toward the center, with the high point at Mt. Kenya. Slashing the length of the nation from north to south is the Rift Valley, to the west is the Lake Victoria Basin, and to the east sliding away to the sea are hills that drift into dry lowlands and finally coastal beaches. Aside from some land on the coast, only the southwest quadrant of the country is fertile; the soils elsewhere in Kenya are leached, alkaline, and poor in quality. Such a diverse topography is accompanied by an equally diverse ecology, illustrated in the range of zones between Mt. Kenya and the Indian Ocean (Figure 2).

In terms of human adaptation, Kenya may be divided into five geographic zones. The *coastal zone* along the Indian Ocean is an infertile lowland extending 10 to 40 miles inland from the sea. A barrier reef parallels much of the 275-mile coast, and several large islands (including Mombasa and Lamu) dot the coastline. The ecology of the zone includes several types of mangrove trees, diverse dune vegetation, and brackish estuaries. Settlement outside the larger communities is in small villages and dispersed homesteads, most located a mile or more inland from

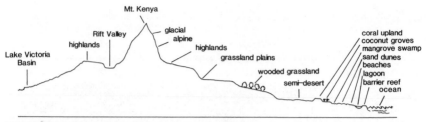

FIGURE 2. Selected Ecological Zones in Kenya

the infertile coral rocks that dominate the coast. Mixed agriculture with maize and cassava as staples is prevalent. The coast is described by sociologists as a "shatter zone" in which slaving, warfare, smuggling, and other nefarious activities have fragmented the indigenous society, a majority of which composes a loose federation of seven ethnic groups called the Mijikenda.

The *arid zone* stretches in a great arc from the southeastern part of the country throughout the north and northwest. The key physical characteristics of this zone are low rainfall, a dry climate, periodic droughts, and vast areas of rock-strewn wasteland interspersed with hilly outcrops and mountains. The soils, particularly in the arid north, are shallow, stony, azonal, and of recent geological origin. Despite poor soils and aridity, nearly all of Kenya's arid region has enough vegetation to support some pastoralists and sporadic wildlife. In the north, such peoples as the Boran, Gabbra, Rendille, Samburu, Somali, and Turkana pursue nomadic or semi-nomadic life-styles, although since 1970 the government has pressured these groups of people to settle so that schools, clinics, and other social services can be provided.

The *highland region*, known as the "white highlands" in colonial days, is a vast, rolling uplands characterized by a cool climate, abundant rainfall, rich volcanic soils with good humic content, and dense human settlement. It is the agricultural heartland of Kenya, constituting only 18 percent of the nation's land mass, but accommodating over 70 percent of the population. Complex flora and fauna and immense agricultural diversity characterize the area. The alpine vegetation on the higher reaches of Mt. Kenya, for example, has subvarieties of bamboo, lichens, alpine grasses, and giant ferns. At such high altitudes the intensity of equatorial sunlight creates conditions that support rare flora and abundant agriculture. The highlands are in two major sectors, dissected by the eastern Rift Valley, which runs from north to south through central Kenya. The eastern highlands north of Nairobi include Mt. Kenya, the Aberdare Mountains, and the high plateaus west of Mt. Kenya, which are made up today of small-scale farms, settlement projects, farms for wheat, maize, coffee, tea, and barley, and cattle ranches. The western highlands with Eldoret and Kitale as market centers are vast wheat-, barley-, and maize-producing areas with somewhat less population density than the eastern highlands. It was these rich highland soils and the healthy climate, devoid of malarial mosquitos and tsetse flies, that supported the first large-scale European farming activity in eastern Africa.

The *Lake Victoria Basin* is an uplifted plateau of fertile land that surrounds Lake Victoria in a half-moon crescent. The area is a rolling, well-watered farmland, interspersed with dry savannahs 1,800 to 2,400 feet above sea level. Kisumu, the third-largest city in Kenya and the major market center for the western region, is situated on the lakeshore and is an important railhead and steamer port. This region is characterized by sandy and loamy soils and a semi-tropical, often humid climate. Most of the area has a high population density. Economic activity includes cotton and sugar production, banana growing, small farming, and a lake fishing industry. Some European settlement occurred in the area but never on the scale of the highlands. Kenya's second- and third-largest ethnic groups, the Luhya and Luo, are the main residents of the region.

The *grassland savannah* of south-central Kenya is a region of lush vegetation, majestic open vistas, and abundant wildlife. Varying in altitude from 2500 to 6000 feet, the area adjoins the highland steppe and the Lake Victoria Basin in the west and gradually gives way to the arid zones of the northeast. This zone includes the Amboseli, Maasai Mara, and Nairobi wildlife areas, a few dozen safari camps and lodges, and the grazing lands of the pastoral Maasai. Islands of similar grassland savannah are also scattered over other parts of the country, including portions of Tsavo and Samburu parks and the Marsabit and Kulal mountains.

Overall, in a nation so dominated by open space and natural beauty, it is curious that the central reality should be one of land struggle, land hunger, and relentless territoriality. For centuries the ongoing law in Kenya has been man's struggle against animals and other humans—a struggle for prime land, for the use of hunting land, for the rights to grazing land, for land to give to loved ones, and the struggle to deny land to strangers. Kenya's quest for prosperity has been related to the land since earliest times.

1

The Colonial Legacy

EARLY TRACINGS

East Africa is currently thought to be the birthplace of man. In Kenya's Rift Valley, around the valley lakes, and in the lush, game-filled savannah lands lived the predecessors of *Homo sapiens*, the toolmaker *Homo habilis* and the man-ape Zinjanthropus. Some descendants of the earliest *Homo sapiens* were still in parts of Kenya when, in the first millennium A.D., three groups of invaders converged on the scene. From the Horn of Africa in the northeast came Hamitic pastoralists speaking a Cushitic language, gradually moving south in search of improved range conditions. From the Nile Valley came other pastoralists, the Nilotic peoples, and from the south and west were beginning to arrive Bantu agricultural people.[1]

The trade and exchange patterns between these groups are unknown, save for the speculation that the two groups of pastoralists coexisted peacefully and engaged in some trade while Bantu-pastoralist relations, though in theory having a basis for good trade of foodstuffs for livestock, in fact were violent, particularly concerning rights to territory. By A.D. 1500 these three distinct peoples were in place largely as they are found today. They assimilated the original inhabitants or possibly, as in the case of the Sandawe people, drove them south into Tanzania.

It is from about A.D. 1500 that the first roots of Kenyan inland trade and entrepreneurial activity can begin to be traced. Both the inland, long-distance trade linking kingdoms in Uganda to the sea and the maritime trade along the coast were well established. The mixing of Arab and African blood along the coast had led to the rise of an Islamic Swahili people who had become avid slave traders, businessmen, and caravan managers.

Networks of trade linked inland peoples with the coast. The Kamba, for example, living 200 miles inland, had become highly skilled elephant hunters and ivory traders, their expeditions ranging hundreds of miles from their home territory. Farther west, Kikuyu entrepreneurs living near Mt. Kenya had overcome ethnic hostilities and developed a sophisticated trade with the Maasai over the Aberdare Mountains, trading in iron goods, beads, cloth, and items they had obtained from the coast. Trade along the shores of Lake Victoria was well established long before Europeans ventured to the lake, some of it linking to the long-distance trade via Ukerewe Island through Tanganyika to the coast. Skins, hides, salt, forged iron, and beeswax were basic trade items.[2]

The stimulus for much of the early trade came from coastal ports like Gedi, Malindi, Mombasa, and Zanzibar, enclaves that had been part of an ongoing Indian Ocean maritime exchange. Arabs in galleon-like *dhows* from the Arabian Peninsula sailed the monsoon winds to and from the East African coast. As the traffic increased in the eleventh and twelfth centuries, the key ports took on the status of city states, replete with Arab merchants, soldiers, and administrators. Aside from slaves and ivory, exports from East Africa included tortoise shells, dried fish, mangrove poles, and thatching and building materials; arriving from Arabia were salt, metal goods, beads, furniture, tools, and cloth.

Two important by-products came from the trade. First, the Swahili language, essentially a trade language, emerged as a lingua franca in Kenya. Based on a Bantu language structure and heavily larded with Arabic terms, it was well in place by the eleventh century. Second, with the language developed a distinct coastal Swahili culture, an Arab-African admixture of architecture, art, poetry, cuisine, manners, and social customs in which commerce was the highest priority. As the language and culture moved inland along the trade routes, so, too, did the strong mercantile ethic.

A new era in commercial activity began in 1498 with the arrival in the Indian Ocean of the Portuguese sea captain Vasco da Gama. Trade and military control were the twin objectives of the powerful Portuguese, and within a short time they dominated the western Indian Ocean. Imposing Fort Jesus, with its high ramparts and turrets overlooking Mombasa harbor, was built in 1593 specifically to give the Portuguese military control of the coast and to pacify the Omani Arabs. The strategy worked only in part, and over the next hundred years the fort fell to Arab invaders on several occasions.

Considering that the Portuguese were on the Kenya coast for two hundred years, it is remarkable that they had so little impact on Kenyan culture. Aside from a few words in Swahili, the Portuguese are popularly believed to have left nothing behind. One reason is that they were not settlers—not interested in the hinterland, their troops were there to maintain the garrison, to help resupply vessels, and to stimulate trade. Theirs was a maritime, sailor-on-the-beach mentality, not a settler's mentality.

Even so, the "gone without a trace" idea is not accurate. The Portuguese contributed significantly to Kenya's food crops, probably bringing the first maize, potatoes, and cassava root.[3] They had an important influence on naval architecture, navigation, sailing techniques, and modes of warfare of the region. Yet the reality is that the Kenyan coast was an Islamic Arab-Swahili culture when the Portuguese came, and when they left it returned to Islamic control. The Portuguese represented an alien, Christian culture that the Moslems took particular care to eradicate.

Trade and slavery characterized the second Islamic period in Kenya between 1700 and 1880. Slaves were needed throughout the Arabian Peninsula to man Arab armies, to perform manual labor, and to serve as servants in homes and eunuchs in harems. The trade in slaves was international, stimulated particularly by Arabian merchants of the Gulf who controlled the traffic and organized the *dhow* transport. Kenya-based Arabs organized expeditions and either led them or relied on Swahili middlemen. The onslaught of slave hunting shattered indigenous coastal societies and caused enormous suffering throughout East Africa and the eastern Congo. Throughout the 1700s the traffic flourished, the first international control coming in 1807 when the British legally abolished slavery and began the long process of forcibly trying to stop the trade. A key personality in the Indian Ocean anti-slavery movement was Sayyid Said, the Sultan of Oman. Partly because he needed British naval support to clear pirates in the Gulf, and partly because he needed help to withstand enemy land forces, Sayyid Said was persuaded to sign an anti-slavery treaty covering his Indian Ocean domain in 1822. The sultan was not enthusiastic about the treaty and in reality lacked the power to enforce his own decree. Slavery continued, and in some areas increased.[4]

It was not until Said's successor, Said Barghash, took stronger pro-British measures that the trade began to diminish. A total ban occurred in 1873, but because the measure was still extremely unpopular with coastal merchants and traders, some clandestine slaving continued. If slavery promoted entrepreneurial qualities in the early Swahili middle-men, its abolition became the central concern of another group of entrepreneurs.

Christian missionary preoccupations of the time were to stamp out slavery and to instill good moral, businesslike (usually Protestant) ethics. The task was formidable, given the entrenched Islamic beliefs along the coast and traditional religions inland. The first mission station in Mombasa was opened in 1846 under two Swiss Germans, Johann Krapf and Johann Rebmann, although it was not until after Sultan Barghash's ban on slavery in 1873 that missionaries began to speak out strongly against the practice. Even then widespread opposition surfaced because slavery was still a profitable business and because the Muslim Swahili population resented Christian teaching. Missionaries such as Krapf, Rebmann, David Livingstone, and hundreds that were to follow became legendary in their opposition to Islam.

What is less well known is the "commercialization of Africans" approach that Livingstone inspired in the hundreds of missionaries that followed him. The basic idea was that commerce would pave the way for Christianity, that profit and a wage labor system would end the slave and compulsory labor systems still in practice. This approach began to be put into practice in the 1870s and 1880s as all European traders and travelers, particularly in the Uganda caravans, came under "moral pressure" to pay fully for their porters and to avoid compulsory labor. The policy, as Livingstone predicted, carried the message of commerce into the black society and historically is one of the important underlying reasons for modern-day entrepreneurialism. Certainly some free-labor practices as well as compulsory practices were in place before European missionaries arrived; it was the emphasis that changed. Through the missionaries came the twin ideas of God and good commerce.[5]

THE EUROPEAN PENETRATION, 1880–1910

The "second coming" of the Europeans to East Africa, unlike that of the earlier Portuguese, was characterized by the moving inland of people who intended to settle. The underlying reasons for this penetration were religious, economic, and political. The missionary movement by 1880 was bringing pressure on British authorities to "truly join" the anti-slavery movement by protecting those missionaries venturing inland.

More globally, the economic reality of the region had been dramatically changed by the opening of the Suez in 1869. Kenya was now closer to Europe, its harbor at Mombasa a more strategic port on the European route to India and the Far East.

The changing nature of industrialization in Europe also opened intense rivalries, allowing Germany and France to challenge Britain's industrial dominance. New railroad technology in particular allowed penetration of the African continent from the sea and in turn stimulated demand for markets. It was Germany's move into Tanganyika, just south of Kenya, that awakened serious British interests practically overnight. An energetic German fortune hunter named Karl Peters had journeyed inland, obtained land treaties from Tanganyikan chiefs, carried them back to Berlin, and influenced Chancellor Otto von Bismarck to consider colonization. When Germany declared the area under its protection the scramble for East Africa was on. Without consulting the Sultan of Zanzibar, whose domain it supposedly was, the British and the Germans simply divided the territory, laying out the present Kenya-Tanzania border.

The British strategy for Kenya was to allow commercial interests to take the lead. In 1888 a privately financed trading company, the Imperial British East Africa Company (IBEAC), was awarded a royal charter to develop trade in Kenya. IBEAC was structured like its counterparts, the Royal Niger Company and the British South African Company, but unlike these companies, the Kenya venture was not based on new mineral concessions or quick agricultural profits, and the company, seemingly without direction or policy, drifted into poor financial straits. The situation led the British government to assume control of the company in 1895 and to establish the East African Protectorate, a territory that included present-day Zanzibar, Kenya, Uganda, and a portion of southern Somalia.

It was during this time that British policy began to focus on Uganda as the key to its strategic interests. The logic today seems tortuous: if

Queen Victoria did not control Uganda, then the headwaters of the Nile
(at Jinja on Lake Victoria) could be dammed by another nation. This
would halt the bountiful river, bring Egyptian agriculture to its knees,
cause peasant uprisings, threaten the Suez Canal, and close Britain's
access to the East. India, the Pearl of Empire, and the Far East trade
would become inaccessible.

The fallacy surrounds damming the Nile, a feat that would have
meant moving large equipment to Jinja, 500 miles inland, through
country with no roads, across rivers, and thereafter building a dam that
was technologically still years beyond the competence of the Victorians.
Nevertheless, the scare tactic worked. Britain moved to safeguard her
interests and declared Uganda under the Queen's protection in 1894.

At this point a curious carrot-and-stick situation existed. Britain
had an inland colony that needed protecting. The only way to insure
its protection was to take control and administer the area; the only way
to administer it was to secure supply lines to Uganda. Kenya became
strategically important, not so much in its own right but because it
happened to be between Uganda and the sea and just north of suspicious
German activity in Tanganyika.[6]

The Uganda Railway and Early Settlement

If one looks for the roots of Kenyan capitalism, the coming of the
railway is an important factor. To secure the territory, to make it pay,
and to attract settlers, the Victorians in 1896 began building a railroad
500 miles into the uncharted heartland of East Africa. It was a strategic
undertaking designed to make the Uganda journey a matter of days
rather than months, thereby protecting Uganda and the source of the
Nile.

The construction problems were staggering. Not only was there
little technical knowledge of the soils, the grades, and the rivers that
would have to be crossed, but there was also little knowledge of the
labor force that would be needed. Because Africans were not interested
in the grueling tasks of railway building, the British imported 32,000
workers from India as indentured laborers. It was these workers who
suffered in the sweltering heat, and it was they who were the occasional
victims of the man-eating lions of Tsavo in the present-day park area
(Figure 1). As unanticipated technical and financial problems mounted,
the enterprise quickly became a political issue in Britain, dubbed by
critics the "lunatic line." Defenders argued that economically it was a
sound venture because Kenya and Uganda could be opened commercially,
and that with the railway would come easy transport of commodities
and trade goods. Skeptics pointed out that there were few commodities
to trade and few goods to move. The eventual solution was to bring
in European settlers to produce the commodities, to stimulate trade,
and to make the railway profitable.[7]

When the railway was completed, 7,000 "Asians," as they were
to be called, elected to stay in Kenya. Most were not railway line workers
but cooks, artisans, and suppliers. They became the core of the Asian

Uganda Railway train near Limuru, Kenya, circa 1905 (courtesy the *Daily Nation*)

community that was to have major commercial impact on Kenya and to add complexity to its class structure.

Although the impetus to the expansion of the Asian population came through the railroad work, it is important to note that some Asians had been in East Africa earlier. From the beginning, the Asians were British subjects brought in by British decree.[8] By the 1880s, on Zanzibar and in Mombasa, Asians had become an important entrepreneurial force that significantly affected the region's commercial patterns.

The route of the railroad followed older caravan tracks that led through dry bush country near Mombasa, gradually climbing toward the 7000-foot Rift Valley escarpment 300 miles from the coast. Near the escarpment a caravan resupply point had developed called Ngongo Bargas, a place where the forest-dwelling Kikuyu and grassland Maasai met to trade with passing caravans. It was near here that the railway would eventually build its repair shops and where, after 1905, the good climate and clear water would attract settlers to establish the city of Nairobi.

Events around Ngongo Bargas in the 1890s, however, would not have hinted of such developments. The area was a trade point and resting place for Uganda-bound caravans. Kikuyu women traded food-stuffs needed by the caravans for beads, cloth, and small manufactured items. Gradually Ngongo Bargas became a major stopping place and undoubtedly a place of early entrepreneurial experience for the Kikuyu.

To the north of Ngongo Bargas at about this time, a baby boy was born who would later call himself Jomo Kenyatta.[9]

Lord Lugard, who was to have great influence in shaping British administrative policy in both East and West Africa, came to Ngongo Bargas as a young adventurer in 1890, and thereafter lived for some time with the Kikuyu to the north. Despite the Kikuyu reputation for violence, Lugard reported them peaceful, helpful, and eager to learn European ways. A few years later, Francis Hall was to press farther north into present-day Muranga District, encounter "treachery and violence," and proceed to pacify the area by raiding villages with heavily-armed Swahili soldiers. In 1894, the first missionary, Stuart Wall, with his wife and five children, arrived at Ngongo Bargas to set up a mission station, after walking the 300 miles from Mombasa.

Two factors made the economic opening of central Kenya relatively easy for Europeans. First, two senior chiefs, a Maasai named Lenana, and a Kikuyu, Waiyaki, were induced to cooperate with Europeans. Lenana in particular opened the way for safe passage through Maasailand, an area that for decades had been dangerous to caravan passages. Although less powerful than paramount chiefs of the Uganda system, some Kenyan chiefs and headmen were strong enough to control their neighborhoods. The underpinnings of "indirect rule" were then put into place: the British controlled the chiefs; the chiefs controlled their people.[10]

Second, European settlement began at a time when the southern highlands were seemingly unoccupied. In 1897 a devastating drought and a major cattle-killing rinderpest plague had decimated both the Maasai and the Kikuyu. The Kikuyu, who inhabited the areas near Ngongo Bargas, had migrated north to the heartland of their territory near Mt. Kenya. Most European settlers coming to the areas the Kikuyu had left believed they had come to unoccupied lands, and some believed they were the first inhabitants ever to use the land. The Kikuyu believed they had departed only temporarily. This misunderstanding was at the core of the land dispute that was to plague Kenya for the next sixty-five years.

Part of the misunderstanding lay in the fact that, as settlers spread north and west into the fertile highlands, they were often welcomed by Africans. Europeans at the time were not seen as a threat or as permanent settlers. Like the Arab caravans and supply expeditions traveling to Uganda, they were expected to leave. In any case, by comparison to the African populations, the number of Europeans was at first small and seemingly insignificant. In 1900 there were only 480 Europeans in all of Kenya, including twenty farming families; by 1903 there were some 790 Europeans, and by 1906, 1,800, a figure swelled by the arrival of 800 Boers from South Africa. The next eight years saw major increases. By 1914 the European population had reached 5,400 and included 3,000 settlers.[11]

From an international point of view, it was in this period that the Marxists' critique of *Empire* was particularly germane to Kenya. The argument was that capitalism, particularly in Britain, contributed to the conversion of parts of the world into agricultural export areas destined to serve only as suppliers to the industrialized nations. For Kenya the theory was to be refined and debated by Marxists and neo-Marxists for the next eighty years.[12] It is doubtful, however, that many Europeans who came to Kenya in the 1890–1915 era had much knowledge of the Marxist critique. Missionaries carried the "civilizing mission"; administrators came to fulfill Britain's security goals, other came to aid Britain's economic growth, a few to aid the British Empire, and most to find profit and adventure. Nearly all would have rejected the idea that the Empire should be curtailed. Left behind in London were isolationists who believed Britain would be better off developing its own society rather than colonies. Others at home opposed imperialism for the tax burden it created, or because they advocated an open "free trade" system. Those who ventured to Kenya talked of law and order, a new civilization, and economic expansion.

What few Europeans realized was that some Africans already had strong entrepreneurial inclinations based on traditional practices. Most indigenous political systems were based on family and clan authority, on elders' councils, or on small chieftaincies. Everyday society for both agriculturalists and pastoralists was more individualistic in Kenya; in the case of agriculturalists, it was more entrepreneurial than the constrained and regulated life under hierarchical chieftaincies in Tanganyika and Uganda.

Pre-colonial African society in Kenya, it can be argued, led to greater individuality, innovation, and opportunism, albeit with less structure and governmental organization. A hierarchical government structure and a ruling elite of chiefs with whom to communicate, traits the Europeans had found appealing in Uganda, did not exist in most of Kenya. When Europeans denigrated the "disorganized natives" in Kenya, they in fact were referring to people who had qualities of freedom and independence that would eventually serve commerical interests very well.

Looking back, changes in the two decades between 1895 and 1915 were astounding. Administratively, a bureaucratic structure was set up and a local government system grafted onto the existing local systems through the chiefs and headmen. Missionaries within twenty years had established schools, clinics, and churches and a community of African Christians. Over 3,000 settlers had brought European farming techniques that some younger Africans were beginning to follow. Asian and European traders had set up businesses that affected Africans by building onto the entrepreneurial practices existent in traditional societies. The first executive and legislative councils were organized, taxes imposed, and an East African (Lands) order imposed that gave legal backing to the idea that "native rights in regard to land were confined to occupation, cultivation, and grazing, and did not amount to a title in the land itself."

Perhaps the most astounding change was the swiftness of land acquisition by Europeans. The original leases were for ninety-nine years, a time period that quickly became a bone of contention between settlers and government. In 1915 the government capitulated and extended leases to 999 years, over half the bygone Christian era.[13]

The way of life the Europeans hoped to put in place for 999 years was agrarian capitalism, via free enterprise for the white settlers. Land was the cornerstone of the dream; it was the issue when World War I began in East Africa. When the troops marched home again four years later, it was still the issue.

WORLD WAR I IN EAST AFRICA

When World War I broke out in Europe, the British in East Africa were at war de facto with German East Africa, the colony immediately to the south. Over the four years 1914–1918, aside from a few German raids into Kenya to attack the railway line and to burn supply dumps, all fighting occurred in German territory and parts of present-day Mozambique and Zambia. The backwater campaign that unfolded was a combination of bloody skirmishes and endless marches in the sun. One of the outcomes was to give 250,000 Kenyans pressed into the African Carrier Corps a long-term basis of political and economic dissent.[14]

At the beginning of the war, European morale was high in Kenya and a quick, decisive victory over the outnumbered Germans was anticipated. However, the allies met one setback after another. The most decisive defeat of a colonial force since the annihilation of the British at Kabul in the 1840s occurred at the battle for Tanga, a seaport in northern Tanganyika that the British tried to take in an attack from the sea. Seasick, untried Asian troops fresh from a crossing of the Indian Ocean were sent ashore to meet a withering hail of German machine gun fire. So humiliating was the defeat that myths of German invincibility born at Tanga were to plague the British for years afterwards. Here, too, old myths about African cowardice and poor soldiery were destroyed. The British were defeated by a totally outnumbered force made up of African regulars (askari) under a small band of German officers. The African askari proved to be disciplined, courageous, and easily a match for the best the British could muster.

Essentially, the "battle for the bundu" (or bush), as the campaign was dubbed, was a slow, slogging, guerrilla war. The German commander, Paul von Lettow Vorbeck, had orders to tie up as many Allied troops in East Africa as possible, thus keeping them out of the trenches in Europe. This he did with hit-and-run tactics that relied on surprise rather than drawn lines and pitched battles. When the war ended in Europe, the Allies in East Africa still had not totally caught up to von Lettow Vorbeck's forces, a situation that allowed the latter to be dubbed "the Germans who never lost."[15]

Casualties on both sides were high for the number of men committed. Since the British had brought in some Asian troops, Kenyan Africans were used less as soldiers and more as porters. Of the 250,000 in the African Carrier Corps for the Allies, over 45,000 never came home, victims far more of illness than of German guns. The Allied losses from all causes were 967 officers, 17,650 from other fighting ranks. The German losses were approximately 740 officers, 1,460 from other fighting ranks, and 7,000 carriers. Total fighting troop commitments were 160,000 Allies and 15,000 Germans.[16]

World War I had many after-effects in Kenya. The myths of the "invincible white man" and the "undisciplined African" were beginning to fade. African *askari* were broadly praised for steadfastness and uncommon valor under extreme combat conditions. In the British ranks, African stoicism and good soldiery in both the Carrier Corps and the fighting ranks were the grist for many memoirs. For African servicemen who saw the war in its full horror, perhaps the most searing experience (which would have later political repercussions) was to see Europeans systematically killing other Europeans.

Curiously, those who suffered the greatest humiliation were the Asian troops imported by the British. The Tanga rout was not the only time they broke and ran under fire, to be found cowering under bushes or wandering aimlessly in the sun with neither rifles nor headgear. In fairness, the combat behavior of the sepoys at times was reported as valorous and spirited. The war, however, did little to improve racial feelings against Asians or to reduce discrimination against Asians who had settled in Kenya.

The war also put a significant strain on Kenya's home front. Some 1,987 of the 3,000 European settlers left their farms to fight, and within months many of their farms returned to bush, erasing years of work.[17] African homesteads suffered not only from the absence of men, but also because African livestock had been commandeered for the war effort. Veterinarian services were in such short supply that the remaining domestic stock were decimated. Making matters worse, a serious rinderpest epidemic killed many cattle in 1916, and in 1918 a drought and famine struck Kenya.

Politically the war was a watershed. African soldiers came home with new perspectives on Europeans, on themselves, and on what they wanted for themselves and their families. Those who survived the arduous campaign were far more willing to protest their home conditions. The colonial authorities sensed this immediately. The solution was to bring in more Europeans, because "it was feared that Africans might return from fighting with an idea that shooting white men was a lighter matter than they had previously thought."[18]

In 1919 the new settler infusion began under the soldier-settler scheme, a plan that brought "qualified" British veterans to Kenya. Some 1,053 large farms were sold to the soldier-settlers at nominal costs and another 257 given free. Although the soldier-settlers fanned out across the highlands, much of the land was taken from the Nandi reserves in the western highlands. Nandi tribesmen had fought colonial expansion at the turn of the century, and the new take-overs reopened old wounds. The land issues alone would take fourteen years to settle.[19]

Although seeds of discord were planted by the European influx and the loss of land, the period just after World War I also saw expansion of African entrepreneurship. Black veterans, frustrated by the lack of agricultural opportunity, turned to other ways of finding profits, and a new commercialism was discernible in a myriad of small business activities.

THE INTERWAR YEARS

The Economy, 1920–1940

During the 1920s, European capitalism was firmly planted in Kenya. The process was carried out basically by 21,000 middle-class English who transported Western entrepreneurial ideas and technology into East Africa. From the beginning the system was a highly stratified one of European owner-managers, Asian artisan-traders, and African laborers. Black Kenyans were drawn into the capitalist economy as laborers and petty traders, exposed to Western materialism, yet denied access to it. Taxes were high, and for Africans most consumer items were too costly. The situation meant that a laborer worked for taxes, food, shelter, and little more.

Exactly why Africans accepted the system without early rebellion or withdrawal is one of the mysteries of colonial Kenya. In part, the capitalist system worked because Europeans were able to bring several forms of compulsion to bear. Taxes on Africans were underscored as essential to the society, and African males were "encouraged" to meet the taxes through wage labor. A labor registration system called *kipande* was installed in 1921 that called for every adult African male to carry a certified labor pass, or *kipande*. On it employers recorded the kind of work done, comments on performance, wages earned, and dates employed. European employers had the power to write derogatory reports, and thus had a way of controlling employees. By 1928, 675,000 of the hated passes were estimated to be in circulation.[20]

During these years European-sanctioned squatterism also helped obtain reliable labor for the plantations. In order to be close to their work, African laborers were permitted to build temporary huts and develop small gardens on European farms. The arrangement gave European managers close, cheap male labor, with women and children nearby when extra hands were needed. As African families became more dependent on their huts and gardens, European control over the system grew. African populations elsewhere soared in the home reserves, and land became in short supply, so that many squatters had no place else to go from their plots on European farms.[21]

In the interwar period, differences between the two main European communities in Kenya—the colonial administration and the settlers—became more open and at times vicious. The colonial administration in Nairobi was primarily interested in keeping the peace and in keeping up the volume of exports so that customs revenues might be collected.

Its parallel concern was making sure Africans paid their taxes, a source of revenue that had become the backbone of the colony's finances. As more liberals found their way into the Kenya colonial service, more discussion about the government's "trusteeship" obligations and "proper treatment of the natives" was heard. European settlers, on the other hand, were mainly concerned about their land, their economic superiority over Africans, and their access to cheap, dependable labor. The basic rift was between those concerned with "African rights" and others who hoped to keep Kenya a "white man's country" in perpetuity.

Much of the conservatism on the part of the settlers undoubtedly came from a beleaguered outlook. Despite the boom years in the mid-1920s, European farmers faced serious problems and their condition was often precarious. In 1930 Lord Hailey estimated that Europeans cultivated less than 10 percent of the land they controlled.[22] The inescapable conclusion is that despite preferential treatment from the colonial government, despite farm credit, cheap labor, price supports, extension services, and other aid, European agriculture was often unprofitable, inefficient, and in fact propped up by both private wealth from Britain and colonial aid.[23]

It is important to note that during this time views in Britain about colonialism and about Kenya in particular were not uniform. Critics argued that despite the cheap labor and colonial assistance, Kenya settlers had commandeered the means of production and marketing and had gone about trying to set themselves up on luxurious plantations with very thin economic understanding. Liberal Britons suggested that Kenya's " . . . European settlers as a class more resembled a landed aristocracy than a capitalist entrepreneur group. Their concern with secure leisure, conspicuous display, and a generally gentlemanly status outweighed any tendencies toward maximum reinvestment of surpluses whenever such reinvestment was not essential to the very continuity of the plantation."[24]

A further criticism was that Britain had in fact permitted a major economic reorganization in Kenya to dramatically change the land practices, the labor practices, and how capital resources would be used. By 1939 serious questions were also being asked in London about the forms of production that had emerged and whether they were suitable for the long-term development of Kenya.[25]

Conversely, support for Kenya as a colonial adventure came from both public and private sectors in Britain. When the Protectorate officially became a colony in 1920 there was general agreement that it should pay its own way and be profitable to the Empire. Supporters in the 1930s suggested Kenya was well on its way to self-sufficiency, and that strategic goals had been won. They pointed out that the Imperial Navy had an important port on the Indian Ocean, that Uganda, the Nile, the Suez Canal, and the passage to India were secure. They further argued that agriculturally Britain had an important experimental station in Kenya for commodities that would benefit the entire Empire, including coffee, tea, sisal, maize, cotton, tobacco, copra, fruits, vegetables, and livestock. Other substantial support for the colonial policy came from private manufacturers in Britain who sought the classical dependency exchange with Kenya: raw materials for manufactured goods. Few manufacturers had compunctions about pressuring government for the most favorable conditions, and most of them received preferential treatment in the colonial legislation of the time.[26]

The crucial fact throughout this early colonial period is that settlers were able to use the state to bias the economy in their favor. This protection, seen in favorable land laws, low freight rates, extension services, credit, compulsory labor practices, protection from African competition, and dozens of other ways, was crucial to the settlers' survival. Without this state protection and their reserves of personal capital, many settlers would have collapsed financially. Kenya settlers in these years were state-aided and state-nurtured, a unique form of welfare within a capitalist system.

African Political Activity and the Colonial Government, 1920–1940

Organized African political protest in Kenya began shortly after World War I, based partly on the experiences African soldiers had in the war, and partly on land shortage and other social grievances. The first organized protest began in 1920 in Kiambu, the coffee-growing district near Nairobi. Here a Kikuyu rural association came together to formally protest the alienation of district land. The group included government-appointed headmen and chiefs who sought redress at the risk of losing their jobs. Their tactics were to use petitions and letters of grievance.

When these techniques proved ineffectual, a more militant protest group called the Young Kikuyu Association was organized in 1921. The head of the association and its guiding political light was Harry Thuku, a Kikuyu government employee of extraordinary organizational ability. He led the group not only in condemnation of government policies, but also in protests over compulsory hut taxes, the labor laws, and the detested *kipande* registration system. To enlist support beyond central Kenya, Thuku visited Kisumu on Lake Victoria and successfully rallied mission-trained young men to organize the Young Kavirondo Association, a political movement dedicated to African improvement. The highly successful Kisumu trip was also to be a part of Thuku's downfall.

Shortly after his return to Nairobi in 1922 he was arrested by the suspicious colonial government and jailed for seditious political activity. A large crowd of supporters who gathered outside the Nairobi central police station to protest his arrest was fired upon by the police in what became Kenya's first political riot. When the smoke cleared, twenty-five Africans were dead.

Harry Thuku's work and the killings following his arrest established his place in history as Kenya's first nationalist. In terms of further political activity, however, his career was over. The government exiled him in 1922 for nine years to Kismayu in present-day Somalia. When he returned to Nairobi he had been politically eclipsed by younger men.

In 1925, during Thuku's exile, a newly named Kikuyu Central Association (KCA) emerged as a viable political organization to carry on African initiatives. The issues remained the same: land rights, land alienation, *kipande*, hut taxes, unemployment, and the education of African children. The difficulty in organizing effective political protests on a Kenya-wide basis was the key stumbling block of every nationalist. Travel for organizers was expensive, the *kipande* system restricted movement, and ethnic suspicion still occurred between African groups that had known old animosities. Suspicion was a major problem because the nature of political protest against a colonial power demanded trust, loyalty, and confidentiality. Leaders like Thuku found it much easier to rally their neighbors than to build alliances across tribal lines.[27]

Three years after the KCA was formed, Johnstone (Jomo) Kenyatta became its general secretary. Kenyatta's life from this point in 1928 to his death, fifty years later as Kenya's first president, is a major thread in Kenya's history. During the late interwar period he was a central actor in the protest movement. In 1929 he was sent to London by the KCA to present a petition to the British government for the election of Africans to the Kenya Legislative Council. Again in 1931 he journeyed to England, this time to bring grievances concerning land and work permits before Parliament. In the specific mission he failed, but from 1931 to 1946 he remained in Europe, first traveling on the continent and in the Soviet Union and thereafter settling in London, where he married an Englishwoman and worked as a lobbyist for Kenyan and Pan-African concerns.[28]

One of Kenyatta's key points, as had been Thuku's, was the ongoing loss of land to European settlement. Since 1900, the colonial government had relegated Africans to reserves that, as Kenyatta pointed out, were by 1912 experiencing severe population pressures. The pressures led to an African out-migration to European farms or to Nairobi. In 1912 some 12,000 Africans were engaged outside the reserves; by 1927 the number was 152,000, and by the beginning of 1939, more than 200,000.[29]

Partly in response to political activity of men like Thuku and Kenyatta, and partly in response to European demands for greater security, the colonial government changed markedly in the interwar period. The government structure after 1920 was to give the colonial governor a streamlined system that could be in touch with all Africans. This was done from the governor's office through a chief commissioner and a council of ministers, each with authority over a government department. At the next level of administration were provincial commissioners, and below them district commissioners, district officers, and finally, appointed chiefs and headmen.

Chiefs were the cornerstone of the local government administration. Most were appointed and paid by the colonial authorities, although usually coming to power at public meetings where provincial or district commissioners could be assured of a chief's public support. Few chiefs had traditional legitimacy as rulers but rather served as the "powerful citizens" who could carry out local government functions. The system followed the "indirect rule" format Britain had developed in other colonies. Chiefs were assisted by headmen to collect taxes, keep the peace, carry on civil courts, and organize local development projects. The "native councils" established in 1924, ostensibly patterned after elders' councils, were designed to give Kenyans experience in representative local government.

Important constitutional changes and new land laws occurred in the interwar period. The Devonshire Declaration of 1923 provided a new land policy which included the right of Asians, but not Africans, to own land—the first indication of any flexibility toward non-Europeans. In 1932 the Kenya Land Commission (Carter Commission) investigated African land grievances with on-the-ground surveys and interviews. Their findings led to the return of several large tracts of land to African use, although the African Reserve System, a homelands concept, was maintained on the basis of skin color. Serious inequities remained in the laws, but the interwar years did provide the first hint that some flexibility regarding land might be forthcoming. In fact, the continued inequities over land during this period were the roots of a guerrilla war that two decades later would force land changes. (See Table 1, page 27.)

The world depression affected Kenya in several ways. As demand for Kenyan raw materials and plantation crops fell, so too did employment in Kenya. Kenyan workers, who had become dependent on salaries, were thrown back to the land, often to reserves that had become densely populated. Politically, by 1939 the Kikuyu Central Association (KCA) had emerged as the main organization of African protest. As anxiety over Hitler grew in Europe, however, the political atmosphere in the colonies became more constrained. The KCA was banned in 1940, its newspaper seized, and its activities called a threat to the colony's wartime security. As the colony prepared to join the Allied cause, the political picture was that of a central administration heavily influenced by a conservative core of Europeans who held power. Outside looking in were a few liberal European groups; farther out were small Asian and Arab political associations, and even farther from the power center were the KCA and perhaps a dozen African ethnic associations. Among the latter were political groups formed by the Kikuyu, Embu, Meru, Kamba, Taita, Luo, and Luhya. These were essentially small, proto-nationalist groups that mixed political protest with local level religious activities in such examples as breakaway churches and local prophet movements that combined religion, healing, and politics. During the war years nearly all these fires were banked, partly by colonial decree, but curiously with African cooperation. A political truce was called for the duration of World War II.

WORLD WAR II AND THE MAU-MAU PERIOD

The fact that a large Italian army and air force were deployed in Ethiopia and Somalia caused alarm in Kenya when World War II broke out in Europe. British colonial authorities feared a quick Italian strike could cut off Kenya's communications, its railway and harbor, and shut down the colony as a food source for the Allies. To prevent this move a contingent of the King's African Rifles was locally recruited and deployed throughout the northern areas. Luckily for the Allied cause, Italy was not an immediate belligerent on the European front. The delay enabled the Kenya garrisons to be reinforced by troops from Europe, plus South African, Nigerian, Northern Rhodesian, and Gold Coast contingents.

Kenya was never invaded, although some Italian air reconnaisance missions and occasional shooting did occur over its territory. The colony's food proved important to the war effort and troops from Kenya, both African and European, were later deployed in the Burma campaign in the long struggle against the Japanese.

During the war, land questions continued to be at the heart of Kenyan politics. White farmers who had been pressed into producing food for the war effort argued that to do so they needed more land and more labor. As their demands were met "for the war effort," a growing number of liberals, both in Kenya and in Britain, criticized the colonial government for allowing African interests to be overrun. In particular, Labour MPs in the U.K., led by Creech Jones, voiced concerns about the misuse of wartime powers in Kenya.

One of the major issues debated during this time was whether or not to allow Africans a voice in these wartime affairs. A change came in 1943 when the colonial government accepted the idea that a *European* representative of African interests could be appointed to the government's Legislative Council. The appointment fell to Reverend L. J. Beecher, a spirited activist and well-known critic of colonial abuses. He had been responsible for an inquiry into African tax collection problems in 1936 and had built a reputation of concern for African interests. In fact, his first announcement must have staggered the conservative settlers. He looked forward, he said, to the day Africans would sit alongside Europeans in the legislature and someday replace them. In fact, the first African sat in the legislature within a year. In 1944 Eliud Mathu, a Kenyan who had attended Oxford University, became the first black appointed to the colonial governing body. Through the articulate Mathu, demands grew perceptibly for broader African representation.[30]

By 1945, when World War II ended, Kenya was a very different political society. Greater diversity was apparent in the European community, due not only to a small liberal wing of the settler society, but also to a new influx of missionaries, businessmen, colonial administrators, and discharged officers, particularly from the British Indian Army. Most important, returning African soldiers brought new seeds of discontent and new views on how they should be treated in a post-war era. Again, as in World War I, Africans had seen European soldiers killed by non-Europeans—the Japanese in Burma. The experience, combined with those of World War I veterans, ended forever any white supremacy myths.

It was the return of a single Kikuyu, however, that catalyzed postwar African politics. In 1946 Jomo Kenyatta came home from Britain the undisputed leader of the nationalist movement. In 1947 he was elected president of the newly organized Kenya African Union and within three years had built KAU into a movement of some 150,000 members. Their concerns were land and social inequities. India's independence from Britain in 1947 further inspired Kenyans with hope for their own self-determination.

By 1950 widespread unemployment and landlessness among a large Kikuyu population lent impetus to more militant action. African leaders in the small trade unions, in the vernacular press, and in other circles began calling openly for winning self-government by whatever means necessary. Violence finally erupted in 1951 and was blamed by the British on a secret society called Mau-Mau.

Mau-Mau was more than a society; it was a land rebellion, a violent uprising of Africans, mainly Kikuyu, against European colonial authority *and* against landed Kikuyu "loyalists" and European settlers. The movement's origin is clouded in mystery. Authorities at first believed a fanatic religious group was loose in the land, and rumors of oathings, "barbarous deeds," and other "vile behavior" were rampant. In all likelihood, it was a coming together of several Kikuyu political forces, some of which had been banned from organizing, such as the Kikuyu Central Association. Their common complaints were the land problems that went back thirty years. Kikuyu dissidents recruited Embu and Meru peoples living near Mt. Kenya to join the movement, but few others outside central Kenya participated.

The 1951 violence began with a series of arson and cattle-killing incidents in the central highlands. One particular incident, however, caused decisive government action. In 1952 a government senior chief and prominent British loyalist, Kungu Waruhiu, was assassinated by Mau-Mau. The government's response was to declare a State of Emergency, to arrest Kenyatta, and to request British troops. The Mau-Mau counterreaction was to increase their military campaign. During the next four years violence ebbed and flowed throughout central Kenya, although open combat was rare. Most action consisted of surprise night attacks by Mau-Mau on police posts and isolated farms and of ongoing search and reconnaissance activities by British troops. The authorities at one time had nearly 100,000 Africans in detention camps; as a result of one major sweep in 1954, called "Operation Anvil," some 27,000 Kikuyu, Embu, and Meru people living in Nairobi were sent back to rural villages. Nearly a million Kikuyu were forced to move from their homesteads to stockaded villages. Thousands of homesteads were destroyed to deny them to the Mau-Mau, and hundreds of villages were bulldozed.

As the British military superiority began to tell, some 16,000 Mau-Mau combatants fell back to the heavy bamboo forests of Mt. Kenya and the Aberdare Mountains. Here British military action ground to a halt, except for skirmishes between small foot patrols and raids by

Lancaster bombers that killed more wildlife than Mau-Mau. When the hostilities ebbed in 1956–1957 and the human cost was calculated, the suggestion that European settlers had been the primary Mau-Mau targets was destroyed. Only thirty-two Europeans had been killed, and only twenty-six Asian civilians. However, 1,819 African "loyalists" fell victim to Mau-Mau.[31] On the military side, some 11,503 Mau-Mau combatants had been killed, including their overt support and transport helpers. The British forces lost 101 Kenyan African soldiers, fifty-three European soldiers, and three Asian soldiers.

The financial outlay of the colonial government was £160 million plus a costly deployment of British troops, aircraft, and other equipment. Within a short period a "white paper," the Corfield Report, would detail from the British point of view the causes and outcome of the war. Although it did not do justice to the sufferings of innocent Africans caught up in the violence, the report gave official recognition once and for all to the root cause of Mau-Mau: the loss of Kenyan land to Europeans.

The reaction of the settler community to these findings ranged from hostile rejections to conciliatory attempts at binding Kenya's political wounds. Although the ban against organizing multiracial societies was not rescinded until 1959, liberal Europeans argued for the accommodation of Africans in a multiracial legal state that would see a black middle class, with interests similar to those of Europeans, develop as a force to maintain the status quo. More conservative settlers saw Mau-Mau as proof that Africans would lead Kenya into "darkness and death." The conservatives attempted to use Mau-Mau violence to shore up their political position and to guarantee their rights to the land in perpetuity. As reforms took effect, however, the earlier colonial legislation that had set protective boundaries around 16,700 square miles of "European Highlands" was struck down. The change triggered the first exodus of Europeans, mainly to South Africa.[32]

More broadly, the Mau-Mau war led to major social changes, particularly concerning African land rights and representation in government. Reform began in 1954–1955 when a Royal Commission investigating the land grievances behind Mau-Mau recommended sweeping changes, stating bluntly that the racial basis of land allocation in the colony was not in Kenya's best interests. The commission's work led to the 1955 Swynnerton Plan, which in part called for a change in customary African land-tenure practices to an individual freehold system based on land demarcation and registration. The plan called for consolidating small parcels of property, giving Africans access to credit, to farmer training, to research findings, to technical assistance, and to improved water supplies. The objective was to bring more profitable cash-crop farming to small farmers.

The Mau-Mau war had a second important effect on land issues. The concentration of Kikuyu in stockaded villages during the violence made rapid land consolidation possible. With these populations temporarily clustered off the land, the mechanics of land reform could take

First truck transport company, Kitale (courtesy the *Daily Nation*)

place. By 1959 freehold titles in large numbers had been issued to Africans, new farm supports were in place, and a campaign was underway to employ landless people. The growth of an agrarian middle class had discernibly picked up speed.

Jomo Kenyatta was in exile during this 1952–1959 period. He had been arrested in 1952, brought to trial for complicity in Mau-Mau, found guilty, and sentenced to seven years' hard labor. Government witnesses linked Kenyatta closely enough to early "seditious talk" to make the government's case. Most observers today feel Kenyatta was not involved in the violent wings of Mau-Mau, that he perhaps knew about them and did not use his enormous influence to stop them but could not be charged with leading the violent uprising. In any case, he was in jail before most of the killing occurred. His trial and exile, plus his many years in Europe, kept Kenyatta aloof from local squabbles. He was an untainted person and thus politically attractive to many different African factions. The events that followed between 1959 and 1963 were to build on Kenyatta's "returning hero" image and give him the stature to become the unchallenged candidate to lead the new nation.

Post-War African Entrepreneurial Activity

Stimulated initially by a wartime demand for food to feed Allied troops, African entrepreneurs branched into several activities soon after World War II ended. One avenue was to work as traders in remote areas where communications were poor and Asian merchants had not penetrated. Selling rural foodstuffs to Nairobi hotels, buying Tugen sheep at Lake Baringo for resale in highland towns, selling vegetables to workers on settler farms, or undercutting Asian traders in maize and millet sales were all profitable endeavors. Setting up small shops, tea hotels, maize mills, sugar presses, alcohol distilleries, and truck transport firms were others. In central Kenya, although the age-old Kikuyu-Maasai trade had slackened, the basic economic formula was still valid: Kikuyu food wealth in exchange for Maasai livestock wealth. New entrepreneurs worked the old formula as middlemen by translating Kikuyu food surpluses into the material goods Maasai wanted.[33]

Other forms of entrepreneurship revolved around the informal artisan activities of carvers, carpenters, thatchers, tinsmiths, rope makers, and others outside the regulated, licensed economy. This informal sector had characteristics of a hidden economy, an occasionally illicit form of activity by small, unlicensed entrepreneurs who had other permanent employment but mixed it with "moonlighting" jobs. Other entrepreneurs worked between small industries, serving as traders, agents, suppliers, and salesmen. This informal economic activity grew in the next few decades not only because it was outside government regulations, but also because it was low cost and adaptive, filling a need for inexpensive indigenous goods.

To keep pre-independence entrepreneurialism in perspective, it is important to remember that the political turbulence of the 1950s depressed local capitalism. The Mau-Mau emergency actually sealed off the productive central highlands. Throughout the country the number of new African private companies dropped from 15 percent of the total (in competition with Asian and European firms) to 2 percent in 1953, and zero in 1954 and 1955. As late as 1959, the bulk of the formal economy was still in European hands.[34]

Although African indigenous capitalism was growing and a "middle peasantry" of traders-farmers-businessmen had accrued new savings and purchasing power, African entrepreneurs found serious obstacles. Government regulations, European and Asian competition, and the shortages of capital and technical skills were common problems. Perhaps more difficult, very little commercial trust existed within the African community that could be relied upon for informal business arrangements. The Asian community had its closed mutual-support system and private Hindu language, but the Africans had to create their own old-boy networks.[35]

An overabundance of high school–educated Kenyans also contributed to the rise of entrepreneurship. Some new graduates moved into government and company posts, but many others were excluded. Frustrated by the lack of opportunity, but with high aspirations and often a great deal of determination, they turned to business activity. Most established the classic intermediate businesses that survived on hard work, entrepreneurship, good luck, and little else—an essential step in the beginning of small-scale capitalism.

For younger entrepreneurs, other opportunities opened as independence approached. Commercial constraints were relaxed and some Africans were permitted into the colonial hierarchy and into occupations previously closed to them. Government spending on African enterprises increased, and new venture capital became easier to obtain. Since degrees meant access to jobs formerly held by Europeans, the value of education increased. Also, by 1959 the picture had changed in the Kenyan industrial sector. Foreign manufacturers who wanted small assembly plants and factory outlets began actively recruiting Kenyans, both for their skills and for the protection they would afford in the independence period.

The "unwanted competition" stance by manufacturers in Britain was replaced with an "assembled in Kenya" approach. Foreign firms operating in Kenya began encouraging African traders to carry their products further into the rural areas. Companies like East African Tobacco (BAT), East African Breweries, Unga Flour Company, Shell Oil, and Fitzgerald Baynes were foreign firms with expatriate managers who offered local retailing opportunities. African businessmen began to form joint-stock companies and private companies, mainly for trading in commodities such as flour, charcoal, vegetables, and fuel oil. As the African merchant society grew in size and wealth, so too did a jaunty outlook, expressed by one wealthy African trader as "rich men of all races get on well together."[36]

Looking back over the interwar and post–World War II periods, 1920–1960, African entrepreneurial activity was heavily dependent on key legislative changes, particularly concerning land laws. The crucial developments are the Devonshire Declaration (1923–1924), which basically restated the colonial policy of denying Africans land titles; the Carter Commission, which did the first land surveys and provided some land for Africans (1932); the creation of settlement projects under the African Land Development Organization (1946–1962); and the Royal Commission (1954–1955), which among other things struck down the racial basis of land allocation. As the nationalistic movement gained momentum after 1955, legislative events moved rapidly and opened further possibilities for African entrepreneurs (Table 1).

THE TRANSITION TO INDEPENDENCE

The years 1959–1963 were as turbulent politically as the early Mau-Mau period had been militarily. Influential Africans like Tom Mboya and Oginga Odinga, the Luo leaders from western Kenya, put themselves second to the imprisoned Kenyatta, arguing that his release was a precondition to negotiations for independence. Kenyatta continued to languish in jail as a series of constitutional meetings designed to edge Kenya along the pathway to independence began to unfold. In 1954 the Lyttleton Constitution, named for the secretary of state for the colonies, had opened the political door to African participation. Although still committed to parity between the races, that constitution did allow eight African representatives on the Kenya Legislative Council and did establish a multiracial administrative system. In 1958 the new Lennox-Boyd Constitution raised African participation to fourteen seats. Both Tom Mboya and Oginga Odinga were elected to the council and offered ministerial posts. Both refused their portfolios until the African representation on the council increased.

Beginning in 1959, political events began to move more rapidly. Kenyatta's seven-year term of imprisonment was completed, but he was

TABLE 1
Key Legislative Developments on Land Issues, 1920-1960

Year	Event	Summary of Results
1923-1924	Devonshire White Paper	Restatement of land policy sets up local Native Councils and gives Asians right to own land
1927-1928	District Councils	Seven non-African councils organized for local government
1932	Kenya Land Commission	Carter Commission retains Land Reserve system; first in-depth survey of land use
1944	Legislative Council	First African member seated
1946	African Land Development Organization (ALDEV)	ALDEV established for multiple African land functions, including reallocation, restoration of titles, conservation, range, and extension
1948	African District Councils	Representative local government
1954	Lyttleton Constitution	African participation in government established
1954-1955	Swynnerton Plan	Based on Royal Commission, new plan provides major land reforms in land consolidation, farm planning, and conservation
1958	Lennox-Boyd Constitution	African membership on (national) Legislative Council increased to fourteen
1959	Purchase Plan for European Land	Reservation of land for whites only ends; plan for sale of "white highland" farms established
1960	MacLeod Constitution	Africans gain right to sixty-five seats on Legislative Council; plans for internal self-government established; agricultural ordinance amended

re-detained by the colonial government for "security reasons" at Lodwar in northern Kenya. Two other contentious issues, however, were resolved in 1959: the ban on organizing political societies that had been in force since Mau-Mau began was lifted, allowing multiracial groups to organize on a national basis. Second, the decision was made on what to do about the "white highlands." A basic plan for the purchase of European farms with British aid funds was finalized, and almost immediately the first of the 2,750 farms was offered for sale.

During 1960 protracted negotiations between the colonial government and nationalist leaders were carried out on how the specifics of the land question should be settled. The final agreements included the right of Europeans to recover their investments and repatriate the money; an understanding that this transfer of land would be accomplished in an economically stable way to insure continued growth and production; and finally, an agreement to provide land to the landless, particularly the landless poor, the unemployed, and the squatters.

Meanwhile, in London the Lancaster House Conference led to the new MacLeod Constitution, which gave Africans a majority of sixty-five seats on the Legislative Council and allowed a majority of government ministers to be African. At this point the British government surprised all participants by announcing its intention to grant independence to Kenya in a "short" period of time.

Almost immediately two political parties were formed. The Kenya African National Union (KANU), led by Mboya and Odinga in the name of Kenyatta, was made up ethnically of Kikuyu, Luo, and the old guard of the banned KAU. The second party, the Kenya African Democratic Union (KADU), led by Ronald Ngala, Daniel arap Moi, and others, was a party of some Kamba and several ethnic minorities—Kalenjin, Maasai, coastal Mijikenda, Somali, and other pastoralist peoples.

In May 1960 KANU nominated the imprisoned Jomo Kenyatta as party president, a move quickly disallowed by the colonial government. Undaunted, the KANU leaders stated that Jomo Kenyatta was their undisputed leader and if they were victorious in the forthcoming February 1961 election for seats on the Legislative Council, Kenyatta must lead their party. KANU won over KADU, sixteen seats to nine, and the pressure to release Kenyatta was redoubled. Finally, in July 1961, Governor Sir Patrick Renison agreed to the release. On August 14 Kenyatta was set free and transported to Gatundu, his home near Nairobi, where he received a tumultuous welcome. A triumphant journey through Nairobi and Mombasa followed, and in October, with near-unanimous support, Kenyatta became president of KANU.

It is important to note that as the transition to independence picked up speed, the ruling colonial officials and European farmers were basically bargaining with long-term economic concessions in exchange for retaining some control of the governmental apparatus. Kenyan nationalists first agreed to maintain a private land title and land registration system for the whole nation, a decision that deeply influenced the nation's social structure and affected how the production and exchange of goods and services would occur. The nationalists, in short, accepted a capitalistic, free-enterprise, private property system. They also agreed to buy out European farmers at fair prices, to remain in close economic alliance with the West, to continue to host multinational corporations, to "buy British," and to receive Western foreign aid.

In exchange, the British government and the settlers agreed to peacefully hand over the apparatus of government: the civil service, police, judiciary, prisons, army, and the buildings, equipment, employees, and symbols and legitimacy of government. In so doing, British authorities indirectly agreed to the establishment of a small African elite that would be in a position to garner economic reward at the expense of poorer citizens, a situation that would be potentially explosive and unstable if hard class lines were formed. In addition, despite parliamentary safeguards, the British were in fact handing inordinate power to one man. Kenyatta's broad support and adroitness at "informal" politics gave him the wherewithal to direct the system in any way he chose.

In April 1962 a temporary coalition government of KANU and KADU was formed under a framework constitution. National elections in which the two parties would vie for seats in the first national assembly were set for a year later. The assembly was to be a bicameral system, containing a House of Representatives with 117 seats and a Senate with 41 seats. In the pre-election campaign, KANU's candidates had embraced national unity, centralism in government, African socialism, and a nonaligned approach to foreign affairs. KADU advocated a regional form of government, greater conservatism in finance and welfare, greater latitude for ethnic loyalties in politics, and closer ties to Britain.[37]

The election outcome was close in the Senate (KANU eighteen seats, KADU sixteen, other groups seven). In the House, however, KANU dominated the election with seventy seats to KADU's thirty-two; the splinter groups captured fifteen seats but—ominously—the election was boycotted by ethnic Somalis living in Kenya's northeast arid lands. Their contention was that their territory should be ceded to Somalia.

Following the elections, on June 1, 1963, Kenya attained its internal self-government. Jomo Kenyatta, president of KANU, became the prime minister (later president) and convened Kenya's first cabinet, which symbolically was multiracial.

In September 1963, final agreement was reached in London on the Independence Constitution. Although still setting up a regional form of government, the document had been tempered to be acceptable to both KANU and KADU. On December 12, 1963, in a dignified midnight ceremony attended by the Duke of Edinburgh representing Queen Elizabeth, the British Union Jack was struck for the last time and Kenya's new flag put in its place.

CONCLUSIONS: JUDGMENTS ON AN ERA

Kenya's links with European capitalism began in the late nineteenth century when it became a part of expanded world trade patterns after the 1869 opening of the Suez Canal. From 1900 to 1963, Kenya was an economic dependency, exporting raw materials and importing manufactured goods. In 1963 the reins of government and of economic control passed peacefully from white colonial managers to black Kenyan managers.

Although the end of colonialism was enormously important politically, the economic die that had been cast earlier suggested that Kenya would continue on a capitalistic pathway. So easy was the transition

Pre-independence ceremony showing the Duke of Edinburgh (seated at left), Mayor Charles Rubia of Nairobi (speaking), Jomo Kenyatta (seated at right), and Governor Malcolm MacDonald (seated, far right) (courtesy the *Daily Nation*)

to African capitalism that critics were soon to suggest a black elite had simply replaced the white elite, and that Kenya in many ways remained a dependent satellite of Britain and the West. Others more sympathetic to the system suggested that Kenya could be an economic model for much of Africa, a black-controlled, multiracial state dedicated to individual rights and economic growth.

The reasons behind Kenya's capitalism are imbedded in history. The ground was fertile for such mercantile activity because the Kikuyu, Kamba, Swahili, and others had been entrepreneurs for at least 500 years before the Europeans arrived. Christian missionaries saw the solution to slavery and enforced labor to be the commercialization of Africans, replacing "slave thinking" with Christian ethics of hard work, technical skill, self-reliance, and profit. Colonial administrators were told to govern Kenya so that it paid its own way, a situation that created a demand for profits and the ability to pay taxes. Colonial settlers kept most of the profits for themselves, but provided Africans with farming techniques that were gradually assimilated. Corporate managers in Kenya, using cheap labor and foreign investment, implanted key industrial procedures that Kenyans continued to use after independence, including industrial laws, regulations, accounting systems, and management techniques.

Jomo Kenyatta and Governor Malcolm MacDonald, Independence, 1963 (courtesy the *Daily Nation*)

The historical reasons for Kenyan capitalism are punctuated by a few momentous events. First, Britain's decision to "invite and encourage European settlement" influenced virtually every subsequent development in the colony, including the disposition of African land, labor, and income. Second, colonial policies themselves were instrumental to the shift that occurred toward indigenous black capitalism. In the early period, 1900–1930, the basic evidence is that European settlers, with the aid of the state, retarded indigenous capitalism.[38] However, from 1930–1963 the tide changed and the state and the settlers allowed indigenous capitalism to grow, albeit slowly. The 1929–1935 depression created the need to have Africans producing export crops and paying more taxes. This shift gave rise to an African middle class, which took on many of the values and techniques of the more successful settlers. In particular the indigenous middle class embraced capital accumulation as a good idea and the entrepreneurial spirit as the attending ethic. Real capital accumulation for Africans was not to occur until after independence, but capitalism was under way in the 1930s.

Third, the most important single set of decisions underscoring Kenyan capitalism came in the 1950s regarding land registration and land title. When African nationalist leaders during negotiations with Britain accepted the point that existing land arrangements, that is, private ownership, be retained, they essentially accepted the capitalistic system that goes with private forms of ownership and production.

Finally, the collective settler decision to depart peacefully was crucial to capitalism. For Europeans who had farmed in Kenya for years to be enticed, without violence, to give up their family farms for cash payouts is one of the most remarkable achievements of the independence negotiations. Stability and growth followed for nearly two decades.

Most judgments on the Kenyan colonial era focus heavily on the role of the European settlers, and on what colonialism ultimately did. On both topics the range of judgment is enormous. Were the settlers folk heros or white devils? Was colonialism consummately evil or the harbinger of a new civilization? None of these morality debates has proved very fruitful. The essence of the problem lay in the system, in the colonial structure.

The colonial settlers were neither heroes nor devils. Most were ordinary individuals encased in a larger structure that dictated their behavior. "If they were going to survive as agricultural producers, they had to *take* the land, *coerce* labor, *prevent* peasant production, *bias* the administrative infrastructure and tax system, and *keep* a monopoly on power."[39] The structure of the system set the parameters of settler behavior.

In human terms judgments on the colonial era must be harsh. The pursuit of profit and capitalistic adventure created untold hardships. The subjugation of blacks by whites was extreme, particularly in the taking of land and the exploitation of labor. Five years of Mau-Mau violence was only one by-product.

People in such situations create myths to justify their actions. The great anomaly was that Victorian and Edwardian settlers could so earnestly wrap themselves in myths of moral correctness while remaining largely unaware of what was happening in local African culture. Decisions that carried long-term effects were taken with perilously little knowledge of African society. Blinders occur for different reasons, and in this case part of the settler mentality was the belief that they owned the country. The land represented wealth that had been developed by their own labor, their energy, and their use of technology. In their view, the land was theirs because they had paid for it within colonial rules. But these rules had their origin in Europe, not Africa. The rules set the structure, and the structure dictated the behavior of both whites and blacks.

What, then, did the colonial system ultimately do? Basically the eighty years were a transfer process, a cultural steamrolling that broke down a great deal of the indigenous society and made way for new social and economic patterns.

The process carried high costs in human suffering and cultural decimation. At the same time the colonial structure ultimately left behind some basic accomplishments that helped Kenyans gain new skills. Political awareness was certainly planted by the educational system. In fact, colonialism sowed the seeds of its own demise by encouraging the educational process as it did. African protests, petitions, strikes, and boycotts were led by men educated to what democracy and self-determination were all about.

Given the racial turbulence within the cultural transfer process, it is amazing that the entrepreneurial spirit embued by Europeans was accepted lock, stock, and barrel by Kenyans. Except by pastoralists, the quest for prosperity was never questioned as the basic ethic. It is also amazing that political hostilities between Europeans and Africans were repairable enough to make the independence period as racially tranquil as it was to be. The ability of African leaders to forgive and forget was a part of the largesse of Kenyan blacks, far more charitable in this regard than either Asians or Europeans.

Times change, and acceptable behavior in one period, indeed expected behavior, becomes unbelievable in a later era. There is nothing unique in one system's control of another; it had occurred in Kenya since earliest times, involving Africans, Arabs, and Europeans, particularly in the quest for profits and the control of land. Judgments on the colonial structure and the settlers will always be mixed. History will probably applaud their accomplishments in agriculture, health, and education and their contributions to Kenya's development. History will also decry the unnecessary suffering, the racism, the profiteering, and the blindness to the African condition.

2

Independence:
The Kenyatta Era

INTRODUCTION

Kenya's independence brought new personalities to the political stage, a new structure of power, new patron-client relations, and an affirmation that the quest for prosperity would be on a capitalist path. Whereas many new nations, such as Tanzania, uprooted their colonial economic patterns, Kenyan leaders continued doing essentially what the Europeans had done. They attempted to find wealth and status via material attainments. As in colonial times, these goals were pursued by competing groups that sought control of resources through access to the top echelons of power.

In the first fifteen years after independence, Kenya was dominated by the commanding presence of Jomo Kenyatta. The political beginning of the era was legalistic, constitutional, and full of pronouncements about government "by rule of law." As Kenyatta consolidated his power, an informal system based on favoritism and nepotism emerged parallel to the legal system. The unchallenged seizure of power by Kenyatta and his "royal family" in the late 1960s became the realpolitik of the time. How this era evolved is important to understand, not only because the political institutions put into place by Kenyatta survived him, but also because Kenyatta's actions directly supported the growth of Kenya's indigenous capitalism. The entrepreneurial ethic spread rapidly after independence. For the elite of the region, politics was a way of prospering, both legally and illegally. For the middle and lower classes, opportunity depended on contacts, skills, and participation in the burgeoning patron-client system.

THE TRANSITION YEARS, 1963–1968

The Kenyatta regime was put to the test militarily and politically before the heady celebrations of independence had completely died away. Violence erupted on Kenya's northeastern borders and quickly escalated into a major crisis. Ethnic Somalis, who had asked repeatedly during independence negotiations to have their grazing lands annexed to Somalia, and who had boycotted the 1963 national elections, began launching guerrilla attacks on Kenyan police posts and trading centers. Initially these attacks were attributed to lawless Somali bandits called *shifta*, but soon it became apparent that military support was coming from Somalia itself. Kenyatta finally declared a state of emergency in the north and began the process of securing the area militarily. It was to be a three-year guerrilla war, a tedious continuous gun battle across the vast, arid frontier.

On January 12, 1964, during the Somali crisis, mutiny occurred in the main Nairobi-based battalion of the Kenyan army. British troops helped Kenyatta restore order, but the mutiny badly shook the regime. Reasons contributing to the uprising were slow promotion of indigenous Kenyans to officer rank, the continued presence of white officers, unfavorable conditions within the ranks, and expectations raised by independence that had gone unfulfilled. In moves that would influence civil-military relations for the next two decades, Kenyatta improved barracks conditions and promoted indigenous Kenyans faster. He also infiltrated all services with intelligence personnel who were to alert civilian authorities of any intrigue, and he brought members of the KANU Youth League into army service, thus fostering an element of partisan loyalty to himself and to party members within the ranks. In brief, Kenyatta's moves discouraged the military from again challenging civilian rule.

During 1964 most KADU members, including its leaders, left the party and joined KANU. KADU was later disbanded. Also during this period basic differences between the political left and the political right in Kenya began to surface. Vice-President Oginga Odinga, a political ally of Kenyatta earlier in the independence struggle, assumed leadership of the ideological left stating at one point that "communism is like food to me." As Kenyatta increasingly took anticommunist stands, their collision became inevitable. In June 1965, Kenyatta publicly denounced "communist imperialism" and shortly thereafter reshuffled his cabinet to reduce Odinga's power.

The policy differences between the two camps were based on fundamental disagreement as to who should govern at levels just below the president, how political power should be distributed among dominant groups, and who should control access to opportunities in the modernized sector of the economy. Political differences ran basically along ethnic lines—Odinga found most of his support among Luo and Luhya peoples, Kenyatta among central highlands Kikuyu, Meru, Embu, and Kamba. Ethnicity was not the only determinant, however, and both leaders had supporters in the opposite camps. For example, Tom Mboya, a Luo, was also one of Kenyatta's allies. Supporting Kenyatta was a ruling group of Kikuyu, many of whom were from his home district of Kiambu. The Odinga-led Luo dissenters disagreed with Kenyatta over the centralizing elitism they saw developing—the "Kikuyuization" of the bureaucracy—and over what they perceived as Kenyatta's autocratic control of the economy. Odinga called for nonalignment and accused Kenyatta of close pro-Western corporate connections and of showing little interest in the welfare of the poor.

Throughout 1965–1966, the struggle that went on was characterized by continuous jockeying for position and speech making within the ranks of KANU. Finally Kenyatta, increasingly irritated with the situation, called a national party meeting in March 1966 "to set the mischiefmakers straight." He dominated the meeting and quickly drove KANU's left wing out of the party. Even the moderate leftists who remained with KANU eventually lost their positions.

Odinga responded by resigning from the government and forming an opposition party, the Kenya People's Union (KPU). In the political reshuffling that followed, twenty-nine KANU Members of Parliament left KANU to join the KPU. Kenyatta tolerated opposition during the next two years, but finally in 1968 he moved again. First Odinga was implicated in receiving communist funds with intent to cause national unrest. Bildad Kaggia and other KPU leaders were arrested and detained "for holding a public meeting without a license." Although outcries against the move and against the preventive detention law were heard even from moderate quarters, the purge went on. KPU candidates were disqualified as candidates for election as they had allegedly filled out election forms incorrectly. By the end of 1968 the KPU was declared to have insufficient seats to be an official opposition. In essence, the KPU was driven from the political scene by sheer presidential power, and Kenya became a de facto one-party state.

At this point the Kenyatta government had fully consolidated its power. A single-party system loyal to Kenyatta was in place, and the constitution had been modified to allow a centralized administration. Kenyatta's political opposition had been routed at least temporarily, new contacts with the West opened, and a pro-capitalist philosophy made explicit. In essence, Jomo Kenyatta had centralized the system around himself, and his political personality had become clear. Kenyatta was a master politician and tactician—a man able to be flexible and forgiving at times, but unbending or ruthless when he thought it appropriate. He was without ideological or deep philosophical intent and was not drawn into the great social debates swirling around Africa. Unlike his neighbor, Julius Nyerere in Tanzania, Kenyatta articulated no particular social philosophy. In the early years of independence he showed little interest in Pan-African or international issues that would necessitate globe-trotting diplomacy. The basic reason may have been simply his intense dislike of flying.

Kenyatta's ruling style fascinated political analysts. Henry Bienen described him during this period as one who "has ruled above party by manipulating factions, working through a relatively strong civil service, operating in a rather narrow sphere of concerns, utilizing his ethnic base, but at the same time appealing to all Kenyans with the force of his historical position as 'He who suffered for the Kenya Nation' as the spokesman for Kenya nationalism, as the *Mzee* or Elder of the

Jomo Kenyatta, president of Kenya, 1963–1978 (courtesy the *Daily Nation*)

nation."[1] Perhaps more than any other East African leader Kenyatta actively cultivated the "Father of the Nation" image and built upon the aura of his office. Whether at that stage he could have been called truly charismatic, even in his home area, is debatable, but there was no question as to his mass following and great crowd appeal. Doubts and disenchantment were almost a decade away.

During the early years Kenyatta's personal position on two major issues became clear. He was an African capitalist who would guide Kenya in that direction and rely on a trusted civil service to be the backbone of his regime. The civil service remained loyal to the president because of the status involved and the material rewards. To make this system work Kenyatta expanded the bureaucracy, gave it prestige, and called upon it to lead, to sacrifice, and above all to be loyal. "African socialism" was talked about as a guiding philosophy but soon became an empty slogan, replaced by Kenyatta's pragmatism and entrepreneurial approach. Taking their cue from the top leadership, civil servants engaged increasingly in outside business interests. Simultaneously, independent black businessmen and traders grew in numbers and took their place in the middle class. The two groups fused and formed an economic patron-client system that derived power and resources from the government and garnered support from clients in exchange for a share of the resources.

On the central issue of capitalism, Kenyatta was unwavering. On other policy matters, however, there is little evidence that Kenyatta himself articulated any particular policy. As long as the economic party line was followed, events took their own course or were directed by others in the president's name. The oft-reported pragmatism of the Kenyatta regime was more accurately "disjointed incrementalism," a no-policy policy that operated by dealing with issues as they arose. Kenyatta usually reacted to events largely without offering detailed policies or advanced planning. This system worked because much was done in Kenyatta's name and because of a strong consensus among the elite that capitalism was good for everyone and an ideal way to seek prosperity. For the common folk there were the standard speeches designed to unify the nation, but in fact the rural masses acquiesced because of the expected benefits of the growing patron-client network. Most local neighborhood leaders either received token rewards or were promised some reward via friends (although some were so far from the national resource center that they had little access to its rewards).

Three possible factors may be suggested as to why Kenyatta chose capitalism. First, he was a traditionalist, a conservative man by nature who constantly sought accommodation between the traditional African way and the European colonial way. It would have been out of character for him to break with accommodations he had reached earlier. Second, Kenyatta was away during the nationalist struggle and missed most of the arguments that called for a radical new economic order. In fact, the most distinctive element in Kenyatta's early years was his absence from Kenya's political scene. From 1931 to 1946 he was in England and Europe; from 1952 to 1960 he was in detention in Kenya. While living in Europe he visited the Soviet Union on two occasions. Whatever the experience, Kenyatta was not enamored of the system or ideologically inclined to advocate Soviet Marxism in an African milieu, although this attitude may have sprung more from his personal discomfort in the Soviet Union and lack of contacts than from political philosophy. Finally, Kenyatta may have had procapitalist leanings by virtue of his age. As he was older than most leaders when he came to power, he may have been more willing to accept the economic status quo and less disposed to initiate radical changes. Many of his contemporaries in the older generation of nationalists had similar attitudes, notably Hastings Banda and Felix Houphouet-Boigny. Younger presidents like Julius Nyerere were less staid in outlook, less traditional, less inclined to accommodate an old system, and more willing to embrace change.[2]

Looking back at the 1960s, overall political stability was Kenyatta's main achievement. This stability was accomplished either through design or happenstance, by carrying out some land reform in the highlands, by controlling the provincial administration, by neutralizing opposition, by attracting economic aid from abroad, by keeping the support of the middle economic classes through appeals to their vested interests, and by keeping the politically restive Kikuyu loyal to him and working for the regime. He effectively curtailed the military by keeping the army small and by penetrating the ranks with informants. His patron-client system worked through a combination of favoritism and repression.[3] A buoyant world economy and a steady pace of Africanization in trade and in government also aided stability. Opposition, whether it surfaced within Kikuyuland or elsewhere, was not tolerated. Opponents were either integrated into the system or dispatched by economic intimidation, threats, denunciation, or occasionally by detention.

Formal Political Processes

As the early Kenyatta years passed, it became apparent that a push-pull process was under way between formal "government" institutions that were inherited from the British and informal political processes that were based on ethnic origin, patronage, and economic status. The formal system—the executive, judiciary, administrative, and other branches of government—continued as bureaucratic entities and indeed employed nearly 80 percent of all those who worked for wages in Kenya. At the same time, other institutions that had been set up to reach the people, such as the political party, unions, farmer cooperatives, and local government councils, were either falling into disuse as was the case for the party and unions or were becoming ineffectual because of corruption and poor fiscal control. Their functions were either abandoned or carried on through indigenous organizations such as local churches, the *Harambee* self-help movement, or informal self-interest groups.

Nearly every formal structure of government was changed in the 1963–1968 period to accommodate Kenyatta's desire to centralize power around himself. Some of the most important alterations are described below.

Constitutional Changes. Kenya's Independence Constitution set up a two-house system based on a federal or regional concept that incorporated elected regional assemblies.[4] Kenyatta and his supporters bridled against this system, and in May 1965 an Amendment Act passed Parliament that made it possible to change the constitution by a 65 percent vote of both houses. In December 1966 a major change occurred when the two houses were joined to form a unicameral national assembly; in addition, regionalism was abandoned in favor of a centralized system. This early independence period was also characterized by other testing of and tinkering with the constitutional process. In 1969 a new version of the constitution made explicit the changes that had occurred since 1965.

The only encumbrance to the basic freedoms guaranteed in the "Bill of Rights" came in 1966 with the establishment of a preventive detention law, providing that a person may be "restricted in his movements" if the government's Home Affairs Ministry is satisfied that this is necessary for preservation of public security. Critics have pointed out that there are no limits to this power and "public security" has remained ill-defined. Nor is the government even compelled to reveal the charges against a person being detained. The detainee is not allowed communication rights or automatic recourse to the courts. With a few notable exceptions, Kenyatta himself did not use these powers of detention.

Executive Changes. By using both the symbols of office and the aura that surrounded the presidency, Kenyatta was able to adapt the executive branch to serve his political goals and effectively protect his regime. By law, the Office of the President is vested with sweeping powers. He is head of state, head of the central government and civil service, commander of the armed forces, and the single nominee of the ruling party. His maximum term of office is five years, but he may be re-elected. He has the discretion to appoint any vice-president he chooses. In Kenyatta's case there were three vice-presidents: Oginga Odinga, 1963–1966, who resigned to lead the opposition party; Joseph Murumbi, 1966–1967, who resigned for health reasons; and Daniel arap Moi, 1967–1978, who became interim president at Kenyatta's death and thereafter president.[5]

Kenyatta also had the right to choose his cabinet, which included the vice-president (already noted), the attorney general, and the appointed heads of each government ministry. The only requirement was that ministers must be selected from elected Members of Parliament. During most of the Kenyatta years there were twenty ministers and some twenty-five assistant ministers whom the president also appointed. Through these appointments he controlled the bureaucracy and, often, Parliament.

Civil Service Changes. Kenyatta's pragmatism was revealed early in his relationship with the government administration. In his early years he moved decisively to crystallize power around the central administration and to make it a highly professional, loyal service. As the titular head of the Public Service Commission, Kenyatta had pervasive power. The commission could make appointments, set pay scales, administer discipline, and when deemed necessary, dismiss personnel.[6] The central administrative apparatus encompasses six levels of government. Below the Office of the President are seven provinces, forty districts, and, within each district, divisions, locations, and sublocations, each staffed by civil servants. Kenya's entire territory falls under this central government structure,[7] although from the district level downward, there is a local government system based on elected councils. Kenyatta's control over both these sectors, all the way through to the appointment of top ministers, remained unchallenged throughout his reign.

Local Government Changes. At the time of independence the local government structure was similar to that in Britain, made up of both a district (rural) council and urban councils. All were controlled by laws enacted by Parliament as overseen by the Ministry of Local Government; all were separate from the central administration, although overlapping it at the district level. Councils had permanent administrative staff, as well as elected counselors, ostensibly representing constituents in wards or small neighborhoods. A council's responsibility varied according to its size and financial resources, but originally, at independence, included local road maintenance, primary school operations, sanitary inspection, food and market regulation, licensing, trade regulations, and the like. Revenue was obtained from local taxes, license fees, and grants from the central government. It was in these financial areas that councils ran into difficulty, particularly because of inadequate bookkeeping, loss of council funds by peculation, and theft of council supplies. Beginning in 1968, council budgets were taken over by the central government and their overall powers reduced.

Another difficulty that led Kenyatta to curtail council activity was the seemingly incessant political conflict between local government counselors elected to the various councils and the MPs who represented the same constituents. MPs tended to assume that their powers were supreme, and they freely used their wealth and connections in the capital. But friction with local government counselors often resulted. Other local conflicts centered on small-scale illegalities and favoritism by counselors, examples of which were pointed to by central government officials as a poor way to govern.

Kenyatta's critics pointed out that curtailing council activities undercut basic political rights. The centralization of government increased the distance between people and government. By 1969 the local councils had become powerless "talking groups" left in place simply as a government hand-wave at democratic representation. The central government assumed most of their functions, particularly in rural areas and small towns, and local council funds were increasingly controlled by the central bureaucracy.

Political Party Changes. Aside from the occasional electoral function, KANU was used by Kenyatta in two basic ways: first, to rally support for some cause or in response to some crisis, and second, to "point politicians toward Nairobi"—in essence to help Kenyatta take political activity out of the hands of local politicians and place it under central government control.[8] Except for these functions, the party was largely moribund.

In Kenyatta's early years KANU was in debt, its headquarters disorganized and poorly managed, and it was ignored by the central administration. The 1966 party conference, aside from Kenyatta's move to set the mischiefmakers (party left wingers) straight, was a response to public criticism that the party system was meaningless, and thereafter the party structure was modified to include a national office, an annual conference, and a local branch structure in each district. After 1968, when Kenya became a de facto single-party system, KANU languished as a loose, balloon-like system that could be activated in periods of crisis, for elections, or at times of national celebration. Otherwise the party has become dormant, its local offices padlocked and unused.

The official view of the political party during Kenyatta's years was quite different from the reality. KANU was supposed to be a monolithic, unified organization that worked closely with the government. A key objective of Kenyatta was for the public to see the party as a unified and solid organization, and for open opposition to the party to be prohibited. In essence, the party became the united front behind which political struggles were waged.

Other government institutions and political organizations also underwent changes in these transition years. For example, the judiciary, which was set up at independence to be totally separated from the executive and legislative branches, remained so, but was structurally altered by the Judicative Act of 1967.[9] Political organizations such as the Kenya Farmers Association, the Central Organization of Trade Unions (COTU), the Kenya National Chamber of Commerce (KNCC), and the Federation of Kenya Employees continued to operate as special interest groups but had their power visibly curtailed whenever they opposed any of the president's initiatives.

Informal Political Processes

During the early Kenyatta years an informal political system emerged, partially in reaction to the curtailment of the legitimate political structures. The informal system was fragmented, ill-defined, and largely of a grass-roots nature. Some of the informal political institutions include the *Harambee* self-help movement, local welfare unions, and independent and denominational churches. Moreover, in some areas an invisible *sotto governo* ("under government") essentially ran things. Here the line between legality and illegality often blurred, particularly when self-interest groups formed around a patron who had economic ties to Nairobi.

Of the more open activities, the *Harambee* movement was the most widespread as a substitute political system. *Harambee* means "pull together"; it was both a rallying cry used by Kenyatta and a money-raising system for local self-help projects such as schools, dispensaries, or community centers. Over 50 percent of the *Harambee* projects were educational in nature, mainly concerned with building schools. Before the Kenyatta era ended, thousands of completed projects dotted the Kenyan landscape.

Harambee projects relied on local contributions of money and volunteer labor. In return for doing the construction, many groups extracted promises from the government to staff the enterprises when they were completed. The movements for these projects became political because they involved "big men" in local affairs, extracted funds from the elite for peasant use, and helped achieve community consensus and participation. As Frank Holmquist notes, "They gave the peasants political space." The *Harambee* projects, like the churches, were a free zone in which individuals and politicians could safely interact. They were "good things" to do.[10]

Harambee schemes were also a substitute for many of the mass-based institutions that had been undermined by Kenyatta's centralizing tendencies. The party, cooperative societies, labor unions, and local councils had come under the regime's control. Self-help schemes like charity picnics, were local, and politicians who needed political support were advised to show up and contribute. The schemes flourished partly because Kenyatta engineered them as checks and balances on local MPs who were obliged to pay attention to their local constituencies. The process became one of political brokerage. As villagers began projects all over the country, the result was that they co-opted—often entrapped—

the local elite and forced elected MPs to be concerned not only about a specific project but also many other social issues.

Kenyatta also encouraged the *Harambee* movement as an alternative to an unruly Parliament, in essence saying to the MPs that they should "go build the country, for it is in this way the people will judge you." Another interpretation of Kenyatta's support of *Harambee* was that the MPs should stay out of national politics, spend less time in Nairobi, and leave the centralization of power to the president. In short, *Harambee* became an avenue that neither the party nor other institutions provided to people.[11]

Welfare unions provided other political outlets. The Akamba Union, the Luo Union, GEMA (Gikikuyu, Embu, Meru Association) all were organizations that provided ethnic protection through solidarity in jockeying politically for resources allocated from higher authority. Similarly, churches in the Kenyatta era played an informal political role, although largely through the process of discussion, song, and social ventilation. In western Kenya, where access to Nairobi's resources was diminished by distance, independent churches served as mutual support groups. As for denominational churches, with the appointment of Kenyan bishops and higher officials, the Anglican and Catholic churches in particular became more political in that they had international resources as well as missionary networks that helped to influence parishioners.

In both denominational and independent churches, an element of escapism existed in the suggestion from sermons that the here and now are meaningless, that the situation of one's life should be accepted until one's just reward could be realized in the hereafter. Although not directly political, such messages did tend to de-radicalize churchgoers and reduce dissent. Because Kenyatta was not active in the church it was not a particular avenue to power, as it was in the newly independent Congo, former French territories, and some Latin American states.

The more invisible form of local politics in Kenya was the *sotto governo*, a loose network of local politicians and influentials who operated beyond the government, party, or other official process. These grassroots groups involved traditional political leaders, well-off landowners, traders, and shopkeepers and prominent farmers, plus, in some cases, young entrepreneurs—all brought together and organized ostensibly as social or sports clubs. As groups they may not have had the power to initiate changes from the top, but could block and negate government initiatives from below.

In Kikuyuland, a *sotto governo* phenomenon had existed for decades, often based on the *mbare* or clan system of settlement spread along ridges of the upland terrain. Village-level self-protection was one of the goals. The alliance was largely of older, landholding families who continued to be influential, with younger, entrepreneurial families who had ties to the new business networks, particularly through the local cooperatives and the trading and transportation systems. Similar alliances in western Kenya included African church leaders and local preachers. Some of the prominent men had informal links to business interests in

Nairobi: a function of these ongoing *sotto governo* systems was to tie the grass-roots interests to broader political and commercial concerns. Such systems were the local base of individuals who were influential through claimed or real ties to "big men" closer to the Nairobi power base. The lowest level of the patron-client system tied small communities in a series of leap-frog links to the metropolitan center of power. The crucial element was the use by clients of a patron's connection to higher influentials, a form both of self-help and protection. These alliances that existed outside the government or party structure were the real base of politics of a small community.

The informal political processes had an illegal side that, when active at the grass-roots level, took on a nefarious character. Extortion, theft, and influence-buying were one dimension. Other illegal political activities that reached public attention—the press or the government—included the holding of banned political meetings (particularly among Oginga Odinga's supporters), licensing violations, local bureaucratic illegalities, favoritism in government appointments, nepotism and bribery in letting government contracts, subversion of the customs and excise laws, and the occasional exposure of MPs in illegal business activities.[12]

THE MIDDLE YEARS, 1969-1974

Kenyatta's rule in the period between 1969 and 1974 was characterized by a recession and major drought, new oil price uncertainties, and ongoing land problems. Politically, all of these problems were overshadowed by the nation's worst national crisis, stemming from the assassination of Tom Mboya, the Luo nationalist leader. Mboya, the ally of Kenyatta and in 1969 both minister of economic planning and secretary general of the ruling KANU party, had risen to power as a politician with support across ethnic lines. His power lay in his early trade union contacts, in his Nairobi base of operations, which gave him a trans-ethnic constituency, and in his exceptional organizational abilities. In all he was a serious contender for Kenya's presidency should Kenyatta pass from the scene. As Kenyatta's health and age became an issue, so, too, did concerns about the succession. Kikuyu politicians in particular were worried that power would go to a non-Kikuyu, or worse, a non-Kikuyu from one of the largest rival ethnic groups.

During this period the struggle beneath Kenyatta for his favor and for lucrative priorities in the new economic order was particularly fierce. Since the KPU and the Luo-based Odinga opposition had been banned in 1968, a scramble to fill the vacancies had occurred, particularly among competing Kikuyu politicians. Factions formed and reformed; so, too, did periodic tension within the ranks of the Kikuyu. The basic dispute was over who controlled power and resources in Kikuyuland, but its ferocity spilled into the national scene and provided added tensions to the succession issue.

Mboya's genius was in bridging national factions and in weaving alliances between otherwise competing groups. By 1969 he was truly

Tom Mboya, labor leader and government minister assassinated in 1969 (courtesy the *Daily Nation*)

a national politician, appealing for unity across ethnic lines and serving as a linchpin between factions. His Luo heritage, however, made him an outsider in Kikuyu subethnic politics and a serious threat if his broad appeal hid serious presidential aspirations.

On July 5, 1969, as he stepped from a shop in downtown Nairobi, Mboya was shot and killed by an African assassin. Within hours rioting and violence broke out in pockets of Nairobi and in Kisumu, the main Luo city in western Kenya. Four days later, when President Kenyatta arrived at the Nairobi cathedral to attend the requiem mass for Mboya, his car was stoned by a crowd shouting *"dume!"* (bull), the symbol of the ousted KPU opposition party. Government police dispersed the crowd with tear gas and baton charges, but in the melee two people died, sixty were hospitalized, and three hundred arrested. To that point it was the worst rioting the new nation had experienced.

The burning question was who killed Mboya. On July 21, sixteen days after the assassination, a Kikuyu, Nahashon Isaac Njenga Njoroge, was charged in court with the murder. He was duly tried, found guilty, and reportedly hanged.[13] In the meanwhile, Mboya's assassination had led to ongoing ethnic tensions, particularly between the Luo and the Kikuyu, who then dominated the central government.

In November 1969, apparently in an attempt to appease the Luo, Kenyatta traveled to their homeland to ceremonially open a major hospital in Kisumu. Another violent crisis was to ensue. During his speech he was repeatedly heckled by KPU youth wingers. He reacted by delivering "an angry, curse-laden personal attack on Odinga"—who was seated a few feet away—that included a warning to the Luo that "we are going to crush you into the floor."[14] As the presidential convoy began to leave the area, Kenyatta's car was showered with stones. His personal bodyguards reacted by shooting into the crowd with automatic weapons, reportedly killing eleven and injuring seventy-eight. The unofficial count was higher.

The political outcome of the Kisumu incident was surprising. Rather than inciting the Luo to anti-government uprisings, the crowd killings led to widespread shock and withdrawal. One reason for the reaction may have been the age-old Luo respect for authority, a tradition that would have called for Kenyatta, the Elder, to be treated with respect and to be considered quite justified in administering discipline to unruly youth.

If 1969 was a year of bloodshed, it was also a year in which Kenyatta bound up wounds and tried to accommodate political dissent. Political tension following the Kisumu incident eased when Kenyatta quickly initiated electoral reforms that affected the Luo directly. Nominations for the December 1969 elections for Parliament were reopened to all comers by a decree that candidates could be selected in local primaries. The new decree permitted dissenters to enter the political process if they would simply register as KANU candidates. Most of the detained KPU members were released and permitted to join KANU and stand for election.

Kenyatta's new electoral initiatives were accepted across the country in an astounding reaffirmation of the electoral process: 700 candidates contested the 158 seats in fierce electioneering debates. The outcome was a form of political cleansing. Over 40 percent of the incumbent MPs were defeated, including five cabinet ministers.

Aside from the Mboya crisis, the 1969–1974 period was characterized by political activity in three areas that would resurface in the contemporary period: ethnicity, student issues, and civil-military relations. Ethnicity had always been an important factor in Kenyan politics, but by 1972 two major issues had surfaced that demanded presidential attention. The dominance of Kikuyu people in government was such as to trigger serious complaints from non-Kikuyu. One study showed that in 1972 the Kikuyu, then 20 percent of the population, held 41 percent of the senior government offices. By contrast, the Luo, at that time the second-largest ethnic group with 18 percent of the population, held only 8.6 percent of the senior offices.[15]

Kenyatta's official response to the criticisms was largely symbolic. Secretaries at the University of Nairobi were instructed not to answer the telephones in the Kikuyu language, the "unified nation" speech was made more often, and token appointments of non-Kikuyu were made to government posts. Probably most effective was Kenyatta's pointing to his cabinet as multi-ethnic, a cabinet that symbolized each citizen's entry to higher government, although in fact the Kikuyu "subcabinet" continued to make decisions.

The Asian question was another ethnic matter. Kenya's Asians had long been a mercantile middle class that had remained aloof from African society. As the drive to "Africanize" Kenya picked up speed, Asian tradesmen became the targets of politicians. The main restriction was to exclude Asians who did not hold Kenyan citizenship from trade license renewals. Greater restrictions were debated but not carried out, largely because the constitution protected all citizens, including Asians and other minorities such as Arabs and Europeans.[16] In addition, Kenyatta's capitalistic philosophy protected Asian citizens of Kenya from greater harassment, although in response to political pressures the government made it clear that nationalized citizens could be deprived of their Kenya passports on grounds of "disloyalty." How disloyalty was to be defined was never made clear—an ambiguity that effectively curtailed Asian political expression.

Student relations with the Kenyatta government were markedly more contentious after the 1969 Mboya assassination. Kenyatta, as chancellor of the University of Nairobi, was in a position not only to lecture the students on proper behavior but also to deny degrees and, if necessary, close the university. Constraints were also maintained on students by the formation of a KANU student branch, by appointment of Kikuyu loyalists to higher posts in the university, and by the promise of jobs after graduation. Nevertheless, a series of student protests followed the Mboya assassination, particularly centering on the government's decision not to allow former Vice-President Oginga Odinga to speak at the University of Nairobi campus. The university was closed, students sent home, and prominent leaders not readmitted until they agreed to abandon their protest. Kenyatta's willingness to use force contained student protest for the moment. More serious ruptures were to come over scholarship-support issues and other crises, but in the early 1970s Kenyatta's power held sway.

Civil-military relations came to the fore in March 1971, when an alleged coup d'etat by a group of Luo, Kamba, and Kalenjin military plotters was stopped by the government. Thirteen men were brought to trial, including three who had escaped to Tanzania and then were extradited. The trial tainted several higher officials, including Kenya's chief justice and the army chief of staff. Neither was prosecuted, although both resigned. The convicted plotters were jailed amid long speeches about the proper role of the military and the importance of loyalty to the state.

In conjunction with the army mutiny of 1964, this event led to concern that Kenya was indeed drifting into a situation in which a military government could replace Kenyatta either before or just after he might pass from the political scene. Kenyatta sensed this and caused a number of preventive steps to be taken. These steps were to keep the army small, increase the "intelligence system" within the ranks, make the pay and benefits more attractive, and maintain the British advisory role.[17]

Decade of Land Politics

Undoubtedly, Jomo Kenyatta's great challenge in his first decade as president involved land issues. By 1974, when Kenya looked back on ten years of rough-and-tumble land politics, the basic judgments could be made: land policies had been a political success, in that many of the landless had obtained farms. Economically, however, the break-up of the big European farms for African settlers had caused declines in agricultural production.

The original plan for the transfer of the 2,750 large European farms had proceeded relatively peacefully, and in fact the process was applauded as an enlightened way to end colonialism. The British and Kenyan governments did indeed stand behind their commitment to buy out the Europeans. The costs were high. The government purchase of European farms totaled $28 million, of which $25 million departed from Kenya. The cost of converting estates to African ownership was an additional $30 million.[18]

The land that was purchased by the government for redistribution fell into the category of private freehold land. Nearly all the European farms that were converted to African use were in the highlands, although private freehold property existed at the coast and in other parts of Kenya. Four categories of farms were designated for African use according to their potential productivity: high-density farms, low-density farms, cooperative farms or ranches, and state farms.

Kenyatta's decision to open the large farms to resettlement was a calculated political undertaking. Given the resentment over landlessness in Kenya at the time, the move was undoubtedly necessary, but problems were foreseen not only in the anticipated short-term losses in production, but also in the transition process itself. In fact, a whole new land system was being put into place. Customary African land-tenure practices were being replaced by a system of land titles that were bought or acquired from the government and no longer acquired from the clan or through traditional rights of usage. The title registrations, surveys, and legal processes were costly, and some litigation was to continue for years. Because loans were given in a mortgage-like system, defaulters could lose their land at auction, a system contrary to the traditional land tenure that protected individuals.

Other human problems plagued the system. Most farmers coming to the high-density farms had been not only landless, but unemployed and inexperienced in modern farm techniques. Nearly all lacked capital. Their entry into the system was based on human need, not on economic realities. Indebtedness was enormous, and most of the farmers were forced to borrow to the full value of their land. Yet if the risks were great, so were the potential rewards. Among the new smallholders, some began to prosper.

By 1966 it became obvious that the larger settlement schemes were not financially viable, and that unless default on loans could somehow be redressed, the Kenya government faced a major financial crisis. One of the solutions was to tighten financial management on farms; another was to keep several large-scale European holdings intact, to be run as large state farms. These state farms were operated by government managers who hired farm labor on a wage basis, usually allowing workers to have access to small, two- or three-acre plots for private farming.

By 1973, Kenya's almost 25 million acres of usable agricultural land had been distributed as more than 17 million acres in seven African reserves, where the great majority of African smallholders had individual freehold titles, and almost 7.5 million acres in the former white highlands. Of the latter, settlement schemes accounted for 1.5 million acres, mixed farms sold to Africans more than 2.2 million acres, and more than 3.7 million acres remained as plantations. Overall, smallholder production had exploded since independence, not only because of the land arrangement, but also because new, profitable crops were available, as were extension services and state credit, particularly to progressive farmers. "In short, land hunger, which was quite severe in central Kenya at independence, had been assuaged by the settlement schemes; smallholder incomes were increased; the white farmers had been bought out with over a third of their mixed farms retained for African-owned capitalist farming, to which large subsidies continued to be given; while the plantation and ranch sector was left undisturbed."[19]

It is not difficult to find criticisms of such a tumultuous process, even from Kenyatta himself. The setup and management of the farms was exceptionally difficult for the settlement boards. Among African settlers, boundary disputes, defaulting, contract failures, and litigation were common; among local managers, bookkeeping errors, petty theft, and misuse of funds were constant problems.

Another problem lay in the decision to allow 1.6 million acres of large holdings to remain intact and be sold or transferred to wealthy Africans. Elitism and nepotism charges were leveled against Kenyatta and the settlement managers. Critics particularly pointed out that the larger farms did not provide land for the landless or increase farm employment; in some cases production dropped significantly. Some of the most stinging criticism was directed to absentee landlord practices. It was suggested that the "perks" of being an elite farmer included farm credit, extension research, and even farm price controls. Parallels to the government services to European farmers in the colonial years were invariably drawn. During this time the International Labour Office produced a major study entitled *Employment, Incomes, and Equality: A Strategy for Increasing Productive Employment in Kenya* (Geneva, 1972; hereafter ILO Report). The report recognized the problem and the criticisms and suggested a redistribution of larger lands into more labor-intensive units with a greater focus on poor families. The government's response was noncommittal.[20]

A problem already mentioned lay in the loss of productivity of some of the large European estates when they were broken up for African settlement and a few were kept intact under state management for this reason. Some economists in Kenya, and many European settlers, argued that all or most should be kept intact under African management, a situation that would allow continued large-scale production and thus more revenue for Kenya. Those who understood the political necessity of the process agreed with the policy but were critical of the new management provided by the settlement board. The most critical judgments were levied at the upper echelons of power who commandeered large farms for themselves before these farms could be divided for the poor or made into cooperative farms. Some of the farms were well-run, some were not. Most were managed for the black elite by hired managers, sometimes under subcontract to European farmers. This pattern was to continue throughout the Kenyatta era.

Despite the difficulties, toward the end of 1973 the plan was heralded as at least a moderate success. Some 12 million acres had been systematically reorganized into over 650,000 holdings.[21] Large areas of the highlands were transferred into private farms that gradually had increased in production. Crops like tea, tobacco, coffee, pyrethrum, and pineapples were taken up by thousands of small farmers. Livestock on these farms was upgraded with new strains, new breeding techniques, and improved veterinarian services.

Between 1958 and 1967 the total cash revenue accruing to African smallholders, including those in settlement projects, from both market crops and livestock rose from K£ 7.6 million to K£ 34.04 million in current prices, or from K£ 7.4 to K£ 23.8 million in constant 1956 prices.[22] Although these aggregate figures do not indicate how farm income was divided individually, many Kenyans prospered. If the population growth rate had not been so high, a greater success could have been claimed. Political stability had been maintained, and significantly, by 1973 over half of all African customary forms of land tenure in Kenya had been switched to a system based on freehold title. Most important, the increase in smallholder production that had occurred established a large sector of the farm society as small-time entrepreneurs whose quest for prosperity was beginning to be rewarded.

THE LATER YEARS: A TURBULENT MONARCHY

The years 1974–1978 were characterized by the entrenchment of the Kenyatta family as a potent political force. After his release from detention Kenyatta had remarried. His wife, Mama Ngina, had already acquired a substantial economic domain and was actively expanding it to include large tracts of uncultivated land and working farms, plus businesses involving road transport, ivory, wildlife trophies, and mining. As the state system drew closer to that of a monarchy, nepotism became commonplace, with kinship ties to the "king" as the most important

Mama Ngina Kenyatta, wife of
the president (courtesy the *Daily
Nation*)

single factor. A large number of extended family members and others
profited by their favored positions.

During this period Kenyatta's age and health were topics of constant
discussion. Despite widespread predictions that turmoil could engulf
Kenya when Kenyatta passed, the president refused to groom an heir
or to show any concern for what would happen when he departed.
Suggestions went unheeded that he name a prime minister, which was
a constitutional possibility, and thus use his enormous power to insure
a peaceful transition.

During 1974, criticism of Kenyatta's modus operandi—the nepotism,
favoritism, and in-group corruption—became more open, particularly
as growing economic hardship plagued the country. The oil-based world
recession and a drought beginning in 1973-1974 curtailed growth and
cut severely into the government's promise to improve the lot of the
common man. How long the average citizen would have tolerated the
combination of recession and political corruption will never be known.
Another macabre political assassination plunged the nation into renewed
crisis.

J. M. Kariuki, a flamboyant MP and outspoken critic of the Kenyatta
regime, had for several years been rising in popularity as a political
defender of the poor. An ex-Mau-Mau detainee, and a populist and
inveterate gambler of considerable wealth, Kariuki had risen to become
a powerful MP and eventually leader of the unofficial opposition in
Parliament. Although at one time close to Kenyatta, serving as the
president's secretary, he increasingly disagreed with Kenyatta and the

J. M. Kariuki, Member of Parliament assassinated in 1975 (courtesy the *Daily Nation*)

Kenyatta loyalists, arguing for wider distribution of Kenya's wealth and greater equity for the poor. He was well on the way to becoming a common man's champion and had unquestionably attained a mass-based following.

He was taken from a Nairobi hotel in March 1975 by senior police officers and murdered by unidentified assassins. When his body was found and finally identified, under conditions that suggested a cover-up by the government, student riots broke out, Parliament revolted against the government, and an internal Kikuyu split surfaced openly. Charges of government involvement swept in from several sides.

Jomo Kenyatta, in a move that could well have averted complete turmoil, quickly formed a blue-ribbon commission in Parliament to investigate the murder. This calmed the atmosphere and gained time, but when the commission's report was presented three months later, it rekindled the crisis. The report accused the Kenya police of a massive cover-up and named the commander of the paramilitary Government Service Unit (GSU) as "the person who took an active part in the murder himself or was an accomplice of the actual murderer or murderers." The report went on to ask for the resignations of the commissioner of Kenya's police and the director of its Criminal Investigation Division (CID) because they had refused to cooperate with Parliament or give the commission access to police files.

The report was tabled in Parliament on June 3, 1975. The debate that followed was turbulent, at times vicious, and again led to strong countermeasures by Kenyatta. Those critical of the government who held government positions were simply dismissed, or told to resign. Outspoken John Keen, assistant minister of works, was one of the first. Others were arrested and detained, including Deputy Speaker Martin Shikuku and MPs Mark Mwithaga and John Seroney.

The key element in this second phase of the Kariuki crisis, as in the Kisumu incident following Mboya's assassination, was the unbridled display of power by Kenyatta. As an open warning to Parliament, the arrests of Deputy Speaker Seroney and his colleague Shikuku were carried out in broad daylight during a full parliamentary session. Uniformed police simply marched into the chamber, arrested the MPs, and escorted them out.

In a clear threat to other dissenters, Kenyatta discussed some of the events before a massive audience in his annual Kenyatta Day speech. "The hawk is in the sky," he said. "It is ready to descend on chickens who stray from the pathway." Within a few days open opposition waned. Kenyatta's show of force had won in terms of holding his government together and avoiding further bloodshed. This crisis, however, would plague him until his death.

Probably most damaging to Kenyatta's reputation at the time was a series of revelations about the regime published in the *Sunday Times* of London.[23] Written with detailed inside information, the three-part series first laid out the Kariuki affair, focusing on his threat to the governing elite, the cover-up of his murder, and the power plays used to control the crisis. Details of the extended Kenyatta family landholdings were exposed as a testimony to corruption. The article concluded that the murder could not have occurred without the concurrence of very highly placed people. Articles that followed detailed the landholdings of the "royal" family, particularly the wealth amassed by Kenyatta's wife. Profiteering at the expense of wildlife and the Kenya ecosystem was also examined, using as examples the large-scale ivory poaching and the destruction of many of Kenya's rain forests to make charcoal for sale to the Gulf states of the Arab world.

The articles further suggested that the regime was entangled in corrupt activities, including the acceptance of bribes from European businessmen, and that as a few Kenyans were getting extremely rich, the masses were getting poorer. Parallels to Latin America were drawn. The series concluded that the lesson of the Kariuki affair was straightforward: any opposition that seriously gets in the way of this system will be eliminated.

Officially Kenya reacted with outrage. British diplomats were handed notes of protest, and the articles were denounced as distortions aimed at besmirching the president. A broadside of rhetoric to cleanse Kenyatta's image flowed from the government, and official efforts at national reconciliation were launched. Even during the press revelations no one doubted Kenyatta's continuing ability to protect his central establishment.

Coffee pickers and managers, Thika (courtesy the *Daily Nation*)

Among the factors that helped stabilize the regime after the Kariuki crisis were profits from exceptionally high coffee prices in 1976–1977, following a disastrous frost in Brazil. Because of the world shortage of coffee, not only were enormous profits made on Kenyan coffee, but Kenyans also profited in the illegal transshipment of Ugandan coffee to the coast. So widespread was the smuggling in 1977 that price quotations for Uganda coffee were available on Nairobi streets. A great many coffee barons were made, and a great many other Kenyans profited indirectly from the boom, enough to curtail open political dissent. Not even the collapse of the East African Community in 1977, an event that would close the Kenya-Tanzania border and have long-term economic consequences as noted below, dampened the enthusiasm of the coffee-boom years.

Another internal political event in Kenya during this period was the attempt to change the constitutional provisions regarding presidential succession. According to law, the vice-president automatically assumed the office of president for three months should it fall vacant. Some Kikuyu-led politicians feared that this interregnum would give the vice-president ample opportunity to use presidential power to ensure his own nomination for the office, and they sought measures to bar this possibility. The move was stopped by a coalition of Daniel Moi (then vice-president) and Charles Njonjo, the Attorney General, and finally the support of Kenyatta and his cabinet.

Tea pickers near Kericho (photo by David Keith Jones)

Formal and Informal Economic Processes

As the Kenyatta era drew to a close, the economic realities of the time came into perspective. Although growth had occurred and the economy had been stable, serious problems of unemployment, income distribution, and land shortage existed. Differences between a wealthy elite, a growing middle class, and the rural masses caused a lively debate within the intelligentsia. New problems of corruption were discussed openly in Parliament and in the press. A perceptible rise of the hidden economy, both quasi-legal and clearly illegal, was almost-public knowledge. Nevertheless, in 1978 an expansive atmosphere prevailed among entrepreneurs. Foreign investment continued to flow into Kenya, and foreign aid, both bilateral and multilateral, increased dramatically.[24]

Although in the first decade of Kenyatta's presidency there was reason to applaud Kenya's economic performance in such sectors as coffee, tea, and tourism, there were also ominous signs that the economy had major structural flaws. Confirmation of these problems came in 1972 when the ILO Report recommended major economic reforms that would "spread the wealth, benefit the poor, and open jobs in the rural and 'informal' manufacturing sectors."[25] The report unequivocally stated that the major problem group in Kenya's rapidly growing population was the "working poor," the underemployed and underpaid. Their status, the report said, was related to major inequalities in access to education and other needed facilities such as health care, in differences between geographic regions and social groups, and in inequalities between the sexes.

The Kenya government in 1973 officially accepted the recommendations, but in practice only a few policies changed. The most visible were changes in licensing laws, with less harassment of hawkers and less restriction of the informal manufacturing sector. Probably as a result of the ILO discussions, Kenyatta increased the minimum wage in 1974 and further redistributed settlement-owned farms. The actions served to contain discontent among farmers and urban workers and undoubtedly contributed to the political stability of the time.[26]

Overall, however, the ILO Report was not broadly implemented and the more open economic system it called for was rejected. Although it would have been in the "enlightened self-interest" of the elite to instigate such reforms as long-term protection of their position, such reform did not come, simply because it called for greater sacrifices than the elite deemed necessary.[27] The full reforms would have penalized the elite and middle-income groups in favor of the lower economic strata, apparently an unnecessary sharing of the wealth in the view of Kenyatta's advisors.

Because Kenya was open to field research and because the ILO study had stimulated so many questions, a wave of new data began to appear about income distribution and the nature of economic life among the masses on smallholder farms. Crawford and Thorbecke, for example, assessing urban-rural and modern-nonmodern income, revealed that the urban population of 12 percent earned 30 percent of the national income, and the rural population of 88 percent earned some 70 percent of the national income. Seen in terms of modern versus nonmodern activity over both urban and rural areas, 17 percent of the population were judged to be working in the modern sector, earning 48 percent of the national income, and 83 percent of the population were working in the nonmodern agricultural and "informal" areas, earning 52 percent of the national income.[28]

Another major finding from the smallholder data assessed where farm families actually got their income. An astounding 41 percent of their income was estimated to come from off-farm sources such as migratory work, casual local labor, and other business. This high figure immediately raised two questions. In terms of the class debate, was there a true "peasantry" when only 59 percent of farm income was derived from the farms? Seemingly, rigid stratification of income was not occurring if approximately 40 percent of this group (corresponding to 41 percent of the income as off-farm) were off-farm workers. Second, this economic pattern placed a large burden on urban sources of income that could shrink quickly when recessions occurred. Cushioning resources possibly did not exist on farms to the degree expected by analysts. The conventional wisdom about rural resilience—the ultimate fall-back for the urban unemployed—could in fact be called into question by the data.

If these were perplexing problems for leaders within the Kenyatta regime, little evidence of their concern emerged. Throughout the era the mercantilistic, capitalistic atmosphere was pervasive; class issues were not open to debate. Messages coming from Kenyatta were clear. The national policy was to applaud free enterprise, to allow business expansion wherever possible, and to minimize national control. An occasional hand-wave at equality and proper socialist behavior in the sharing of wealth was made but not taken seriously by the regime. The rise of government partnerships in foreign-owned companies and the growth of government-controlled parastatal bodies tempered the free-enterprise claims.

The reality was that the Kenyatta doctrine was pervasive; anyone venturing into the market economy above the village level would be hard put not to become a capitalist. "Economic pragmatism," "free enterprise," and "innovation" were the economic slogans of the time. The Kenyatta elite had reached an informal consensus on the desirable economic direction and simply took the economy in that direction. Entrepreneurial activity, ranging from small-time gardening in rural areas to big-time gambling in Nairobi, was part of the search for prosperity.

Nevertheless, the economic class and social-equity debate that began in the early 1960s continued throughout Kenyatta's era, particularly at the university. The issues were how the Kenya class structure was differentiated, how wealth was being accumulated, how it was being used, and what was happening to Kenya's masses in economic terms. On the last issue, three basic positions were articulated. The first argued that Kenya was developing along the class lines of a capitalistic state: the wealthy getting wealthier, the poor getting poorer, and a basic class confrontation between them growing probable. The second position was that a "middle peasantry" was emerging in agriculture and in trade that had a modest accumulation of capital and that, being tied to the land, was a stable, acquisitive force that would reduce class tensions. The third position held that no real class confrontation was under way, but rather everyone, including the well-off, faced a downturning economy.

Kenyatta was oblivious to the class debate. When it surfaced as protest, for example at the university or in the Odinga controversy, it was seen as "radicalism" and was dealt with by either overt or covert force. One reason Kenyatta could ignore such issues was that no class-based opposition had surfaced, although J. M. Kariuki may have inspired confrontation had he lived. In place of such confrontation, strong economic alliances existed along ethnic lines. Within the all-important Nairobi urban setting, ethnicity as well as one's education, economic position, place of work, and political aspirations differentiated people. Class-based issues were crosscut by factions that had all kinds of people in them. Factions were more important than classes in the struggle for influence, and they kept forming and re-forming in response to the rewards the regime offered. Those strata that did emerge, the wealthy and the middle class, were never challenged by the rural poor.

Nowhere was Kenyatta's support of capitalism more apparent than in the favored treatment given foreign investors and multinational corporations (MNCs). Even before independence, Kenyatta had reassured investors that the independent Kenya government would not be a "gangster government" or deprive people of their rights and properties, but rather "We will encourage investors to come to Kenya . . . to bring prosperity to this country."[29] The inducements included financial encouragement, loans, equity participation arrangements, joint state-private undertakings, and other forms of subsidies. The Foreign Investment Protection Act of 1964 guaranteed foreign investors the right to repatriate both capital investments and profits. Although the law was changed in 1976 to curtail corporate profit taking, the new restraints led mainly to more sophisticated ways to repatriate profits, such as double invoicing or overvaluing inbound raw materials for tax advantages.

The scope of multinational activity is discussed later, but in Kenyatta's time it included plantation ownership and agricultural processing, mineral extraction, petrol distribution, road transport, advertising, banking and commerce, and subsidiary manufacturing.[30] In manufacturing firms with more than fifty workers, MNCs dominated such industries as leather, footwear, cigarettes, soft drinks, petroleum refining, chemicals, paint, soap, vehicle assembly, cement, and metal products. By 1972 the MNC investment in Kenya was estimated at approximately $364 million, over 20 percent of the nation's gross national product.[31] Overall the important point about the MNCs was that they were very much a part of the business elite's quest for prosperity during the early Kenyatta years. A growing number of businessmen, largely from Kikuyuland, formed alliances with foreign investors, and in many cases Kenyans "actually constructed the machinery through which to control foreign capital in the interests of indigenous accumulation."[32]

Aside from encouraging investment by multinational corporations, Kenyatta sought to increase the inflow of foreign aid and to entice UN agencies to locate in Kenya. The aid picture changed from that of a largely British-Kenya relationship to an expanding inflow of monies from bilateral and multilateral sources, over 90 percent of it from the West or the World Bank. By 1976 the World Bank alone had provided $333 million in loans and $146 million in soft credit, at that point ranking Kenya as the leading recipient of World Bank money on the African continent.[33] In 1972 the United Nations Environment Programme, (UNEP) established its headquarters in Kenya. In 1978 Habitat, the UN Center for Human Settlements, followed suit. Emphasizing the open-door policy, Nairobi also became a headquarters for international foundations, corporations, and nonprofit organizations serving Eastern Africa and the Middle East. Tourism increased significantly, by 1972 accounting for more than 40,000 jobs, compared to 90,000 jobs provided by all manufacturing activities.

In contrast to the formal economic processes under way in the modern sector—those activities that could be tabulated, analyzed, and accounted for—an important underground economic sector existed, as earlier noted. The ILO Report paid particular attention to the "informal" part of this economy, suggesting that "informal" meant essentially small-scale, urban-based manufacturing and services such as tinsmiths, open-air garages, unlicensed taxi drivers, and shoeshine and parking boys. The informal sector as a part of the underground, hidden economy was important in the Kenyatta era as an alternative form of income for an estimated 200,000 workers by 1978.[34]

The informal sector of the underground economy was only part of the larger hidden economic structure that combined legal and illegal, public and private, and large-scale and small-scale financial activity— all outside the formal, tabulated economy. It is important here to sketch at least those large-scale, public and private illegal activities that were under way in Kenyatta's time in order to understand what the Moi regime inherited. The following seven examples were openly discussed by Kenyans, often reported in the press, and criticized in Parliament.[35]

Royal Family Dealings. Essentially these family dealings involved the use of presidential influence to obtain private-sector contracts, favors, and business advantage. International trade activities through multi-national corporations were combined with business activities in ranching, farm properties, gemstones, hotels, film, insurance, advertising, pipelines, transport, casino management, commodity trading, wood products, and wildlife products, particularly ivory.

Illegal Land Seizures by the Elite. Seizures of land intended for smallholder farms became widespread at the end of the Kenyatta era. Land speculation by groups of wealthy Kenyans enabled government land to fall into the hands of the elite instead of going to the intended landless population.

Civil Service Irregularities. Illegalities included bribe taking; dispensing favors, tips, and confidential information; and giving privileged access to jobs and contracts. Bureaucratic corruption was periodically condemned by the government itself in such activities as the 1978 conference for civil servants on "The Kenya We Want." Aside from attacking corruption, the conference posed resolutions against personality cults, nepotism, and tribalism in the civil service and called for public officers to register their private interests.

Corporate Irregularities. In both multinational and local companies irregularities surfaced occasionally as influence buying, payment of protection money, payment of bribes for import licenses or work permits, and payments to bureaucrats to sabotage competitors by red tape— slowness and inefficiency on crucial clearances. Illegal accounting and invoicing practices to avoid taxes also occurred.

Election Campaign Irregularities. Particularly in the 1969 and 1974 campaigns, the buying of votes, the use of intimidation to deliver votes, and election rigging at the local level occurred.

Smuggling Activities. These activities included not only the lucrative Uganda coffee traffic but also manufactured goods, wildlife products, and in the 1970–1975 drought periods, relief foods that had entered the illegal commodities market and found their way out of Kenya to Ethiopia,

Somalia, Sudan, and Tanzania, thereby creating greater food shortages in Kenya.

Poaching of Natural Resources. Poaching of forest products for charcoal making, mainly for Arab markets, and mangrove poles, also for Arab markets, was widespread in 1967–1977. Animal poaching for ivory, rhino horn, spotted cat skins, giraffe tail trinkets, elephant's foot footstools, and colobus monkey skin carpets flourished until the international pressures and a hunting ban became effective in 1977.

Overall the impact of these activities in the Kenyatta era was to create sizable wealth for a small elite, to redirect monies from public coffers to private channels, to oil the patron-client system, and to set up new informal rules for how wealth could be won. These underground activities were elite undertakings, tightly controlled by regime leaders and not open to even the middle class. Proliferation of these activities, particularly in the civil service, would come later. It is important to note that corrupt activities, although criticized in the Kenya press and in Parliament, were not universally condemned in the society unless the activity involved sending wealth to Swiss banks or illegal activity by Asians. Others who spent their illicit money locally often took on a ward heeler's mystique, dispersing largess, creating jobs, and supporting a network of relatives and followers. The illicit activities were a major source of jobs, new enterprises, and a new class of patrons who quickly gathered clients.

It is also important to stress that the "informal" hidden economy is complex, both in its makeup and in some of the questions of legality. Its exact makeup today in manufacturing worth is unknown; its scope includes those manufacturing and service activities that, according to the ILO Report, are largely ignored, unregulated, unsupported, and often discouraged by the government. Available information suggests that the main characteristics of the informal sector are such things as easy entry, lack of formal training, family ownership, labor-intensive processes, adaptive technologies, and reliance on indigenous resources. Other characteristics include an unregulated market process, emphasis on repair and improvisation, and the use of scrap materials and locally-made tools.[36]

Added to the unmapped nature of the informal economy and much of the greater hidden economy is the uncertain nature of public criticism about illegal activity. Crimes that are "equal" under the law are often not equal in the public view. Small-time smuggling or illegal hawking and beer-brewing usually carry little public scorn; poaching is only slightly more odious. On the other hand, outright theft by a civil servant, peculation in local cooperative societies, circumvention of trade or road laws (which can give one an enormous economic advantage), are considered "bad" practices. The more overt the theft, the greater the public outrage. Mob beatings of suspected thieves, when caught in the act, occur periodically in Kenya.

CONCLUSION: JUDGMENTS ON AN ERA

The death of Jomo Kenyatta on August 23, 1978, was a dramatic moment in Kenya's history. There followed an outpouring of emotion from around the nation, eulogies from around the world, and on the day of the funeral, a great show of pomp and ceremony. Tributes, hymns, and Christian pronouncements were beamed over the radio to every corner of Kenya. Undoubtedly the ordinary Kenyan was moved by the passing, and at the end, despite his tarnished image, the president continued to be held in great awe. The corruption and exploitation that had marred his last years seemed forgotten. Jomo Kenyatta was the Father of the Nation, the *Mzee*, the honored Elder. He was buried with dignity and solemnity.

To understand Kenyatta's era it is necessary to understand the way the informal political and economic process worked. Prosperity was the main concern of most Kenyans who, aside from pastoralists, defined prosperity as material rewards, land security, job status, and education for one's children. The quest continued on nearly all economic levels between 1963 and 1978 as the central reality in Kenya. In Kenyatta's regime all major decisions flowed to the top and were taken either by Kenyatta or by his close lieutenants. The inner circle that held real power was the family. There was an ongoing petitioning and patronage process, questionable in a legal sense, but in fact, the way things were done. Any real or imagined tie to Kenyatta was tantamount to political power, and a great deal of business moved on the basis of "the wishes of the president." Kenyatta's word was law, and no one was prepared to challenge him directly.

Aside from governing, capital accumulation was the basic objective of the people close to the regime. The private business interests and private wealth of the inner circle grew to astounding levels. Those Kenyans who wanted to play for high stakes in land, road transport, manufacturing, mining, commodity exporting, and shipping needed an entrée to the inner circle. To gain it they had to petition the family with proposals and promises. In the process Kenyatta and his family received a constant flow of couriers, messengers, and emissaries.

Assessments of this period must consider both the favorable and the unfavorable. Jomo Kenyatta brought the nation to independence; he was the "Father" of the state; he maintained the constitutional government, kept the economy stable, and made some strides toward unifying an ethnically divided country. On the other hand, he was at times autocratic and ruthless. On several occasions he instituted repressions and curtailed the basic freedoms of critics, and as the years passed, he was either unwilling or unable to curb the exploitation carried out by those around him. Part of his government, and by implication he himself, either condoned or looked the other way in the assassination of J. M. Kariuki and thereafter participated in a cover-up on a parallel with that of the Watergate scandal in the United States. Kenyatta permitted the use of his name in dozens of business and land schemes, some of questionable legality. His regime at the end took on the guise of a monarchy, replete with royal trappings, sycophancy, nepotism, favoritism, and great intrigue around a fading king.

In terms of freedom, Kenyans undoubtedly enjoyed more basic freedoms under Kenyatta than most citizens of black Africa. Except for a few periods, Kenyatta's government was tolerant of public criticism. The right of the people to speak out against their leaders and the government, as protected in the Kenya Bill of Rights, was usually maintained. The press remained basically free to criticize the government, although this freedom was occasionally fettered. Members of Parliament were usually able to condemn government actions and call for changes, and students continued to be able to demonstrate over political issues. In Kenyetta's last years a loose alliance of students, Parliament, and the press was spoken of as an informal political opposition. Human rights were by and large protected, although the use of the preventive detention law and heavy-handed police methods did occur. When those incidents came to light, criticisms of government were voiced openly.

The darkest days of Kenyatta's Kenya in terms of freedom were undoubtedly those following the Kariuki murder. The president's attitude toward criticism stiffened dramatically, and there was obvious muzzling of critics and a shutting down of the relatively open system. Detention was abusively used, as was pressure on the press and on the judiciary. Unquestionably, interspersed through Kenyatta's years were two or three periods of abject oppression. Overall, however, Kenyans had from Kenyatta a system that provided basic freedoms and an opportunity to grow.

How did he accomplish this? Kenya's stability under Kenyatta was based on the president's adroit manipulation of the informal processes as well as the formal powers of the presidency. Kenyatta built an edifice around himself that effectively carried out the stabilization process. Disruptive elements were eliminated or folded into the establishment, and the country was controlled by the sheer weight of the president's office. Showdowns with Parliament, the press, students, or any organized opposition were consistently won by the regime, partly because of its centralized structure, but also because of its support among the middle and upper strata. Factionalism was always a problem, but nearly always contained. A clear patron-client relationship existed between Kenyatta's cabinet members and a network of supporters in their home areas who benefited or hoped to benefit by their ties to those in power. Cabinet posts and subcabinet posts in key ministries were plums that carried the wherewithal to provide jobs, lucrative contracts, and other resources. Some of the strongest patrons were the provincial commissioners and remote district commissioners who supported the regime as nearly autonomous barons. Even Members of Parliament were immersed in the system. Public complaints were lodged against MPs who were too involved with business to attend Parliament.[37] In short, Kenyatta relied on strong supporters to keep his system in place. Kenya's stability was based on effective patronage.

In terms of political ideology, opinion on the Kenyatta years varied widely. Writers on the political left were severe in their criticism of the country's inequity, of the class cleavage, corruption, unemployment, and poverty, blaming Kenyatta for what has been dubbed "frothing black capitalism." They point to the gap between rich and poor and blame Kenyatta's alliances with international business as basically establishing an avaricious mentality in the upper economic strata. More conservative observers have looked at the economic stability and growth, applauded Kenyatta's economic attainments, and pointed to the multiracial aspects of the society. In this view, the regime was to be congratulated as one of the most stable in Africa.

On balance, one must underscore pragmatism as the essence of this era. Inequity, unemployment, and corruption were part of it. Aggressive black capitalism left many victimized; alliances with international businesses helped establish an enormous advantage for the economic elite. Simultaneously, however, economic stability and growth occurred; most Kenyans improved their life-styles, and a multiracial society continued to operate. Jomo Kenyatta balanced a tough, ruthless, sometimes corrupt system to keep some freedoms alive, to keep Kenya peaceful, and to avoid military rule. Kenyatta's era was a kind of democratic monarchy that faded with age. There was a parallel to Mao Zedong's last year in China when senility and old age allowed injustice to be perpetrated in his name. As with Mao, Jomo Kenyatta was venerated despite the last years of turmoil and heavy-handedness.

3

Modern Society

INTRODUCTION

Kenya today is a highly fragmented and differentiated society. It is a land of social contrast and contradiction that has been shaped in part by the competitive free-enterprise ethic and in part by the forces of its history and environment. The nation's rich human mosaic is divided in several ways. Among African Bantu, Nilotic, and Hamitic peoples there are over forty ethnic groups such as the Kikuyu, Luo, and Maasai—each with its own geographic region. Linguistically the groups are divided into over 120 subcultures that share a vernacular dialect. In addition, Asians, Arabs, Europeans, and Africans from other nations each have established communities in Kenya.

For the rural Kenyan, ethnic affiliation is paramount, but one's place in modern society is also determined by clan membership, age and sex, education, occupation, family status, and in some areas, religion and home location. One's broader social affiliations are also important, and such diverse organizations as breakaway churches, secret societies, night meeting groups, hunting or threshing societies, self-help groups, welfare unions, and sports and social clubs dot the landscape.

The Kenya entrepreneurial ethic has influenced the modern society in many positive ways. Wealth has been generated, some Kenyans have prospered, and a great many have attained a far better life-style than thought possible three decades ago. At the same time the quest for prosperity has carried penalties: an increased stratification by social class, greater differences between rural and urban Africans, discrimination against women and some minorities (particularly pastoralists), and major differences in access to health and education. Not all these problems can be blamed on the Kenya ethic, but it can be argued that the free-wheeling, open, occasionally corrupt system has created a "we versus they" reality. The "we" are the upper economic echelons who benefit from a patron-client system; the "they" are those on the lower rungs of the economic system or those who are not in the system at all.

Less concrete but equally important conflicts occur in religious and cultural values. Many Kenyans lament the passing of traditional culture, and some criticize the Western materialistic values dominant in Kenya

64

today. Similarly, religious diversity causes tensions, not only between Muslims and Christians, but also between dozens of splinter groups that build their movements on mixtures of traditional beliefs and Christian tenets. Land issues embody many social and cultural values and represent the major area of social conflict in the years ahead. Underlying all of these issues is the ultimate social question: What are the characteristics of the society in terms of population, and what is the demographic outlook?

POPULATION: THE DEMOGRAPHIC REALITIES

Kenya's population in 1983 was thought to be growing at 4 percent per year, and although the total population of 18 million is small by world standards, the dramatic growth rate overshadows all social issues. At 4 percent it is the highest in the world and means that Kenya's population will double within seventeen years.[1] The data are also sobering because Kenya initiated the first major family-planning program in sub-Saharan Africa. Millions of dollars were given in aid monies to develop effective family planning. The urban, educated woman does use the services somewhat to curtail her fertility. Her rural cousins, on the other hand, more than make up the difference; their fertility remains exceptionally high. As Kenyan writer Micere Mugo has said, it was as if a great prophet had sent forth the message: "Go, ye, and multiply."

The background of the modern population reality began after World War II when medical advances reduced fatal diseases such as cholera, malaria, and yellow fever. The advances came through expanded health services, new clinics, new medications, and new programs of inoculation and health information, particularly in the fields of nutrition and child care. As a result the Kenya death rate declined more rapidly than that in any other developing country, to its present rate of 14 per 1000 population.[2] At the same time, the nation's birthrate rose to its present level of approximately 53 per 1000 population.[3] The combination of falling death rate and rising birthrate has given Kenya its unprecedented population increase (Table 2).

Key trends that emerged from the 1979 census data are the increased growth rate from 1969 to 1979, from 3.3 to 4 percent, the increased fertility rate from 7.6 to 8.1 percent, and the increased life expectancy, from approximately 47 to 51 years for males and from 51 to 56 years for females. In the same period infant mortality rates dropped from 126 to 116 per 1000 population (Table 2).[4]

What are some of the social implications of these changes? First, the Kenya population is exceptionally young. Over 51 percent in 1983 were under age 15. This group, added to the elderly (some 4 percent are over age 60), constitutes a major dependency burden for the working population (Table 3). A minority of the population must work to support the majority for the foreseeable future, a situation that has unfortunate economic implications for individuals and for national growth. Second, the population trends also indicate that the nation is outstripping its

TABLE 2
Population Indicators for Kenya, 1969-1983

	1969	1979a	1983b
Total population	10,942,705	15,322,000	17,800,000
Crude birthrate	51/1000	53.4/1000	53.2/1000
Crude death rate	18/1000	14.2/1000	14/1000
Rate of natural increase (%/year)	3.3	4.0	4.0
Infant mortality	126/1000	116/1000	115/1000
Life expectancy at birth (years)	46.7 male	51.2	52
	51.2 female	55.7	56

a 1977 estimates

b estimates by author for mid-1983

Source: Republic of Kenya, Economic Survey, 1981, 1982, and UNICEF, Country Profile: Kenya 1981 (Nairobi: UNICEF, East Africa Regional Office), pp. 2-3.

ability to create jobs. Of the 6.6 million economically active Kenyans in 1979, only 1.9 million were wage-earners; the majority of Kenya's 4.7 million working population were involved in non-wage rural work. Of these, 2.5 million were women.[5]

Third, in spatial terms, Kenya's population is highly concentrated in the southwest, a pattern that has been reinforced by the location of industry and of such services as water supply, electric power, roads, and communications. For example, rail, road, and air traffic are concentrated in a 620-mile southern corridor from Mombasa to the Uganda border. Fourth, these spatial realities have in turn influenced urban

TABLE 3
Age Structure of Kenya's Population: 1978, 1983, and Projected for 2000

Age	Number (in thousands)			Percent		
	1978	1983	2000	1978	1983	2000
Under 15	7,600	9,000	20,700	49.7	51.2	53.7
15-59	7,100	8,600	16,800	46.4	45.1	43.5
60 and over	600	700	1,100	3.9	3.7	2.8
Total	15,300	19,100	38,600	100.0	100.0	100.0

Source: Roushdi Henin and Susan Mott, "The Impact of Current and Future Population Growth Rates on the Short Term Social and Economic Development in Kenya," Population Studies and Research Institute, University of Nairobi, September 1979.

growth and migration. Some 14 percent of the national population is presently located in cities, which are growing at an average rate of 7.4 percent per year. Although Nairobi and Mombasa are growing less rapidly (at 5 percent and 3 percent respectively), other smaller cities such as Thika, Machakos, and Busia have recorded around 30 percent growth per year. In 1979 Kenya's seventeen main cities and towns accounted for 1.9 million people.[6] Migration patterns reflect both a flow to the cities and a flow from one rural area to plantation work in other rural areas. Most migrants are younger men, but females also migrate in search of work and to fulfill marriage arrangements.[7]

Finally, rural-urban differences are also related to the crucial question of fertility and to womens' attitudes about children. Fertility in rural areas is higher than in urban areas, 8.1 children per woman as opposed to 5.6.[8] Reasons for the differences are complex but include the fact that rural women remain dependent for their security on traditional early marriages. Their husbands are often older men, a situation that causes early widowhood. Under these conditions children provide security for mothers who have little other welfare to look forward to in their old age. By Kenyan law, men may practice polygamy, and widows often have no rights to property or inheritance, which increases their dependency on children. The Kenya Fertility Survey of 1977–1978 revealed that only 17 percent of the women who had ever been married wanted no more children.

A mother's educational level is also related to fertility. As might be expected, a Kenyan woman's fertility drops as she attains ten to twelve years of education. It is highest, however, not among totally uneducated women, nor even among those with one to four years of education, but among women who have had four to six years of school. The reasons are unclear, but speculation centers on healthier mothers in better living conditions, mothers in a slightly better economic stratum, and the abandonment of breast feeding and postpartum abstinence.[9]

Overall, are there any hopeful signs in the demographic picture? Possibly a few. On the average, young women under age 25 who have never been married want fewer children than their counterparts a decade before.[10] As urban expansion continues, the fertility rate for new city dwellers will drop, partly because of greater access to family-planning services. As early as 1955 a private volunteer organization offered family-planning services. The movement became the National Family Planning Program in 1967, the first in continental Africa. By 1973 some 220,000 women out of a married female population of 1.7 million had visited family-planning facilities. Data available in 1978, however, showed that only 6 percent of Kenyan women were using family planning, and some 12 percent did not know what it was. One of the reactions to this information was the launching of a $120 million family-planning campaign.[11]

Looking ahead, the demographic projections carry major problems for the society (Figure 3). By 1989, as compared to 1979, there will be 1.9 million more children under the age of five to care for and 2.6

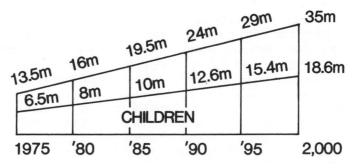

FIGURE 3. Projected Population Growth for Kenya at 4 Percent
per Year (1979 rate), Assuming Declining Mortality

Source: UNICEF, *Country Profile: Kenya 1981.*

million more children of primary and secondary age needing school
places. Primary pupils alone will require 52,000 more classrooms and
53,000 more teachers. The labor force will have to absorb 3.2 million
more people of working age, and there will be 8.1 million more people
to feed, to house, and to care for when they become sick.[12]

Kenyan leaders are concerned about the population issues, but
there is little agreement as to what should be done and little public
thinking about what will happen to the society. If the overall population
as of 1979 is expected to double in seventeen or eighteen years, the
population of Nairobi is expected to double in only ten years, to about
1.7 million in 1989. If the migration and fertility patterns continue,
other urban towns will have doubled in population in four to fifteen
years.

How Kenyan society will cope with the population pressures is
unknown. Government planners are aware that as the population builds,
increased land fragmentation occurs and greater pressures are placed
on marginal lands. Both situations have long-term ecological implications,
including soil erosion, that will reduce the ability of the land to produce.
In urban areas, planners are also aware that most major services such
as police, water, fire, sanitation, road maintenance, power grids, and
telephones will come under enormous stress if the cities double or triple
in size. The major hope is that the economy will grow fast enough to
accommodate the needed changes.

The probability is that the government will be unable to provide
the needed services. Under these conditions new social patterns will
emerge. One might be an urban exodus, forced or voluntary, that leads
urban dwellers back to the rural areas. Ethnic ties would be reemphasized,
local contacts reopened, and life redefined as farmers or pastoralists. In
fact, Kenya's ethnic realities are very much a part of the population
picture.

ETHNIC COMPOSITION

The forty African tribes or ethnic groups in Kenya constitute 98 percent of the population, with Asians, Arabs, Europeans, and non-Kenyan Africans making up the other 2 percent.[13] Ethnic labels in the past generally connoted peoples who share a vernacular language, common customs, a basic political and economic system, and some sense of common history. Beyond this, ethnicity today is largely based on one's geographic homeland, loyalties, and affiliations. Confusion occurs because some ethnic groups, such as the Kalenjin, Mijikenda, and Luhya, are each clusters of seven or more smaller clans or groups that at times are individually distinguished. Historically most ethnic groups have been in a state of flux, the clans within them breaking away to form new alliances with those who share some language and cultural affinities. Ethnic labels today are more flukes of history than accurate names of early Kenyans. Many names simply mean "the people" in a local vernacular; some are old clan names and others are labels given to a people by their neighbors, who happened to be encountered first by the Europeans.

In terms of population size, three groups who live in agriculturally high-potential areas constitute over 50 percent of Kenyan society. The Kikuyu (3.2 million in 1979) of the central highlands are agriculturalists who experienced European culture in depth through both white missionaries and settlers. Most other ethnic groups consider the Kikuyu to be the most aggressive and entrepreneurial of Kenyans. They occupy many of the highest government posts, many top military posts, and are heavily represented in the business elite. Their home districts, Kiambu, Muranga, and Nyeri, contain some of the highest population densities in Kenya. Serious factionalism exists between the northern and southern Kikuyu, and historically there has been animosity with the pastoral Maasai to the south and west. Conversely, good relations remain with the nearby Meru and Embu peoples who are considered ethnic cousins— and to a lesser extent with the nearby Kamba.

The Luo (1.95 million) of the western Lake Victoria Basin, who are Nilotic in origin, combine agriculture and pastoralism in a sedentary life-style. They are part of the western Kenya peoples who use Lake Victoria as a source of fishing, trade, and communication. Luo men are well known as migrant laborers, working far afield in Nairobi or Mombasa, at coastal sisal estates and hotels. They make up 13 percent of the Nairobi population.

The Luhya (2.1 million), also of western Kenya, are Bantu farmers, partially surrounded by Nilotic peoples. Parts of Luhya country have the highest population density in Kenya, up to 1200 people per square mile, and all their region is thickly settled. Like the neighboring Luo, they migrate a great deal to Nairobi and other urban areas for employment. Sixteen subethnic groups make up the Luhya cluster.

Fishing boats, Lake Victoria, western Kenya (photo by David Keith Jones)

A few other ethnic groups, the Kamba, Kisii, Meru, and Kalenjin, are significant politically. President Daniel arap Moi comes from one of the Kalenjin groups, the Tugen. The largest pastoral groups are the Kenya Somali, Turkana, and Maasai, although many of the nation's smaller ethnic groups are also pastoralists, such as the Boran, Gabbra, Rendille, and Samburu. Aside from Kenyan Africans, the 1979 census noted that 71,818 Africans of non-Kenya origin were resident in the

Boran child, northern Kenya
(photo by Norman Miller)

country. The non-African populations included 78,600 Asians, 39,909 Europeans, and 39,146 Arabs.[14]

SOCIAL ISSUES

Who are the wealthy of Kenya? How did they succeed in the competitive quest? Who are the poor? How poor are they? Other key questions touch on the nature of Kenya's urban society, on women today, and on issues of health and education. A basic theme touching all social issues is that the fragmentation and diversity found in Kenya are exacerbated by the differences in wealth and the prevailing entrepreneurial ethic. The result has been both positive, in that a relatively stable middle economic class has developed, and negative, in that many remain poor while some have obtained exceptional wealth.

Stratification: Wealth and Poverty

Modern social stratification in Kenya begins with the wealthy black elite who govern the nation. Below them is a black urban middle class, an urban poor, and in the rural areas both a stratum of moderately well-off farmers and below, the mass of rural poor.[15]

First, who are the black elite? Most are educated, "self-made" individuals who have attained wealth and position within one generation. They are urban dwellers, lawyers, doctors, businessmen, civil servants, government ministers, clergymen, and high-ranking Kenyan employees of the multinational corporations, the UN, and the international aid agencies. As a group they share a desire for the good life, for personal security, for their children's education, and for items the Western material culture can provide. Some are known as *wabenzi* (from *wa*, "people," and *Benzi*, "Mercedes-Benz"), as compared to *wananchi*, or common folk:

> The elite began to regard themselves as a cohesive group that deserved prestige and economic well-being. There were variations in income, but members of this elite were clearly distinguished from the poor and the lower middle class not only in income but in style. They adopted British standards in clothing, housing, furniture, and entertainment. They lived in red brick tiled bungalows with well-tended gardens in Nairobi's residential sections. They played tennis, drank whiskey, and owned high-priced cars. In fact the new African elite who had joined or replaced the white elite not only copied their life-style but often adopted their outlook. They would still help their poor relatives, in conformity with traditional African values, but many of them tended to keep aloof from less favored citizens. They were accused, especially by university students, of perpetuating the dualistic social system of colonial days and of favoring a system of mutual accommodation with the remaining whites. They did not yet constitute a hereditary upper class, although their children might one day do so. Most had been born of poor parents in simple country dwellings, and their achievements were the result of their own efforts.[16]

Second, the urban African middle class are owners of small businesses, government employees at middle levels, nurses, artisans, mechanics, supervisors, and skilled factory employees. The middle class are the "haves" compared to the unemployed and underemployed, and most subscribe to some form of the Horatio Alger myth. Most want to "make it" and are willing to keep working toward an improved life style. Very little political dissent is heard from this sector. Conventional wisdom suggests that the *wabenzi* and the would-be *wabenzi* are a stabilizing force in Kenya because of their stake in the system.

Third, the discontented urban-dwelling, lower economic stratum is the greatest civilian threat to political stability. These people are the underemployed, but not necessarily unemployed—the drivers, clerks, laborers, cooks, waiters, scrubbers, and domestic employees who in 1982 were making less than 300 shillings ($30) a month. Others in this group are the casual day workers, the unemployed urban poor, the shanty dwellers, and the landless and squatter elements within twenty miles of Nairobi. Most of these people live in abject poverty, and most are unreachable by various welfare or aid agencies. Many have either been forced to the urban areas or trapped there by poverty at home. They have all the stresses common to life on the septic fringe of an African city, plus the economic incentive to drift into petty crime simply to feed themselves.

In Kenya's rural areas two basic strata exist. A middle class of farmers and farmer-businessmen has emerged that has variously been called a "middle peasantry," a "rural bourgeoisie," and a class of "farmer-entrepreneurs." They are individuals who have some savings, some surplus, who deal in the national cash economy because they have had some success at accumulating wealth. They may be full-time farmers, farmer-traders, or farmer-politicians. Many have second jobs as local officials. Many others are in essence managing an extended family business that generates up to 40 percent of its income from off-farm activity, either in an actual outside business or as cash generated by working members of the family.

Below the rural middle class is the stratum of the rural poor, made up of small-time farmers, farmer-herders, pastoralists, some hunters and fishermen, and a sizable landless, near-destitute population. These people are farthest out on the nation's periphery in terms of wealth, education, and access to health or government services. They are less mobile, less communicative, less participatory in a political sense, and more alienated from the central system than any other stratum except the urban poor.

Overall, the basic point is that Kenya's unbridled quest for prosperity has created major inequities in wealth, although at the same time allowing a significant middle class, both urban and rural, to emerge. The wage and income picture for the five strata delineated above shows this disparity. The elite, estimated at 3 percent of the population, had annual incomes in 1981 ranging upwards from 60,000 Kenya shillings ($8,000). Two African physicians discussing wealth in 1981 estimated there were at least 500 black millionaires in dollar terms within Kenya, most of them with their wealth abroad.[17] The urban middle class ranged from 3,750 to 60,000 Kenya shillings ($500 to $8,000), with the average earnings for both private- and public-sector employees in 1981 at 15,400 Kenya shillings ($2,050). The urban poor had incomes of from 1,500 to 3,750 shillings ($200 to $500), their earnings coming largely from casual labor in the informal sector. The average income per capita in Kenya at the time was estimated at $380.

For rural Kenyans, income distribution is quantified on a household basis, not individually, although the key point about the wide range in income is still maintained. In 1974–1975 only 18 percent of all rural peoples were members of households with incomes over 6,000 Kenya shillings ($800), the group classified as the rural middle class. The rural poor included 55 percent of all rural peoples with household incomes below 3,000 shillings ($400), 12 percent of those with incomes between 3,000 and 4,000 shillings ($400–$533), and 14 percent of those with incomes between 4,000 and 6,000 shillings ($535–$800).[18]

The disparity becomes more graphic when seen in terms of "modern" versus "nonmodern" economic sectors, that is, those working for wages versus those who were not. The modern portion of Kenya, estimated at 17 percent of the population, commands 43 percent of the national income and has an average household annual income of $1,137. The nonmodern economic sector is estimated at 80 percent of the population and has 47 percent of the national income, with a household average annual income of $473.[19]

Looked at from a different perspective, these rural-urban differences reflect Kenyans who are "advantaged" and those who are "disadvantaged." In gross terms, 45 percent of the Kenya population in the mid-1980s could be considered relatively advantaged. These people include the wealthy, with some capital accumulation (about 3 percent); wage earners in the modern sector (12 percent); and smallholder farmers and rural businessmen in favored economic regions (30 percent). The disadvantaged, a total of approximately 55 percent, are basically small-scale and subsistence farmers (37 percent), pastoralists and nomads (8 percent), and the landless squatters, both rural and urban destitute (10 percent). Much depends on how poverty is assessed.[20]

Establishing baselines of poverty has been attempted periodically in Kenya, mainly as a way of delineating the "poorest of the poor" for aid and welfare. Depending on the measurements, the picture changes. On the basis of income, several studies suggest a sizable portion of the population, up to 39 percent, is below the poverty line, defined as under $250 a year income per capita. Other indicators are that in pockets of poverty, Western Province in particular, up to 50 percent of the population is below the poverty line. Seen in a nutritional sense, "poverty" may be measured in terms of minimum daily caloric intake (a minimum of 1,800 calories a day). Indications are that as many as 40 percent of all Kenyans are below this "poverty line." One study indicates that 50 percent of Nyanza people are inadequately fed.[21]

Another basis for assessing poverty is to consider a family's access to land, and the quality of that land. There are shadings in such measurements from those who control the fertile, high-rainfall areas, to those who hold moderately fertile and marginal lands, to those who essentially rely on pastoralism in the arid regions, to those who are landless or squatters.

Landlessness is important in any rural society, but in Kenya, with only 18 percent of the land either of high or medium agricultural potential, it is a compelling social issue. Over 80 percent of the Kenyan population is rural; in 1980 an estimated 400,000 were landless and countless others farmed on tiny, inadequate plots. Population expansion and old-fashioned techniques of farming increase the fragmentation of the land and reduce its productivity. The price the society pays is measured not only in terms of productivity, but also in other terms, of serious environmental deterioration, soil erosion, and soil depletion.[22]

Poverty, at the heart of it, is a question of who suffers, whose ox is being gored. When one looks specifically at poor families, however, there is a marked variation in the quality of life of family members. A person's access to food and other resources changes with his station in life and his ability to fend for himself. Inequity is related to age; often the very young and the very old suffer the most. Under famine conditions, for example, "stress groups" include young children, pregnant and lactating women, and the elderly. Others simply have easier access to whatever food is available.

Family attitudes toward poverty are also important. It is a myth that rural homesteads are egalitarian, cooperative, and mutually supporting, or that poor urban households are so sharing. When resources become short, many forms of self-interest and anomie surface. Herdsboys steal milk from goats while herding; men spend their last few shillings

Nairobi city center (photo by David Keith Jones)

for their own food. Women hoard food for themselves or a favorite child, and secrecy about food between family members does occur. One member of a family may be significantly more healthy than another. In urban areas one family member may earn money from casual labor and spend it on food or drink before he returns home. In the end, no one really knows how much economic punishment a poor Kenyan family is taking. Nor is there an accurate gauge on what the limits of tolerance really are.

Urban Society and Urban Minorities

Nairobi is the hub of the nation, a place of government and commerce, a supply point for eastern Africa and an international meeting place for nearly 400,000 overseas visitors a year. As a city of nearly 900,000, its population comprises 5 percent of the nation's population and includes a majority of the Asians and Europeans resident in Kenya.[23]

Nairobi attracts a constant flow of Kenyan migrants who come seeking work or simply the excitement of the city. For job seekers, the chance of employment is less than one in ten, and the realities of urban survival are harsh. A low-cost room in one of the city's transient areas will have problems of water, sanitation, and security. Food is expensive, fuel hard to obtain, and living conditions rudimentary. Even for the new migrant who finds work as a vendor, hawker, sweeper, cleaner, or houseworker or construction worker, life is not easy. The place of work may be miles from where he or she can afford to live. Starting at the low end of the scale and virtually without job security, the new worker is immediately a target for relatives coming to the city who make demands for food, shelter, and hospitality. Traditional etiquette is in direct conflict with the need to survive. If famine or a poor crop season has impoverished the migrant's home area, the human flow from there increases.

The new migrant worker automatically competes with workers from other ethnic groups who may have better contacts or longer traditions of urban migration. Luo, Kikuyu, Luhya, and Kamba peoples have traditionally been mobile, adaptive, city-wise workers. Men from the coast, the north, or parts of the Rift Valley who do not have a strong migratory tradition can encounter bewildering obstacles in an urban setting and on the job. Over 30 percent of Nairobi workers must settle for being "self-employed" as day laborers; they have no other jobs.

Nairobi newcomers, whether new migrants, incoming middle-class or elite Kenyans, or newly arrived Asians and Europeans, encounter a city that is divided into distinct neighborhoods. Radiating from the city center in roughly concentric circles are the apartments and maisonettes of the Asian and African middle classes, followed by the larger homes and gardens of the elite. Farther out are the African low-income housing, a mixture of permanent and impermanent buildings. Segregation is by income, not by race, although there are neighborhoods in Nairobi that are overwhelmingly Asian or European because of the housing patterns laid down in colonial times: Parklands for Asians, Karen and Langatta for Europeans, Muthaiga for the diplomatic community, Mathare Valley or Kawangware for newly arrived African migrants.

In terms of minorities, Nairobi is the main residence of Asian and European communities; Mombasa, Malindi, and Lamu on the coast are centers for the Arab community. The Asian society is made up of people with roots in present-day India and Pakistan; roughly 70 percent are from Gujarat, 20 percent from eastern Punjab, and 10 percent from Goa. About 10 percent are Christian, 25 percent Muslim, and the remainder of some branch of Hindu. Most are second- or third-generation descendants of original immigrants who came to Kenya during the building of the Uganda Railway. They are the grandchildren and great-grandchildren of Gujarati merchants and artisans, Goan clerks, and Punjabi soldiers. Some came as new brides, apprentices, shop clerks, or craftsmen needed in newly established family businesses. Over time, strong family ties have united the Asian community. In some circumstances the closed family networks and use of the Hindu language are seen as clannishness, a social pattern that has engendered resentment, particularly from Africans in the lower economic strata.

The European community has historically been divided between farmers and nonfarmers. Few Europeans are farming today, but many former settler families have remained in Kenya, some in business, others as lawyers, doctors, or as retirees in Nairobi, Naivasha, Nanyuki, or along the coast. Some of the retirees are among the 4,445 Europeans, mostly of British origin, who have been granted Kenya citizenship. Of the remaining 35,000 enumerated in the 1979 census, most are missionaries, teachers, or members of the international community that includes businessmen and short-term residents who work in embassies, UN offices, and foreign aid programs. Included in the European population in 1982 were an estimated 8,800 U.S. citizens resident in Kenya.

The Arab community is about the size of the European, some 39,146 in 1979; just over 19,000 are Kenya citizens. Being an Arab in Kenya is largely a matter of self-identification, since a high percentage of the coastal population has some Arab blood, most often dating back to the period when Arabs and Africans intermixed to form the Swahili culture. Some with strong Arab blood ties in recent years have found it expeditious to be classified by census takers as Africans. Other old Arab families trace their ancestry on the Kenya coast to roots in the Gulf states to the north and have continued to identify themselves as "true Arabs." Arab Kenyans are Muslim, and most are in trade or business, often in shipping, export-import, or ship supply.[24]

Interactions between the three minority groups and the larger African population are congenial enough along business lines, but rigid and episodic on social lines. Commercially a form of three-colored capitalism prevails. Asian shopkeepers, African traders, and European businessmen "do business," and the multiracial state envisioned by some nationalists does exist in this economic sense. Most social exchange, however, is highly stratified. Asians remain close to their subcommunities and rarely marry outside them; European social patterns follow British etiquette and for long-term residents revolve around one of the established clubs. Other newer Europeans drift into social networks largely by nationality. Arab social patterns are based on strict Islamic tenets that close the society to outsiders. African social interaction in Nairobi is still ethnic in its patterns, with specific bars and restaurants known as Kamba, Kikuyu, Luo, or Maasai meeting places.

The Role of Women

Kenyan women, particularly rural women, are at the center of their local economic systems—essential in their role in the bride-price institution and as the individuals who do the majority of routine manual labor.[25] Although their role in society is improving, they still have relatively little control over their own destinies. Bride-price, the system wherein the groom's family pays the bride's family for marriage rights, is practiced today. Payment is not necessarily in cattle as in the past, but rather in cash, plus symbolic gifts such as cloth or household goods. The system was criticized by Tom Mboya as alien to one's right of free choice. Bride-price and the practice in some ethnic groups of female circumcision, which President Daniel Moi has criticized, are pointed to as examples of rural women's second-class status within the society.

Female-male work distinctions cost Kenya millions of lost labor hours per year. Women do the majority of the routine farm work, tend babies, and manage the hearth; men's farm work is animal husbandry and occasionally heavy tasks such as clearing brush or building roads and waterways. New cash-crop schemes such as coffee or tea planting are usually taken on by men, often through lessons learned at farmer training centers. Women in this situation normally continue to take care of food crops, a basic inequity that allows men to control the main family earnings.

In terms of poverty, if one could pinpoint the group that is most disadvantaged, it would be Kenyan rural, uneducated women in the 18–48 year age group. They have less than men and less than educated women in terms of health and well-being, less in terms of living space available to them in huts, less in terms of the size of their gardens, their access to food, clothes, shoes, a radio, mobility, new ideas, education—even, it might be added, less in terms of the right to survive if born crippled. One sees only deformed male beggars on the streets of Nairobi, rarely females. Given the bride-price system, a deformed female child would have little economic value and often simply does not survive.

For women who come to work in Nairobi or other urban centers without at least a primary education, employment is very difficult. They may find work as house servants or child governesses, but these jobs are dependent on close ties to a kinsman working in the household. Even then the situation will be less than ideal: cramped quarters, few women nearby, and insecurity about their possessions. If they have children, they must leave the children behind in the rural area, and they must allow their farms to be cultivated by someone else who may claim future rights of cultivation. For totally uneducated single women, the few jobs available include work as vendors, scrubbers, office sweepers, barmaids, and prostitutes.

Education for women in the last two decades has reduced some of the blatant discrimination, and Kenyan women overall have greater opportunity than women in any of the neighboring East African countries. Part of this is due to the Kenyan ethic that encourages women as entrepreneurs and gives responsibility to women to run the home business. In fact, part of the debate in the educational community centers on what special efforts should be made to further female educational opportunities.

EDUCATION FOR WHAT?

Kenya's formal education system is organized under two government ministries, Basic Education and Higher Education. Both are centralized, hierarchical systems that together employ more than 128,000 teachers and serve more than 4 million students. Education is the single largest budget item in the central government's expenditure, amounting to about $360 million in 1980. In most years this is between 24 and 30 percent of the total budget, depending on how it is calculated. Some 64 percent of the education expenditure is spent on primary education.

Changes in the education sector have severely taxed the government's financial resources. From 1977 to 1981 primary school enrollment rose from 2.9 million to 4.1 million. Secondary school enrollment in 1981 reached 464,671, an 11 percent increase over the previous year. The teaching force in 1981 was 127,580, up 8 percent over 1980. (A total of 102,489 primary school teachers and 15,914 secondary teachers were employed in 1980.)

In post-secondary education the growth has been slow. In 1981 some 2,596 students were enrolled in primary teachers' colleges and 8,827 at the two university campuses, the University of Nairobi and its affiliate, Kenyatta College. New projects have also been launched to combat illiteracy through about 2,200 adult education centers. Literacy rates for the population as a whole are estimated at 25 percent in English, 33 percent in Swahili, and 46 percent in a vernacular language.[26]

Because education is so important as a way to find status and prosperity, it is a particularly contentious area. Part of the Kenya ethic of entrepreneurialism is tied to the idea that education is status. Officially education is a *right* at the primary level. In fact, at independence, universal education was held out as the noblest human investment, a grand goal, the panacea for Kenya's development problems. Today these hopes have faded and Kenyan skeptics point to at least five anomalies that collectively pose the question: Education for what?[27]

First, education is losing its economic meaning in terms of employment. For a great many primary and secondary students there are simply no jobs on the marketplace. The national economy is growing too slowly to accommodate even those students with higher educational attainment. Second, enlightenment gained through education gives students hopes that can never be fulfilled and conditions them to expect a way of life that is impossible. Third, educational discrimination exists against girls and young women, against pastoral groups, against poorer students, and against politically weak ethnic groups. In the underserved areas, facilities and supplies are unavailable. Elite families, on the other hand, can use education as a means of maintaining privileges and legitimizing a higher status for themselves and their children. Fourth, education can breed incompetence. Even for those who complete required courses there is a growing realization that much "learning" has been by rote with little competence developed in creative thinking, initiative, problem solving, or technical intuition. Finally, the expenditures on education are increasingly beyond the nation's ability to pay for them. The costs are staggering, both in terms of the proportion of government funds and in terms of unrest and social discontent.[28]

One of the government's efforts to alleviate the inequities has been the *Harambee* (self-help) school building projects. The Kenyatta government in the 1960s and 1970s encouraged *Harambee* projects as a way of solving local education problems as well as gaining grass-roots participation of citizens and their local politicians. To retain his influence a politician usually had to contribute one of the bigger gifts to the *Harambee* movement. The *Harambee* schools, although built with locally

Primary school teacher, Marsabit (photo by Norman Miller)

Secondary school classroom, Marsabit (photo by Norman Miller)

raised funds and volunteer labor, often had commitments from the government for staff and maintenance. By the time Daniel arap Moi came to power, however, more schools had been built than the government could support. As a result, some of the secondary schools and many others had become private operations that took students unable to find places in government-backed schools. In 1980, some 920 of Kenya's 1,700 secondary schools were *not* government maintained or aided; a majority of these were *Harambee* schools.[29] Overall the outcome has been to provide some educational opportunities, but at the same time to perpetuate elitism in education because *Harambee* school graduates are competitively disadvantaged.

Critics of education in Kenya also point out that the nation's educational policies do not concentrate on basic self-reliance skills as much as, say, the Tanzania system. The critics argue that a new social reality is emerging in Kenya, which will make it essential for young people to spend less time in school and more time farming, herding, or fishing, simply to stay alive. School becomes a luxury when basic food and money are scarce. In fact, the population boom and rising energy costs have probably ended the hope that anything beyond a primary education could become a *right*.

There is also a challenge to the assumption that the well-educated are better citizens—more law-abiding and less rebellious than uneducated elements in the society. In fact, revolutions could well be led by the educated unemployed who see themselves as social outcasts with nothing to lose.

Against all costs and criticism, however, education remains central to the society's basic ethos, particularly the opportunity structure as perceived by Kenyans. Despite unemployment and a scarcity of wealth, the demand for education remains high. This demand, plus the fact that jobs are increasingly competitive, keeps Kenya operating as a kind of meritocracy. Whether this is totally realistic is unimportant. As long as education is thought to lead to opportunity, it serves as a cement in the body politic. The fundamental problem is that Kenya can no longer afford to expand its educational system and thus the whole ethos is coming under strain.

HEALTH: MODERN MEDICINE VERSUS TRADITIONAL HEALING

In reality, health is related to wealth.
Those who have wealth, have health.
                    Missionary doctor
                    Marsabit, Kenya, 1983

A major social issue in Kenya today concerns the health sector's ability to deliver equitable services. Kenya's health policy is to provide free access to health care for all citizens. In reality, because of the geographic remoteness of many communities, transport costs, and high costs of personal and medical supplies, health services are episodic. Traditional healers are still the first line of defense against illness for an estimated 75 percent of the population, and a great many Kenyans have no access to Western medicine.[30]

Despite this problematic health picture, significant advances have occurred in conquering many diseases, as evidenced by population growth. Life expectancy has risen, and death rates, including infant mortality rates, have fallen. In the eight-year period 1970–1978, acceptors of family-planning services rose from 77,100 to 295,000. During the same period government health expenditures rose from $21 million to $57.3 million, an increase from 6.8 percent to 7.5 percent of all government expenditures, or an increase on a per capita basis from $1.80 to $4.03. The number of practicing physicians increased from one for every 12,770 people to one for every 7,889 people; the number of hospital beds, from one for every 770 people to one for every 737 people. Kenya's per capita income rose from $140 to $340 in the same period.[31]

Kenya has both a public health care system and a large private system operating on a fee-for-services basis. Tertiary care facilities are available in the larger cities, including provincial capitals such as Nakuru and Kisumu. The government's health system, like its education system, is hierarchical in nature, officially emphasizing Western, high-technology, curative medicine. In 1980 some 1,581 hospitals, clinics, and dispensaries provided health services for over 16 million people in what is basically an upward referral system.[32] Under the government umbrella are also mission-run and other private volunteer facilities. In 1980, 1,800 physicians were registered in Kenya, 600 of whom were Kenya citizens.[33]

Those rural Kenyans who are relatively wealthy and can afford to travel may gain access to higher-level government hospitals or to care in the private sector; those who are not rely on rural government dispensaries or traditional healers. Although traditional healing is still extremely widespread, there are basic conflicts between Western and traditional approaches. Western-trained doctors disparage traditional practitioners as "bush healers" who are unsystematic, unsanitary, usually ineffectual, and occasionally dangerous. Because there are many types of traditional practitioners—herbalists, diviners, counselors, general practitioners—a degree of confusion exists. When supernatural beliefs about healing are brought into discussions or when exotic and bizarre cases are reported in the press, misunderstandings increase.

Those who express some sympathy for traditional healing point out that Western services are often not available, and that they are expensive and sometimes terrifying to rural people. Local healers are readily accessible, may have knowledge of the patient's family, are culturally comfortable, usually inexpensive, and are particularly useful in problems of anxiety, stress, and mental anguish. Psychosomatic illness in African societies, as in the West, is a major element in perhaps 75 percent of the patients seeking treatment. Traditional healers can treat these problems better than Western physicians. Advocates also point out that some synthesis with Western practices could elevate the healer to the level of an auxiliary health worker. These suggestions have not been pursued in Kenya, as they have in Tanzania and elsewhere, mainly because so little is known about Kenyan traditional healing in Kenyan medical circles, where only one in three doctors is a Kenya citizen. In general, Western-trained physicians usually know very little about the positive sides of traditional healing.

Traditional healing is a pillar of African culture, and in most ethnic groups has the status of an art that has evolved over centuries. Traditional concepts of disease suggest that the body has been invaded by evil spirits and that both divination to discover the cause of the illness and exorcism or cleansing to heal the patient are necessary processes. Sophisticated systems of diagnosis and treatment have been developed in some local societies. Techniques include cupping, bleeding, massage, tattooing, minor surgery, incisions with medicine rubbed into tiny wounds, and the use of a vast array of herbal preparations. Counseling is a large part of a healer's work.[34]

The economics of traditional medicine are a further source of conflict between the two sectors. Western-trained physicians are suspicious of the ingredients used by local healers, and critical of the illegal means used to obtain them. Zanzibar, Uganda, Rwanda, and Zaire are important sources for a trade that criss-crosses Kenya. Dried animal intestines, crocodile gall bladders, horns, plant roots, herbs, dried leaves, and bark are all part of the traffic.

Although the traditional pharmacopia is a full-scale industry, a veil of secrecy exists about most of it. Part of the reason is the illegality of using poisons and animal products, and part because the preparations are family recipes. Like healers, many herbal traders have learned preparations from their fathers and grandfathers, and the closely-guarded family secrets permit monopolies to be maintained. Overall the economic reasons for the survival of the trade are the relatively low cost of the products compared to that of Western drugs, the low cost of the services, the ease of access to the products, and the efficiency of the local market system.

SOCIAL VALUES

Since independence, Kenya has become a far more open and free-wheeling society. Western material values have been embraced, greater mobility attained, and laissez-faire attitudes acquired. The new freedoms have carried benefits in terms of income and learning, but the society has also paid a price for the rapid change in social values. The authority of respected elders who once controlled community behavior has been eroded. There has been a significant rise in crime, an increase in security problems, and an increase in juvenile delinquency including teenage theft and promiscuity that represents a shattering of traditional authority. Absenteeism, school-girl pregnancies, and adolescent VD are major concerns of Kenyan parents. Alcoholism affects families in both rural and urban areas, and the "bachelor town" syndrome found particularly in Nairobi causes long separations and erodes family cohesiveness. Anomie and loss of identity are talked about by Kenyan sociologists as problems of modern society.

Fading Cultural Values

Many of Kenya's social problems are blamed on loss of identity and cultural values. Writers Bethwell Ogot and Ben Kipkorir point out that many age-old values have disappeared and others changed dramatically in one or two generations. Traditional etiquette and decorum have disappeared in the cities. Marriage, birth, and child-naming ceremonies have changed. Even customs surrounding death have been altered. Burial ceremonies today reflect Western notions of emotion and mourning, and a burial feast for an important person may be delayed a year in order to be organized as an extravaganza, a practice unheard of two generations ago.

The basic criticism is that Kenyans have chosen aggressive Western materialism as a national ethic, a choice that is counter to Kenyan traditions of sharing and mutual support. Kipkorir blames colonial rule, which he says was by its basic nature at war with African culture. Colonialism was a political steamroller that left Kenyans sadly lacking in meaningful values. It was a process of domination that depersonalized Africans, misinterpreted their history, and demanded the learning of another language.[35]

Most writers admit that complex forces contributed to Kenyan cultural loss and most are aware of the argument that colonialism brought some "good" in the areas of literacy, technology, health, and agriculture. The tragedy in their view is that few Kenyans were able to select the positive elements from the Western values and simultaneously maintain their own integrity. One consequence is that the black elite who have wholeheartedly embraced Western values are alien from their mother culture, a situation that contributes to the gap between rich and poor.

Kenyan writers like Micere Mugo and Ngugi wa Thiong'o suggest that the independence period has been no better than the colonial period in promoting cultural values.[36] Nationalism rushed Kenyans toward the creation of a nation-state without establishing any unifying cultural institutions, and as yet a national culture has not crystallized. The drift is away from a common indigenous heritage to either Western commercial values or forms of shallow cultural exotica that Micere Mugo calls the "drumming, dancing, jumping with spears business for tourists."

Kenyan leaders have shrunk from embracing the past. Despite their rhetoric in support of African heritage, Kenyatta, Mboya, Kariuki, and other Kenyan nationalists did not believe that Kenyan cultural values were the key to development. Western religion, medicine, and free enterprise were each emphasized over the indigenous systems. The practice continues today. Modern politicians not only bypass indigenous values, they openly use Western dress, automobiles, and forms of entertainment as status symbols, particularly as a way of distinguishing themselves from the masses.

Religious Values

As cultural values have changed, so too have religious ideas and practices. Kenya today is a meeting ground for Christianity, Islam, and traditional faiths, and each has devout followers. Christianity is estimated to account for the religious beliefs of 54 percent of the population (38 percent Protestant, 16 percent Catholic), Islam some 6 percent, and traditional faiths 40 percent.[37] The estimates are speculative. Religious conversions, cross-overs, and the tendency of some people to embrace two faiths simultaneously make quantification impossible. Part of the problem lies in establishing just what constitutes a traditional religion. Historically each of Kenya's ethnic groups had well-established religious tenets that interpreted life, provided rules, and lent authority to political leaders and ritual healers. Although eroded by education and conversion to Christianity or Islam, these indigenous systems still have currency in some areas, particularly among older Kenyans. Generally these systems embraced beliefs in a god or creator, a spirit world, and a human world wherein spiritual attacks could occur and spiritual protection was necessary. Most systems honored ancestors as links to the spirit world and some venerated animals, rocks, and trees as embodiments of these spirits.

The mixing of indigenous religious ideas with Christian and Muslim tenets has gone on in Kenya for generations. The outcome has been an array of messianic churches, prophet movements, and Christian breakaway sects that borrow ideas from each other. The process may include belief in a black Jesus, the mixing of African prophet names with Biblical names within newly drafted scriptures, the use of local place names in Christian hymns, or the use of drumming and traditional dancing as part of the basically Christian service. Other forms of this syncretism include the use of Islamic robes and turbans in Christian sects.[38]

The Kenya entrepreneurial ethic, or at least the opportunistic elements in it, is also seen in the shifts of religious affiliation. In drought-prone areas, "posho" (cornmeal) Christians increase in numbers when the churches provide famine relief. In other areas, affiliation with the churches may be in name only, and carried basically for economic association, particularly where most businessmen are Christian. Anyone who has attended a mission-run school is inclined to claim that denomination as his own, even though he may not have been to church since school days. Twice as many people as the Christian churches had on their rosters claimed the Christian religion in the 1962 census.

Despite the opportunism and uncertain affiliation, religion in contemporary Kenya is a major force. President Moi is a devoted Christian, and biblical virtues are a part of his national oration. The Christian church hierarchies, particularly through Anglican and Catholic bishops, have significant political power. Missionary support of hospitals, clinics, schools, and other development establishments gives the church further influence in the society.

Independent local churches are extremely important institutions of social control and political outlet. As for Islam, although small in terms of total population, it has influence on the coast and in urban areas where Arab and Asian Muslims are members of the business elite.

Indigenous religions are clearly being eroded, but their tenets still .have currency in healing when supernatural forces are thought to be active, or in questions of fortune and misfortune. When a child dies or a disaster strikes, age-old ideas of supernatural cause may be embraced. As in all faiths, there are attempts to explain the inexplicable.

LOOKING AHEAD: LAND VALUE, LAND FEVER

Land issues are central to Kenya's social system and will be for years to come. A land fever grips Kenyans and intertwines both modern and traditional values. No other issue is so political or so explosive. Who has land, who gets land, who buys and sells land—and when and for what price—are the perennial sources of discussion at all levels of the society. The deep-seated consciousness about land is based on land shortage, landlessness, and the social inequities bred by land problems. Land offers basic survival opportunities in an insecure world. Land is welfare when there is no welfare system. Land is wealth when no other forms of wealth are available.

Status and honor are obtained from the land. The qualities that distinguish one person from another are related to the earth. It is honorable to have a large *shamba*, to cultivate it well, to make the soil produce and have a bountiful harvest. To own the land, to be the "father" of the land, gives a man status. To cultivate well, to be successful with the soil, gives a woman distinction. In small communities these distinctions are important. People struggle to control land. Without it, a person is of less consequence.

Religious taboos and supernatural explanations are part of the land picture. In some Kenyan societies the fertility of women is linked to that of the land. Large families and large harvests are thought to be related and, conversely, pollution, spoilage, and contamination of the land are thought to be caused by malevolent people, often infertile women. Supernatural ideas of vengeance and anger may be tied to barrenness and landlessness. Women who are believed to have super-natural abilities are thought to have the power to harm the land, to destroy crops, cause floods, hail, drought, or other misfortune.

Land issues influence behavior among pedestrian people who live in small, closed communities. The location of a new homestead in relation to the economic center of a village can depend on land-tenure practices. If a young, newly married farmer acquires land close to a village center he will increase his chances of social exchange and barter, of gaining economic information, and of eventually acquiring more wealth and status. Land also influences ideas about time, about human rhythm and the pace of life. Kenya's two rainy seasons a year allow double planting of some crops. The entire agricultural cycle can thus occur twice a year. An individual is bound to the land for each process—plowing, planting, weeding, and harvesting. Although the work day, particularly for men, is often short, there are no longer seasons of inactivity that could encourage travel, learning, or leisure activities.

Land issues are behind many problems that erupt between neighbors. Conflicts over land use, exact boundaries, land ownership, or rights of pasture are all conditioned by the need to have and to control land. In western Kenya, over 50 percent of all local court cases have been estimated to be land related. The dynamics of an entire village can be changed by land conflicts, particularly when costly litigation forces kinsmen and friends to take sides.

Looking ahead, land issues will continue to dominate Kenyan society. Population projections are sobering for Kenyan planners, but the core of the society's problem is not population, but the inequity of wealth and income, particularly as reflected in land ownership. For large baronial estates to be owned by Kenya's black elite when nearly 25 percent of the society is landless is part of the problem; for women to be shackled to the land and expected to work it alone is another. For the entrepreneurial ethic to reward some but condemn others to the status of impoverished squatters is a more general statement. Poverty is not the result of population growth, as is fashionable to suggest; rather it is the result of unequal opportunities, unequal education, unequal access to health, and unequal application of the laws of the land. In reality, every Kenyan cannot expect to have land today; every father cannot expect to pass on a parcel of land to each of his sons. Yet these are the abiding hopes of most people. Land and inequality are intertwined, and they are the driving forces behind Kenya's current politics.

4

Modern Politics: The Moi Era

INTRODUCTION

In Africa most of the political rights that nationalists fought for at independence have been eroded or lost. The rights to a free press, free parliament, and independent judiciary, and the rights to organize politically, to form labor unions, and to criticize the government openly have given way to closed authoritarian systems, often of a military nature. "Peasant power" and political freedom have been circumscribed. The avenues of political action through political parties, councils, cooperatives, or other associations have been undermined and replaced by centralized control. In their place have grown alternative, informal systems of political action and dissent, including exile parties, underground cells, welfare groups, and politicized church activities.

Kenya has been fortunate on these scores. Periodic repressions have occurred, and government action just before and in the aftermath of the attempted coup of mid-1982 eroded some such freedoms, but overall the basic rights of citizens, of the Parliament, and of the press have been maintained. In comparison to neighboring Ethiopia, Somalia, and Uganda, Kenya has been a paragon of freedom and political stability.

In the early 1980s Kenya's political system was fundamentally unchanged from the Kenyatta era. The political structure had been kept intact, the government's modus operandi was similar, and most of the elite were still the elite. In his first five years as president, Daniel Moi changed several top government officials and periodically reshuffled his cabinet. But in terms of political policies, the nation remained conservative and pro-Western. Kenya had evolved to a modified parliamentary system with a de facto and then de jure single party, a centralized administration, a strong presidency, and an independent judiciary. Kenya's economic pathway continued to be capitalistic, and despite recession and political upheaval the basic entrepreneurial ethic remained firmly in place.

In the Moi years, the entrepreneurial ethic in the ongoing quest for prosperity has been a double-edged sword. Support that sustained the regime came from the wealthy elite and the middle classes who wanted the status quo maintained. Support also came from the West through the multinational corporations (MNCs) and through massive infusions of foreign aid. Kenya's patron-client system continued to work, partly from resources that filtered down from the aid. On the other hand, the entrepreneurialism unleashed destabilizing forces. As the 1978–1982 recession deepened, illicit economic activity became more commonplace, and corruption proliferated. As resources became scarce in the patron-client networks, dissent and unrest increased. The stability of the regime became the basic issue, second only to the issue of its very survival.

THE FIRST FIVE YEARS

Although the government structure was kept in place by Daniel Torotich arap (son of) Moi when he became Kenya's second president in November 1978, in fact a dramatic new political era had begun.[1] The Kenyatta years had set the mold. The constitutional and parliamentary systems were in place, the rules were known (if not always obeyed), and the old problems well understood. Kenya was poor, rural, dependent on cash-crop exports, and closely tied to the Western economies. As Moi came to power, so too did a new set of problems. The country faced a continuing energy crisis, foreign currency was in short supply, interest rates were rising, the nation's ability to feed itself faltered, and within months of Moi's ascendency came the sobering news of the 1979 census and of Kenya's exceptionally high population growth rate, the highest in the world.

The first five years of the Moi era may be seen in three parts: a honeymoon period, 1978–1979; then a period of economic decline and political turbulence, 1980–1981; followed by a period of upheaval surrounding the attempted coup of mid-1982 that gave way to the relative stability surrounding Moi's reelection in September 1983.

1978–1979

First, as vice-president under Kenyatta, Moi automatically assumed the presidency for a three-month interregnum when Kenyatta died. A plot to unseat him never fully developed, and before the end of the three months it was obvious he had marshalled enough support to win KANU's nomination. Part of the reason for Moi's success was that he moved swiftly to consolidate his position, bringing two Kikuyu leaders, Charles Njonjo, the attorney general, and Mwai Kibaki, the finance minister, into his close confidence. By the time the KANU nominating convention met to pick candidates there was no effective opposition. His election in November 1978 was more a national celebration than a contest of power. The national parliamentary election a year later, on November 8, 1979, ousted most of the old Kenyatta guard, brought to power many candidates sympathetic to Moi, and in effect gave him a sweeping mandate.[2]

Because he had been vice-president of Kenya for eleven years, Daniel Moi was well known in government and diplomatic circles. His reputation was that of a congenial, hardworking civil servant. Born in

Daniel arap Moi, second president of Kenya (1978–   ) (courtesy the *Daily Nation*)

1924 in Sacho location, Baringo District, in the Rift Valley Province, Moi was a member of one of Kenya's smallest ethnic groups, the Tugen of the Kalenjin cluster. He was educated at an American mission school in his home area and thereafter turned to teaching. In 1950 he entered politics, first as a member of the District Council and thereafter as one of the Kenya Legislative Council in 1957. He was one of the first eight Africans elected to the Legislative Council. He split from Luo and Kikuyu colleagues in 1960 to help lead the opposition party, KADU, rejoining KANU in 1964 when KADU disbanded. Between 1961 and 1967 he was successively minister of education, of local government, and of home affairs, becoming Kenya's third vice-president in 1967.[3]

After Moi's election to the presidency in 1978, nearly every political faction in Kenya joined the new system. Kikuyu politicians, although ostensibly reduced in influence because the president was no longer Kikuyu, accepted the new regime. The Luo, the second-largest political force, were elated by the new political order. The senior Luo politician, Oginda Odinga, was given a parastatal post, and many of Odinga's supporters were again allowed to stand in the 1979 election. Most were victorious.

In the honeymoon phase of his regime, Moi vowed to end political factionalism and corruption. As he toured the country to build support for his new regime, his political style gradually emerged. It was that of an amiable, avuncular school teacher, an abstemious man who neither drank nor smoked, a person given to homilies and biblical pronouncements.[4]

To build unity Moi released a dozen detainees who had been held by Kenyatta, abolished school fees, initiated a national literacy campaign, and went to the hustings on the corruption issue. He denounced smugglers, hoarders, and bribe-takers in several open meetings, and behind the scenes moved to clean up the bureaucracy. Police Chief Bernard Hinga, his assistant David Nene, and five senior provincial police commissioners resigned or retired. Two MPs were tried and found guilty of coffee smuggling and sentenced to five years in prison. Land speculators were warned, the Ministry of Works and several government parastatals were singled out for corruption, and some attempt was made to limit unbridled use of funds in election campaigns.

In international affairs, Moi openly embraced a pro-Western course. Kenya withdrew from the Olympic games in Moscow in protest over the Soviet invasion of Afghanistan and continued to denounce the Soviet Union as a major threat to the Indian Ocean "zone of peace." In domestic affairs, a new Five Year Development Plan (1979–1983) was launched, calling for an economic growth rate the first year of 6.3 percent and a major campaign against poverty. The plan's objectives reflected Moi's optimism and his support of free enterprise and the Kenya ethic, although the economic realities of the time were not encouraging. Coffee and tea prices were falling in the world market, manufacturing and tourism were slowing, and a maize shortage was developing.[5]

During 1979 Kenya experienced a spate of strikes that also curtailed the president's optimism. In a Labor Day speech he warned that "legal" strikes could occur only after all other avenues of negotiation had been exhausted and that "illegal" strikers would be dealt with seriously by the courts. On another initiative, Moi tried to improve student-government relations. Late in 1979 the party established a KANU wing at the university, a move that was initially applauded as a way to end the adversarial relationship between students and the government and to enlist students in national development problems.

1980–1981

The second short period in the Moi era was characterized by economic decline and a shift in the central power structure around Moi. The country experienced a new series of strikes and threatened strikes by doctors, students, bank employees, and even professional musicians. Capping these problems were uncertainties about the economy, particularly the food supply. Revelations of major pilfering of the national grain reserves surfaced, as did news of mismanagement in agricultural credit, storage, and transport. In 1980 alone oil costs jumped from K£ 145.7 million the year before to K£ 226 million. During 1980 the nation registered an economic growth of less than 4 percent, and in 1981 the picture grew worse. Sugar, rice, milk, and meat prices rose.[6]

Political turbulence paralleled the two-year economic decline. In early 1980 splinter groups, made up partially of those who lost the 1979 election, became active. Moi's public denunciation of the groups led to a wave of loyalty pledges to him and the government. In February 1980, to strengthen the bureaucracy and gain greater control in Parliament, the president reshuffled his cabinet and expanded the number of ministers from twenty-four to twenty-five. By also increasing assistant ministers and exercising the right to nominate a few MPs, he raised the number of government's members in Parliament to over 50 percent of the chamber, effectively curtailing opposition. The broad ethnic composition of the government ministers was again hailed as an example of democratic process in Kenya. Despite this, Moi continued to receive information about dissidents within the government.

In February 1980 student riots at the university were blamed on poor food, broken cutlery, poor academic organization, and an unsympathetic university administration. The university was calm for March and April, but in May the students went on a destructive street rampage in support of a threatened nationwide doctors' strike. Ominously, demonstrations also occurred in outlying high schools. In one incident students at Kabaa High School wrecked their cafeteria, diesel plant, and headmaster's house in protest over water shortages, textbook shortages, inadequate food, and being forced to wear short pants.

During 1981 Oginga Odinga drifted from favor after suggesting that the reign of Kenyatta had been land-grabbing and malevolent. Government spokesmen quickly attacked Odinga for his "slanderous assertions" against the regime. Other signs of political unrest in mid-1981 included an inconclusive treason trial of a civilian trying to buy arms from the army and a government ban on tribal unions such as GEMA (Gikikuyu, Embu, Meru Association), the Luo Union, and the Abaluhya Association. The government stated that it did not wish to limit legitimate cultural activities or ignore ethnic differences but wanted to eliminate negative tribal groups who engaged in divisive politics.

In 1981, Moi again reshuffled his cabinet, elevating inner circle loyalists G. G. Kariuki and Nicholas Biwott to cabinet posts as he looked for ways to keep political dissent under control. To bolster the regime, Moi expanded the army in 1980 from 12,400 to 14,750, increased military salaries, and formed a new infantry battalion named the "Moi Battalion." To underscore Kenya's military readiness, both internally and externally, Moi hosted Mengistu Haile Mariam, the Soviet-backed Ethiopian leader. During the convivial four-day visit, Somali military irredentism was jointly condemned.

As 1981 drew to a close, violent tribal land clashes erupted in the Nandi-Luhya border areas of western Kenya, the product of long-standing boundary tensions. This violence and the food shortages in many rural areas suggested that Kenya's festering political problems were not only urban but cut broadly across the society. In December 1981, while presenting 2,654 degrees at the university graduation, Moi warned against agitation, wayward ideologies, and "ivory tower" reactions. He stated that the university was free to perform its functions, but emphasized that such freedom must be respected by students and faculty.

Through this two-year period, Daniel arap Moi became sterner, more paternalistic, less flexible, and far less jovial. He lectured against social disobedience and repeatedly called for loyalty to the government. The unanswered question of the time was whether Moi's sterner style came from his belief that he was in total control and could be more harsh, or whether it reflected his fear that society was crumbling and that an authoritarian rod was needed to sustain his regime.[7]

1982-1983

In the third period of the Moi era, the president's reelection and the coup attempt of August 1982 were the major events. The coup attempt was a national trauma, and some historic perspective on the event is needed. Although the recent Moi years had been difficult, there were still no deep ideological splits in Kenya. Sympathy for the populist views of the late J. M. Kariuki and the now out-of-favor Oginga Odinga did exist, but radicalism—advocating the violent overthrow of the government—had never occurred. What apparently happened in 1982 within higher government circles was a fear of plots, an increased suspicion of writers, lecturers, and students, and a growing uncertainty about the government's stability. How much of this was accurate and how much was paranoia will never be known. Certainly these events occurred in a broader context of tensions that included the effects of the world recession, periodic lawlessness in Kenya's border areas, problems in both university and secondary schools, and large-scale overspending in both the health and defense sectors.

Political tension rose perceptibly in May 1982. While in London, Oginga Odinga criticized Moi's government and suggested it was time to form an opposition party. Moi labeled Odinga's actions divisive and destructive. On June 9, under pressure from Moi loyalists, Parliament passed legislation that made Kenya a de jure one-party state, an action that banned any organized opposition to the government. During this time Moi used the preventive detention law for the first time against four university lecturers, a former MP, an attorney, and a former deputy director of intelligence. Tension further increased when an alleged plot by students and lecturers to buy guns for dissidents was revealed. On July 21, the editor of the *Standard* was dismissed for an editorial that criticized the regime for detention without trial, intimidation, and "causing fear and insecurity in the body politic."[8]

Kenya's bloodiest uprising and most serious threat to civilian rule began at 3:30 A.M., August 1, 1982, when Kenya air force personnel seized the radio station, the post office, two air bases, the international airport, and several other strategic points in Nairobi. The first radio announcement by the "People's Redemption Council" stated that the reason for the coup was that "rampant corruption and nepotism have made life almost intolerable in our society. The economy is in a shambles, and the people cannot afford food, housing, or transport."[9]

Army troops loyal to the government counterattacked rebel positions after dawn, and by noon the government announced the rebellion had ended. This was accurate for Nairobi, but fighting continued for several days at the Nanyuki Air Base near Mt. Kenya. During the upheaval students at the university had been forced out of their dormitories by rebels to demonstrate for the Redemption Council; some did, while others hid or slipped out of the fracas. Almost immediately looters had begun breaking into Nairobi shops, and for the next two days indiscriminate looting occurred. To restore order, army troops were ordered to shoot looters on sight. When civil order was restored, the official tallies listed 159 killed, $3 million in goods lost, and extensive property damage. Unofficial reports put the death toll between 600 and 1,800, including one Japanese tourist, an Asian United Nations employee, and countless bystanders. A number of Asian women were raped.

In the immediate aftermath of the uprising, some loyal troops began a protracted search for rebels, while others returned truckloads of looted goods to the Kenyatta Conference Center. Moi reassured the nation by radio and asked everyone to resume work. All air force personnel were arrested, and shortly thereafter, the entire air force disbanded. The university was closed, some students arrested, and an investigation into the uprising begun. Two air force enlisted men, believed to be key instigators, fled to Tanzania by small aircraft and were given asylum by the Tanzania government.

In the ensuing months military courts gave jail sentences ranging up to 25 years to several hundred airmen. By March 1983, six officers and two enlisted men had been sentenced to death, although no executions had been announced. In civilian courts charges against all but a few student leaders and other civilians were dropped. One explanation suggested that the attempted coup was a whimsical, episodic event without deep social roots and largely the work of malcontents on a binge. This theory points to air force personnel all over Africa as jaunty,

Kenyatta Conference Center tower, downtown Nairobi, viewed from Uhuru Gardens (photo by David Keith Jones)

arrogant, and highly educated men who often believe they can do anything with their awesome military power.

A second explanation ties the putsch directly to social causes, particularly the economic decline, citing falling incomes in tea and coffee, energy costs, population problems, and food shortages in urban areas. The rebels' first radio broadcasts stated that the "people cannot afford food, housing, or transport" as evidence of this thesis. Others who take this position point specifically to political issues. Smith Hempstone, a writer with long experience in Kenya, noted that the rebels essentially charged Moi "with imposing a one-party state, censoring the press, violating human rights, indulging in corruption and nepotism, and mismanaging the economy. In effect, the have-nots were rising against the haves, and there was more than a little truth in the charges."[10]

A third explanation portrays the uprising as a series of misfired plots. The central theme here is that the air force plot was only one of those underway, that plotters in the air force, army, and police were cooperating, but that due to fear of exposure, the air force group attacked prematurely, failing to bring army and police with them. It is suggested that Kenyans in the army, air force, and police knew of these plans two weeks before the event, and that in fact Kenyan intelligence officers knew of the plot but did not inform Moi.[11]

Whatever the exact reasons, the civilians' behavior during the uprising pointed to serious social tensions. The nearly instantaneous looting by thousands of urban dwellers, even if deliberately organized

Charles Njonjo, minister of constitutional affairs and former attorney general, shortly before being eased from office (courtesy the *Daily Nation*)

by the coup leaders, spoke dramatically of social malaise just below the surface. The unbridled attacks on Asian shops, and by some troops in the aftermath on Asian women, underscored the resentment many low-income Africans have for the Asian trading class. More broadly, the uprising challenged the governmental system. The unanswered question throughout late 1982 and early 1983 was whether the regime would be able to respond to the social discontent, to ease the malaise and let some dissent exist.

Two events in 1983 gave partial answers: Charles Njonjo and the political faction he headed were eased from power, and Daniel Moi was reelected president in a rousing national election that saw over 900 candidates stand for 156 seats in Parliament.

Njonjo, 63, former attorney general, minister of constitutional affairs, and chairman of his local KANU branch, had been an early confidant of Moi when he came to power; indeed, Njonjo helped Moi consolidate his position in the transition period. Although without a strong local constituency, Njonjo, a Kikuyu, had built a powerful following at the national level and was one of the few possible challengers to Moi's power. Factional fighting behind the scenes among Njonjo forces, other Kikuyu forces, and Moi loyalists apparently began before the 1982 coup attempts. One afterthought about the coup suggests it was perpetrated

Mwai Kibaki, vice-president of Kenya (1979–   ) (courtesy the *Daily Nation*)

against Moi because he was moving so slowly to ease Njonjo from power.

Whatever the case, Njonjo's departure was unique in Kenyan politics. The only other Kenyan leaders who commanded large followings and posed threats to the central establishment, Tom Mboya and J. M. Kariuki, were assassinated. Njonjo was simply forced out of office. He had quickly become the focus of speculation when President Moi announced that a "traitor" was plotting with a foreign country to overthrow the government. Moi immediately made it clear that Vice-President Mwai Kibaki was not the suspect. Njonjo was accused of being the culprit in Parliament by several MPs. The informal charges against Njonjo included connections with South Africa, possession of large foreign bank accounts, and vague allegations that he was in league with other countries, perhaps Israel, the United States, or the United Kingdom, which would aid his ascendancy to power. When Njonjo later resigned from Parliament, rejoicing broke out in the chamber. President Moi, who had been silent throughout the crisis, ordered that talk about the affair be stopped, citing the Biblical passage "Let him among you who is without blame cast the first stone."

During the Njonjo affair, national attention turned to the up-coming national election that had been set for September 1983, a year earlier than necessary. Standing unopposed for both his Baringo parliamentary seat and the presidency, Moi quickly won the party's nomination. For the national parliamentary election, all but four applicants were cleared by KANU to stand (a contrast to earlier elections when many candidates had been declared ineligible by the party). Moi had made it clear that the "traitor" issue should not be at stake in the election, but in fact, the survival or demise of Njonjo's supporters was one of the key issues. Great interest was focused on whether Moi could use the ballot box to legitimate the departure of Njonjo by ousting Njonjo's supporters from Parliament.

The results of the balloting September 26, 1983, were inconclusive as far as Njonjo's former supporters were concerned. Some were defeated, but others were returned, and a few of Njonjo's critics, including John Keen, were defeated. More conclusive was the prompt appointment by Moi of his new twenty-three-member cabinet, which was made up of Moi loyalists. The only European standing for election, Philip Leakey, became assistant minister of foreign affairs. Those dropped from the new cabinet included Stanley Oloitipitip and Charles Rubia. Three ministries were eliminated by reconsolidation. As a result of the elections and the Njonjo affair, Moi's power was consolidated and Kikuyu power in the national arena was, for the moment, significantly diminished.

POLITICAL CHARACTERISTICS

Looking beyond immediate events, the Moi era by 1984 could be termed Kenya's "cyclical" period, as compared to the "dynastic" period in Kenyatta's last years. The dynastic phase was essentially a broad form of nepotism and government by the "family," wherein any remote tie to the Kenyatta family, either real or imagined, was tantamount to political influence that could magically win contracts, acquire land, and find favored treatment. The cyclical period under Moi was characterized initially by the rule of law, constitutionality, open elections, a relatively free press, and government by regulation. It was a time that reemphasized the constitution, the Kenya Bill of Rights, and the protection of the common man under the law.

Gradually, however, the events of 1981–1982 had begun a new, cyclical process. Politics became confrontational, more aggressive, and more extreme. Dissidents, whether Luo groups, university students, or elements of the military, were pitted against the central regime with the common purpose of replacing it. The regime in turn became more protective, more beleaguered, and more bunkerlike. Compared to the relatively open system of 1979, Moi's government in 1982 had shut down many avenues of criticism. The concern became one of shoring up the government, not focusing on ways to accommodate protest or aid the sagging economy. The preoccupation was in dealing with active dissent, which had become a major characteristic of the society. Following the coup attempts and the departure of Njonjo in 1983, the pendulum swung again to a period of "good feeling" and post-election euphoria that found the regime pointing with pride to the new stability and the "new democracy." The basic difference between Kenya's two independent regimes was that Kenyatta was a political monarch, Moi an astute political survivor.

In other respects political characteristics of the two eras remained remarkably similar, particularly concerning political values that underlay the entrepreneurial ethic. The Moi regime kept the same government structure, the same policies, and even the same informal process that saw much of the day-to-day politics carried out by special-interest groups. Economic policies continued to center on national growth and expansion. Despite expressed concern for the poor, the Moi government elected to pursue growth of the whole "economic pie," rather than the more equitable distribution of its pieces, in hope that growth of the economy would be good for everyone.

Informal political processes that emerged in Kenyatta's time continued into the Moi era. Churches and welfare groups, ad hoc social organizations, and, to a lesser extent, the *Harambee* movement continued to be the focal points of political activity at the grass roots. As occurred periodically in the 1960s and 1970s, "night meetings" reemerged as a political phenomenon in the 1980–1982 period. They included clandestine dissent groups, and most seem to have been known to the central authorities. In tandem with these informal political processes was a proliferation of informal and underground economic activity as described in earlier chapters. Much of this activity was illicit.

Politics continued to be based on patron-client relations, on alliances and factions that have continued to exist throughout the system. For example, the Kikuyu people, over 20 percent of the population, have dominated the "central alliance" made up of themselves, Embu, Meru, and some Kamba peoples. A "western alliance" of Luo, Luhya, and Kisii also exists on many political issues. Outside these groupings in recent years has been a Rift Valley alliance made up of Kalenjin and some Maasai. Farther out politically are the Mijikenda of the coast, who form a loose alliance. Peoples of the north and northeast, such as the Turkana, Boran, Samburu, and Somali, are politically fragmented and basically without alliances.[12]

The informal rules of politics also remained remarkably similar in the Kenyatta and Moi eras. In the view of a Kikuyu elder and former politician in Nyeri District, who preferred to remain anonymous, they boil down to three suggestions on how to survive: "Honor the top," then "pay tribute," and finally "use your *matatu* man."

"Honor the top" is a prescription to support the governing elite, to allay their insecurities and to avoid political threats of any kind. In Kenyatta's era and in the early Moi era, most political activists abided by this rule in exchange for a degree of openness and economic opportunity in the system. The rule is based on the clear elite-mass distinction in Kenya politics. In the Moi era, the elite core consists of the president and his inner circle, prominent people around them, and high-level government bureaucrats who act as power brokers. This top echelon has included Mwai Kibaki, G. G. Kariuki, Nicholas Biwott,

Simeon Nyachae, and, until his fall from power in 1983, Charles Njonjo. Near the core are other cabinet ministers, MPs, some central administrators such as permanent secretaries and provincial commissioners, a few lawyers, academics, church people, and wealthy businessmen.

"Pay tribute" is a prescription to share profits with those in powerful positions, in exchange for business opportunites and business protection. The rule underscores the patron-client system that has operated in stages between the central core and the national elite, between the national elite and the regional elite, and between the regional elite and their district and village clients. The crucial link is to the district level, where the common features of politics continue to be bossism and allegiance to a few local big men who have contacts upwards. These local big men may be traders, entrepreneurs, kinsmen of urban elite, local MPs, or counselors, but their influence stems from ties to the capital. Their power lies in their ability to allocate rewards, assign jobs, get contracts, waive fees, and make business contacts. They are themselves brokers, or are closely tied to the go-betweens who link the system. As in any part of the patron-client system, there is interdependence; each link needs the others.

"Use your *matatu* man" refers to the use of brokers or rural taxi (*matatu*) operators who serve as go-betweens to bring the system together. In the Moi era, as factions and alliances have proliferated, the go-betweens have included some small-scale politicians. *Matatu* men engage in a circuit-riding process, usually between Nairobi (or a provincial capital) and a local area. They are mobile couriers who may be traders or transport owners, taxi drivers or traveling part-time farmer-politicians. It is a diversified system that allows an individual to play in both national and local arenas. The *matatu* men are brokers between the elite and the common folk, between clients and their patrons, between the formal and informal systems. The "rule" of using your *matatu* man, like the other "rules," enhances the status quo and promotes stability. How long these "rules" will be followed in the face of greater dissent and new confrontations is unknown. Much depends on events outside Kenya in the arena of world prices and world politics. Much also depends on what specific issues arise to affect the body politic.

POLITICAL ISSUES

Analysts could focus specifically on a dozen issues in contemporary Kenya that affect its political stability: exploitation by the elite, land issues, political corruption, political repression, election rigging, or the lack of political participation, to name but a few. In the aftermath of the 1982 uprising, the political roles of the military, the press, and university students are perhaps most germane to understanding contemporary Kenya.

The Military

First, Kenya's military policy has been to develop an elite force of highly trained light infantry, supported by a small, combat-ready air

force (now disbanded), a naval patrol force, and an independent paramilitary police (the Government Service Unit or GSU). At the beginning
of 1980, Kenya's total military establishment was small, particularly
when compared to that of its neighbors. The army was estimated at
14,000, while Somalia's army was 120,000 and Tanzania's 60,000. Since
1980, a build-up has been underway with U.S. and British assistance.[13]

Aside from a mutiny in 1964, a sedition trial that implicated some
officers in 1971, and the "*Ngoroko*" plot of 1978 surrounding the Kenyatta-
Moi transition, Kenya's military had not surfaced as a political force
until the 1982 putsch. The reasons for this include the small size of the
military, emphasis on professionalism and the separation of civil and
military functions, selective recruiting, and checks and balances within
the ranks to keep it out of politics. Under Kenyatta, the services had
been deliberately structured to be multiethnic, so that no single tribal
group became dominant. Thus a commander could be a Kamba, the
second-in-command a Kikuyu, and the third a Luo. In addition, the
GSU, which is totally self-contained and has its own equipment, served
as an independent counterweight to the army. If necessary it could
operate as a deterrent to the army in support of civil authorities.

Other reasons for noninvolvement of the military in political issues
included the fact that Kenyans seek military careers; the military is an
all-volunteer force whose life-style is considered good. The personnel
are well paid and have their own housing, food, medical, and recreational
facilities. The spheres of military activity are well defined. The army
has been kept out of police actions and riot control and there is no
mixing of army and police. (The GSU is specifically trained for riot
control and does help the police when called upon.)

In terms of training, Kenya's military forces have been considered
highly professional; army officers, for example, are often graduates of
Sandhurst in England, and noncommissioned officers are well grounded
in special courses. Traditionally, promotion has been through the ranks,
and many of the first Kenyan officers served in the colonial forces. The
army has a tradition that traces its history to the battalions of The
King's African Rifles that fought in both World War I and World War
II.

Yet the factors behind the 1982 attempted coup suggest that no
matter how well paid its troops, or how stirring a battalion history, the
military is always a potential problem. Not only in Kenya but in many
other nations the rule, rather than the exception, has been that when
economic and social conditions become difficult, and when rumors of
corrupt practices in the civil leadership prevail, military personnel may
see it as their "duty" to save the nation. Kenya's brush with military
rule followed this pattern. Because the coup attempt failed, the civilian
leaders initially had a relatively free hand to reshuffle the forces and
to insure loyalty. What remained uncertain in the aftermath of the
uprising was the relative strength of the army leadership and the civilian
leadership in Kenyan politics. Military influence was unquestionably

greater than at any other time in the nation's history. How pervasive it was occupied public debate for months following August 1982.

The Press

Second, the press is politically important in Kenya because it is still relatively free and has the power to sway opinion.[14] Both the Kenyatta and Moi regimes, however, have put pressure on the press to be restrained, and both governments have either expelled foreign journalists or arrested and detained Kenyan editors and writers. The key concern in the government's view is irresponsible reporting, or sensational articles that can destroy confidence in the regime. Criticism of the president is unacceptable, as is reporting what might harm Kenya's international image. To debate fundamental freedoms, such as the *Standard* editorial did in July 1982, would be acceptable in tranquil times but was unacceptable when the government was under criticism.

Press freedom is cited in the national constitution, but details of how the freedom is to be guaranteed are lacking. There are no laws specifically protecting the press. For this reason, pressures from the government do have influence and a good deal of press restraint occurs. The one legal outlet that gives the press opportunity to criticize government policies is reporting on debates in Parliament. Since Parliament has often been the scene of vociferous, back-bench criticism, the government does not escape untouched.

University Students

Third, students are an important political factor. Kenya's university students are an elite. They have survived a grueling series of examinations that have eliminated their former school classmates. Unlike students in societies with more universities and broader employment opportunities, however, Kenya's students are constrained by the government. Some of the constraint is financial, in that the government awards scholarships for support. Some is psychological in that most students are looking forward to high-status employment, which is usually in the government. In the past, few students were willing to jeopardize their futures by being labeled troublemakers. A geography professor teaching at the university estimated in 1980 that of 8,000 students, fewer than 200 could be considered "radicals," and most of these would become "liberals" as soon as they got jobs within the establishment.

Although student demonstrations occurred during the Kenyatta era, particularly surrounding the Mboya and Kariuki assassinations, the university atmosphere was generally calm. The Moi period has been different. In 1979 there were demonstrations over the government's decision to ban some KANU election candidates. In 1980 the student riots over poor food and other complaints led to closure of the university. In 1981 student riots occurred over government changes in election rules. In 1982 unrest at the campus followed the detention of seven lecturers before the coup attempt; after the putsch, the university was closed and some students were arrested. Under Moi there was little tolerance of "misbehavior"; student demonstrators were on each occasion dealt with swiftly, with arrests made and "outside agitators" implicated. The message was always the same: the Moi regime would brook no open student activism that criticized the regime.

Although the issues that bring students into the streets are usually political, the underlying causes for unrest are more complex. The heavy control of government over their lives and futures is one factor. The necessity to conform, the need to find good jobs to support less fortunate family members, periodic exam pressures, and for some, cultural conflicts between home life and university life are other factors.

Students also have difficulties reconciling some of the inequities they see in Kenyan society. It is common to chastise the elite for their big cars and suburban homes, yet most students have accepted the Kenyan entrepreneurial ethic and are on the same career path as the elite. Like most university students around the world, they embrace "modern" values. They play tennis, dress in fashionable clothes, listen to "in" music, and shun traditional ways of doing things.

Conflicts for students exist when they became a part of internal university issues, particularly when drawn into factions that exist within the faculty. The university has been crosscut by Kikuyu-versus-Luo cleavages, particularly over faculty appointments and scholarship funds. In broader relations with government, a mood of confrontation goes back at least to the late Kenyatta years, when students formed an "unofficial opposition" in league with the press and Parliament's back-benchers.[15]

There are still other important reasons behind student unrest. The location of the university in the capital, near the government and near large, poor settlements such as Mathare Valley and Kawangware, make students constantly aware of government activities and of the inequities of the system. The management of the university at times has been severely criticized by those outside the institution, as well as by students and faculty. The fact that no tradition of student participation in the running of university affairs exists is a further source of frustration. Such frustration is often cast in ideological terms.

INTERPRETATIONS OF POLITICAL LIFE: REALITY AND IDEOLOGY

Kenya's political economy may be described as a special brand of African capitalism carried on by a black elite, a complex urban middle class, and a rural middle class of farmer-entrepreneurs, each aided in part by infusions of international capital. Although there is a wide private debate on where the economy is heading and what can be done to improve the society, ideological issues have not been discussed publicly since the demise of the KPU opposition party in 1969. Neither Jomo Kenyatta, in his later years, nor Daniel Moi has encouraged such debates.

The reality today is that Kenyan leadership is essentially in two philosophical camps. The dominant leadership is conservative. It embraces

ideas of free enterprise, foreign investment, and fiscal controls acceptable
to the International Monetary Fund. The second group is best described
as a "populist" minority. It is made up of individuals who talk of the
"interests of the people" and "what's good for the common man." Most
of these leaders including Oginga Odinga, J. M. Kariuki (until his
assassination), Martin Shikuku, and John Seroney have accepted the
private sector and many capitalist elements. Their ongoing concern has
been to spread the wealth and create social reform.

Standing back from the reality, dozens of writers, artists, and
academics have offered analytical interpretations of the Kenyan political
economy, and at least four positions along an ideological spectrum are
found.[16] First, on the far left, are Kenyan Marxists who believe that a
major class conflict is brewing in Kenya. Because capitalistic forms of
ownership, production, marketing, and supply have evolved, Marxists
believe there will inevitably be a class war, or revolution, which is seen
as necessary to change the Kenya system. Kenyan and expatriate Marxists
writing about Kenya argue that a rich elite controls the economic
apparatus, and that this elite shares relatively little with other Kenyans
and in fact creates greater poverty and economic misery. Most Marxists
are academics, although a few playwrights and artists are also of this
persuasion.

Second, Kenyan socialists usually believe that a class confrontation
is not inevitable, that peaceful change is possible particularly if government ownership and economic control are more efficient. Many find
sympathy with the British Fabian movement in advocating public ownership of the means of production, distribution, and supply. A moralistic,
humanitarian, nonconformist element, such as that found in British
Fabianism, is also articulated in Kenya, mainly by academics and other
writers. Other Kenyan socialists are stimulated by Scandinavian agrarian
reform thinking. They advocate stronger cooperative and marketing
arrangements, greater local autonomy for farmers, and greater equity
and land reform. Kenyan socialists usually advocate a mixed economy
wherein a private sector works under government controls. Class differences are seen as important but are not usually defined in strict
Marxist economic terms.[17]

Third, Kenyan liberals support the mixed-economy idea with socialists, but see advantages to greater free enterprise and foreign investment. They see class distinctions as unfortunate, but perhaps inevitable, and a greater degree of mercantilism as acceptable, if restrained
by government. Most younger civil servants are in this camp, advocates
of the profit motive for themselves and for individuals in general. Some
influential writers and press people, including the editors of Kenya's
Weekly Review, are liberals. It can also be argued that the Kenya
government, despite its conservative verbal pronouncements, is in this
camp. Government is the largest employer; it embraces a "mixed-
economy" approach in that free enterprise is permitted, but regulated
by parastatal organizations, while at the same time the government

owns the railroad, airline, communication system, and portions of many private corporations.

Finally, Kenyan conservatives call for more private ownership, more free enterprise, and less social control, arguing that as the economy grows, nearly everyone will benefit. The conservatives reject the class argument as crucial to the economy and suggest that inequity in Kenya is a part of the soil, of the land, of the accident of birth. The conservatives are entrepreneurs or would-be entrepreneurs; they support multinational investment in Kenya and applaud foreign aid (striving to be in a position to benefit from it). Most African lawyers, doctors, businessmen, and other professionals are in this camp, as are some military and many high-level government officers. Most of the wealthy Kenyans who have large land holdings are by nature conservative; most have become rich in one generation.[18]

Although a number of issues discussed earlier swirl continuously through ideological writing and debate (corruption, equity, land reform, and the income grab, to cite only a few), four issues in particular have had currency in the Moi era. These are the issues of class, dependency, corporate transnationalism, and the status of peasants.

On class issues there is no consensus. Marxists are split over what economic categories are essential to discuss. Socialists and liberals admit there are class problems in Kenya but do not define them as strictly economic, rather as social strata determined largely by education, occupation, tribe, religion, and income. Conservatives are not concerned with class issues, except to protect their own principles.

On dependency, again there is little consensus. The notion that Kenya is a dependent satellite of the West has been abandoned or modified in recent years because it does not explain very much. The current focus of the problem is that dependency is not so much a geopolitical issue as one of economic networks, groups, and individuals who are caught in a historical process that is difficult to change. The argument centers on the idea that nations do not exploit other nations as much as do less-defined business groups operating in complex economic relationships. International mining, manufacturing, trade, and agriculture have their own forms of dependency. If exploitation occurs it is not one nation doing it to another, but rather individual arrangements in different subsectors of the world economy.

On multinational corporations (MNCs), Marxists and socialists differ. They disagree about the need for the MNCs, on the benefits they bring, on whether the industrialization process brutalizes Kenyan workers, and even on whether Kenya's scarce materials are used for the manufacturing of nonessential items. Liberals argue that MNCs are useful if they pay their way. Conservatives suggest they are crucial to the development of Kenya and for the transfer of technology in a modern economy; the exploitation and brutalization arguments are rejected with evidence of the high taxes paid to Kenya by the MNCs and the employee benefits and wages they provide.[19]

Concerning the status of the Kenyan peasantry, or rural poor, three arguments prevail. One is that peasants are gradually improving their lot, some are doing well (such as those in Kisii or Nyeri districts), and the future is moderately hopeful. Another is that there is major differentiation within the peasantry, some getting poorer, some getting richer. This camp holds that a "middle peasantry" is evolving as a form of rural middle class, engaging in some export crop production, hiring some casual labor, feeding themselves from farm produce, and keeping some surplus to trade locally. They are not yet "managers" owning estates, or well-to-do "kulak" farmers, but an emerging rural middle class. The third argument holds that there is no differentiation, that the trend is downward, that only the elite and the "kulaks" are getting rich, and that the peasantry is sliding into greater poverty and greater misery.

To put this debate into perspective it is important to remember that public ideological discussion in Parliament or in the press is not Kenya's way. Certain issues such as corruption or the role of multinational corporations are acceptable topics, within limits, but the main ideological forum has been within academic circles and in academic literature, much of it published outside Kenya.

Kenyan "realists" who count themselves among the elite and urban middle class—the press, civil servants, business people, military personnel, and others—tend to view ideological discussions as largely irrelevant. The suggestion is that such philosophizing is Western ethnocentrism of European extraction, a way of using ideas and labels like "Marxism," "socialism," and "capitalism" as if they easily transferred to the African political landscapes. The realists see the debates as too abstract. The fact that much of the ideological discussion surrounds peasant economic behavior also seems premature. Although there have been a few excellent studies, no one knows as yet what a synthesis of Kenya's many peasant subcultures would indicate. Peasant farmers have their own life views, which are not particularly ideological. In short, from the realists' viewpoints, the intelligentsia may be debating the "peasantry" as a topic, but the peasantry is not debating either the intelligentsia or their ideological concerns.

On balance, criticisms of the ideological arena overlook the fact that academic debates have posed important questions and have in recent years led to several empirical studies.[20] The debates have also led to clarifications and distinctions important to understanding Kenyan politics. For example, today there is general agreement on the historical phases that Kenyan capitalists passed through. The progression starts with the traditional political economy, gives way to broader mercantilism and trade systems, to the penetration of European capitalism, to the transformation of African traditional and mercantile systems into proto-capitalist systems, and finally to the evolution of Kenyan black capitalism. Since independence, the progression has seen further infusions of investment and aid monies from the West, further expansion of the entrepreneurial, mercantile class, and an expansion of government involvement in the economy.

There has also been some new thinking on whether or to what degree the colonial forms of capitalism were truly destructive of African traditional values. There are no hard data but much pragmatic evidence that traditional economic values do survive, people still do live with strong communal bonds, still do value kinship ties, and still do rely on reciprocity and mutual support. The basic economic orientation for most rural people is the family and the neighborhood. An "economy of affection" with friends and family, or, more broadly, an "economy of affinity" for people with whom one is comfortable, is still the basis of grass-roots life. Many traditional values, as Colin Leys, Goran Hyden, and others have pointed out, were complementary to capitalist behavior, for example, such peasant orientations as acquisitiveness, individualism, and thrift.[21]

Finally, the ideological debates have helped focus attention on the nature of peasant politics in Kenya, and a few general insights have emerged. For example, Kenyan peasant politics is based on ethnicity, on patron-client relationships, and on the "big man" phenomenon. Political situations are fluid and changing, and dualities and inconsistencies are common. Alliances change with the issues at stake in a chameleon-like political process. Peasants are autonomous and they do live within tiny cultural boundaries. The overriding "isms" are not Western ideological labels, but communalism, localism, familyism, and pedestrianism. Peasant politics is a neighborhood affair, small in scale and small in the space involved.

Overall it is important to emphasize that although critical public debate on ideological issues is not occurring, discussion is permitted by the government on the "ideal society." In the election campaigns of 1983 "the new democracy" was openly discussed, and the coup attempt was criticized as a heavy-handed, gun-toting approach that is not Kenya's way. Some populist ideas of "what's good for the people" were part of the electioneering, and although no one believed that the lofty speeches set the real agenda of political life, they did help to ventilate and restabilize the system. In fact, political stability was the basic issue under debate by all discussants, whether "realists," "populists," or ideological academics.

POLITICAL STABILITY AND THE
ENTREPRENEURIAL ETHIC

Stability was the fundamental issue in the Kenyatta-Moi transition; it was the question when the Kenya economy declined in 1979–1981, and it remained the basic issue in the aftermath of the attempted coup. Stability for Kenya ultimately means the continuation of the constitutional process under conditions of some economic growth. It means "investment climate," a willingness by Kenyans and non-Kenyans to expand and to put money into local endeavors. Stability means confidence that no

radical change will occur, a continuation of the status quo. For the
business elite, the ultimate economic fear is loss of investment. For the
governing elite, the ultimate fear is loss of their government.[22]

Stability is usually determined by how a regime responds to crises,
but even the most adaptable regime may be dealing with forces out of
its control. Kenya's free-wheeling entrepreneurial system may in fact
carry the seeds of its own destruction. Unregulated entrepreneurs play
at the edge of legality. When resources become tight, boundaries are
overstepped and rules broken, a process that undermines the system
and adds corruption to a leader's problems. External economic and
political events are equally destabilizing. The world recession contributed
directly to Kenya's economic woes. Kenya is drawn into Indian Ocean
politics as a pro-Western state, a fact that leads to arms build-up and
the creation of unstable military forces. Nairobi is a base for exiles and
exiled parties from Somalia, Ethiopia, and Uganda, an unhealthy situation
if exiles and local dissidents interact and feed each other's anger.

A further question concerning Kenya's stability is the role of
charisma. Kenyatta's charisma was based on his "Father of the Nation"
image, which he cultivated and built upon. Kenyatta used it to bulldoze
his way through many crises. To Moi fell the unenviable task of attempting
to solve some very difficult national problems without such an image.
Ultimately stability is determined by a regime's persistence, durability,
and adaptability—the willingness of leaders to be flexible, to give and
take, and allow the system to ventilate, to blow off steam. Kenyatta
had this ability in his early years. Moi took five years to gain similar
control; in fact this was a remarkable achievement in that Moi came to
the presidency with no family network, no great wealth, no ethnic base,
and few well-placed political allies.

On balance, Daniel arap Moi inherited a difficult situation by any
measure. Several factors ran against him soon after the honeymoon
period ended. His regime was criticized for the same excesses as
Kenyatta's, for the continued use of unaccountable power, the continued
protection of the business elite, and for new forms of ethnic favoritism
that highlighted his own Kalenjin people. Land barons seemingly continued to prosper at the expense of land reform for the poor. At the
same time, Moi's lieutenants were not successful at protecting his flanks.
His attempt at gaining Luo support, through overtures to Odinga, failed
when the irascible Odinga embarrassed the regime by first resigning
from the government and then suggesting that he would start a new
party. Some Kikuyu leaders, at the same time, mistrusted the overtures
to the rival Luos, a fact that drew some Kikuyu support away from the
regime and re-ignited age-old bickering within Kikuyuland. Factionalism
grew as Kikuyu forces saw their interests being curtailed.

Kenya politics has always been factional politics. Each of Kenya's
leaders manipulated the factions, Kenyatta from above, Mboya from
within as a linchpin between factions, Moi as one who delicately balanced
factions. If the past is prologue, the most unstable factions affecting the

nation will be those surrounding the political power struggle in the central province within Kikuyu ranks.

Two other flashpoints exist. First, the urban poor in Nairobi—the underemployed and unemployed, the squatter groups, and even the middle-level poor—are politically unstable. As the looting sprees of August 1982 demonstrated, civil upheaval is an ongoing possibility. The second flashpoint is the military. Numerous factors can create problems, but probably the most dangerous are messages of discontent reaching soldiers, particularly messages of poverty and suffering from wives and children in the rural areas. Because the military has grown significantly since 1980, many of the safeguards Kenyatta had installed are no longer effective.

Overall, the factors that dictated political stability in the Kenyatta era are still applicable to the Moi era. The stability equation "rests on a balance within the military system, on the centralization of power within the state structure, and on the neutralization of potential foci of organized opposition."[23] Ultimately, if a regime like Moi's has time to react to crises such as those of an economic nature, it may well survive. It is the whimsical, short-term events that are far more difficult to guard against. Who can predict political attacks, assassinations, attempted coups, or civil riots triggered by isolated incidents? A great deal depends on the state of the economy and how well the entrepreneurial ethic is serving the lower echelons.

5

Modern Economic Realities

Kenya's economic quest has been for growth within a relatively open economic system. Until the mid-1970s the nation's economy fared well, particularly in comparison to other African states. In the nine years from 1964 to 1972, Kenya had a 6.8 percent growth in GDP (gross domestic product), as compared to a 4.5 percent growth for other African countries and 5.6 percent for developing countries. In the final years of Kenyatta's reign, growth was at some 7 percent for 1973–1975, rising to 8.6 percent in the coffee boom of 1976–1978. The Moi years have been marked by recession and stagnation, the growth rate dropping in 1979 to 3.5 percent and remaining at about this level during 1980–1983.[1]

Although the contemporary period has been economically difficult, there are a number of positive factors in the picture. The heart of the economy is agriculture, which is moderately well diversified behind the leading commodities of coffee and tea. Foreign investment has continued and foreign aid still provides a major portion of development spending. The banking and financial community is well regarded internationally, and the Ministry of Planning and Economic Development in particular has been led by some of Kenya's best financial minds, beginning with the late Tom Mboya. A key social factor behind the country's economic stability is the large rural society, which serves as an economic cushion for the unemployed. Another factor is the informal economic sector that provides alternative income.

However, problems abound. Food poses one of the most serious economic problems. Until 1978 Kenya was self-sufficient in food production, but since then has been forced periodically to import maize, wheat, powdered milk, and other commodities. Aside from occasional drought, the inability of Kenya to meet its food needs is blamed on wholesale smuggling to neighboring countries, issues of pricing, corruption, inadequate incentives to farmers, changes in the credit system that farmers have relied upon, and management problems including poor storage, loss to pests, and transport.

110

Although other economic problems common to developing nations are found in Kenya, including high energy costs, shortages of foreign currency, and major inequities in the distribution of income, the central questions in the Moi years are threefold. Can the country politically deal with a long period of economic stagnation at a time of high population growth? Can the entrepreneurial system remain intact during these hard times? Finally, what have been the actual consequences in Kenyan life-styles of the government opting for capitalism?

THE MOI ERA

Because the economic fortunes of a country like Kenya are so closely tied to its political cycles, the same demarcations used to assess the Moi political era (Chapter 4) are useful for economic analysis. Each period has a central theme: for 1978–1979, euphoria and the new five-year plan; for 1980–1981 a reaction to stagnation and recession, and for 1982–1983 a preoccupation with financial reorganization and tight fiscal management.

1978–1979

The euphoria at the beginning of the Moi era was based on the peaceful transition from Kenyatta and the economic afterglow of the 1976–1978 coffee boom. In fact, Moi had inherited a troubled economic engine from the Kenyatta regime and the windfall gains from the coffee boom were diverting attention from the realities.[2] Kenya's economic growth slowed in 1979 to 4.3 percent, exports dropped, and the trade balance was a negative K£ 709 million, the highest ever recorded (Table 4, page 116). Nevertheless, Moi's honeymoon period continued into 1979, based partially on the launching of the optimistic Five Year Development Plan for 1979–1983.

As Kenya's fourth development plan, the "Moi Plan" took on the herculean task of "eliminating poverty" and "providing the basic needs of the society" under a targeted growth rate of 6.3 percent.[3] Four basic strategies were set forth: to increase income-sharing opportunities through the creation of employment in rural areas (an envisioned 1.5 million new jobs by 1983); to expand agricultural development; to revise exports and to standardize tariffs; and to gain greater benefits for the state from private investment without destroying investor incentives.

The planning process undoubtedly heightened awareness of economic issues and forced government ministries to focus on the future, but even Moi's close supporters suggested the plan was too optimistic. Others labeled it unrealistic because it called for an impossible growth performance, inconsistent goals, and failed to address the balance-of-payments problems.

The honeymoon period was also aided by Moi's initial candor on Kenya's economic problems. He instructed Mwai Kibaki and other spokesmen to keep the public informed of the "hard options ahead" and particularly to be open about the food realities. During 1979 Moi instituted import controls and moved to stop the erosion of foreign exchange. Overseas travel was restricted, advance deposits were required for imported goods, and later controls were initiated with hindsight. The measures only slowed the economic slide.

1980–1981

The next two years were characterized by serious recession and stagnation, on the one hand caused by low incomes for coffee and tea, and on the other because imported oil prices continued to rise. The country's foreign exchange remained a problem in 1980–1981, causing further belt tightening on imports and pressures by government to increase exports. In fact, the litany of difficulties seems unending. In trade they included rising import costs, sagging overseas markets, serious balance-of-payments deficits, and low export earnings. In industry the difficulties included falling domestic productivity, shortages of raw materials, shortage of equipment and spare parts, and power fluctuations that curtailed industrial productivity. In agriculture, dry weather hurt production, farm credit problems adversely affected farmer incentives, and questions of mismanagement within the agricultural ministry arose. Production tumbled in tea, cereals, pulses, potatoes, and milk. In some cases actual production increased, as in coffee, sisal, and pineapples, only to have less value as world prices fell.

In 1980 consumer prices rose an average of 13.2 percent and building activity slowed. As the realities of the year became clear, the government reduced the targeted growth rate in the five-year plan from 6.3 to 5.4 percent and initiated other belt-tightening measures.[4] Import licenses were further limited, new emphasis placed on agricultural growth, and new ways were sought to use Kenya's resources in lieu of imports.

The year 1981 saw a slight upturn in the economy. The maize crop came in well, although continued high oil-import costs and low prices of agricultural exports were still the reality. In mid-1981, Mwai Kibaki, the vice-president and minister of finance, presented a "poor man's" budget that was applauded for its austerity but criticized for its failure to address the oil problem. In a country dependent on mechanized agriculture, the oil problem also meant the food problem.

During this period a recurring worry of the Kenya government was unemployment. Kenya's population in 1981 was estimated at 16.5 million, with the potential work force at about 5.9 million. The latter figure included 1,095,000 in all modern-sector wage employment, 3,040,000 in small-scale agricultural employment, 445,000 employed as pastoralists, 1,180,000 in rural, nonfarm employment, and 170,000 in urban informal employment.[5] During that year an estimated 250,000 Kenyans came on the job market, although only 50,000 are thought to have found wage employment. As school graduates flooded the depressed job market in 1980 and 1981, new forms of unrest, aimlessness, and petty crime arose.

1982–1983

The year 1982 began with an inflation rate of nearly 10 percent, a new wave of industrial layoffs, and major restraints on import licensing.

Again the government reduced its planned rate of growth, this time to 4.3 percent. Perhaps most alarming, Kenya's international credit position in relation to other African states began to slip.[6]

The dire economic conditions, particularly food shortages, poor transportation, corruption, and economic mismanagement were justifications cited by air force personnel in their attempted coup of mid-1982. The immediate aftermath of the putsch was a drop in tourism, a flurry of activity to repair Kenya's economic image, and a rush for commercial credit by businesses decimated by looters. Remarkably, within a week a "business as usual" atmosphere prevailed in Nairobi. In fact, rapid restocking of the looted shops suggested that many high-priced items thought scarce had simply been kept hidden by shopkeepers and made available a few at a time as a form of price rigging.

During 1982 and 1983 the government also made two major efforts to overcome its financial problems. First, it commissioned a blue-ribbon panel to make recommendations for sweeping corrective actions in the economy. When delivered, the Ndegwa Report was remarkable for its candor. It unequivocally pinpointed the reasons for Kenya's crisis to be the rapid expansion of government expenditures and, importantly, a "marked decline over the years in standards of management performance and financial control within the government."[7]

The report further stated that efforts to create employment opportunities had neglected productivity considerations, that government investment in commercial and industrial activities had absorbed an excessive part of the budget and often led to losses, and that government projects had often been inefficient in planning, implementation, and control. More devastating to the civil service, the report cited deficient supervision and coordination in activities by local authorities, a reluctance to make hard choices within government, and a resistance to the president's directives within some ministries even after choices had been made.

In addition to the candid Ndegwa Report, a revamping of the economy was undertaken because of pressure from the International Monetary Fund. Kenya devalued its currency by 17 percent in 1982, new government hiring was slowed, and a more inward-looking import-export policy was embraced. The aim was to attain self-sufficiency; the method was to seek more favorable trade agreements that promoted Kenyan products. By the end of 1983 some of these measures were beginning to work, at least to the extent that the reelection of President Moi proceeded without serious economic impediments. In fact, a second period of euphoria occurred, which can in part be explained by improvements in several of Kenya's key economic sectors.

ECONOMIC CHARACTERISTICS: THE KEY SECTORS

During the Moi years six economic sectors have had particular importance in determining the state of the Kenyan economy.[8]

Agriculture

The agricultural sector includes food and export crop production, livestock, forestry, and fishing. Overall it is the occupation of more than 80 percent of the population, the single largest contributor to both the GDP (gross domestic product) and GNP (gross national product). Many development issues such as land use, environment, nutrition, and rural health are intricately tied to agriculture, as are activities of the banking, transportation, manufacturing, and trade sectors.[9]

In order of economic importance, the main crops in Kenya are coffee, tea, sugar, maize, wheat, pyrethrum, and sisal, together accounting for nearly 90 percent of Kenya's marketed crops.[10] Except for maize, which is the nation's most important food crop, and some sugar, all others are exported. The diversity beyond these products is impressive. Beef and dairy production are important for both domestic and foreign markets, and there are growing markets for forest products, coconuts, fresh fruit, and vegetables.[11]

Some of Kenya's current agricultural problems are related to its basic export-oriented framework. The market process and credit, extension, research, and information services are all in support of the large farms. How to extend these services to the smallholder, who accounts for 55 percent of the country's gross market production, is a recurring issue. Conventional wisdom is that subsistence-level farmers are anxious to enter the market economy if their fundamental problems such as storage, transport, and marketing can be solved, and if the government's ability to reach down with credit and farm information can be attained. The key problem has been the failure of extension; the key solutions have been carried out by private enterprises that organize the main stages of storage, transport, and marketing. East African Breweries is an example in the area of barley production.

Solutions to the small farmer's problems are compelling because Kenya's food picture has not been good since 1978 when local production last met national needs. To regain self-sufficiency in maize, the nation's basic food, by 1989, the government estimates that production will have to expand by at least 4.9 percent per year, probably more. Such rates of growth have been achieved in Kenya only during the brief periods of rapid adoption of hybrid maize. There are few examples of countries sustaining such rates of growth in the production of their stable foodstuffs over extended periods.[12] In order to meet demands for the expansion of maize production, almost 2.35 million acres of land must be brought under cultivation for maize, to meet domestic requirements by 1989. An additional 545,000 acres for wheat, sorghum, and millet will be needed, and there will have to be interplanting and double-cropping with pulses and root crops. Where this arable land will be found is unknown.

Livestock production is an important part of agriculture and as an economic activity is in three categories: specialized large-scale dairy and beef ranching, livestock raised as part of sedentary farming activity, and livestock raised by open-range pastoralists.[13]

About 8 percent of Kenyans pursue pastoralism as their primary way of life. Most live on the fringes of the national economy and traditionally have refused to sell cattle except under adverse range conditions. The majority of pastoralists are semi-nomadic Nilotic or Hamitic people who move their homesteads six to twelve times a year in search of grass and water. Cattle, sheep, and goats are the basis of most herds, although camels are milked for human use by the Gabbra of northern Kenya and kept as pack animals by other peoples such as the Rendille and Somali.

Although livestock products as a whole account for some 20 percent of Kenya's marketed agricultural production and 9 percent of its exports, in 1981 the livestock market was small in comparison to its potential. Periodic drought, livestock diseases, marketing problems, and the social attitudes of the free-roaming nomads are some of the reasons. The fundamental dilemma is how to bring pastoralists further into the national economy without destroying their ability to use the dry lands and their genius in adapting to harsh conditions.

The Kenya government's approach to livestock development has been twofold. First, in terms of marketing, the government operates the Kenya Meat Commission (KMC), a parastatal organization that in turn operates abattoir facilities. The abattoirs have been experiencing declines in their livestock supply for several years, due to adverse range conditions that have depleted livestock and to competition from private slaughter houses. KMC handled only about 30 percent of the cattle slaughtered around Nairobi in 1979 and only 7.4 percent of the smaller stock butchered.

Second, since 1968 the government has launched a series of livestock development projects designed to help herdsmen move from a subsistence to a market economy. The objectives have been to increase cattle sales, improve cooperative ranching, and to develop feedlots and commercial ranches to compensate pastoralists for loss of grazing land in wildlife protected areas. Many of these projects have been carried out with foreign aid monies.[14]

Economically, livestock marketing and development projects will depend for their success on whether and how pastoralists work with the national marketplace. A number of problems exist. Pastoralists typify one form of the Kenyan entrepreneurial spirit in their haughty, self-possessed, self-reliant attitudes, complicated in recent years by the government's ambivalence on the settlement issue. Should the free-roaming life-styles of pastoralists be curtailed? Government administrators, military and police officials, missionaries and welfare workers argue that it should because the mobile nomads are untaxable, violent, independent of clinics and churches, and exceedingly difficult to govern. Most officials cannot trek into the rock-strewn deserts after nomad families and therefore government services are either not available, or available only when nomads happen to camp near settled areas. Military

TABLE 4
Key Economic Indicators, 1979-1983

	1979	1980	1981	1982[a]	1983[b]
Population (millions)	15.327	16.661	17.347	18.035	18.748
Growth of GDP[c]	4.3	3.3	5.5	3.3	3.3
Inflow of foreign funds (K£ millions)	199	353	354	340	--
Exports (K£ millions)	413	516	537	569	550
Imports (K£ millions)	620	960	931	945	934
Trade balance (K£ millions)	-709	-444	-394	-376	384
Coffee production (thousand tonnes)	75.1	91.3	90.7	88.4	91.0
Tea Production (thousand tonnes)	99.3	89.9	90.9	95.6	98.0
Maize Production (thousand tonnes)	1,800	1,620	1,971	2,349	2,400
Wage employment (thousands)	972	1,006	1,024	1,038	1,054
Commodity Price Index[d]					
coffee	264.9	238.6	195.8	209.0	--
tea	156.9	162.5	145.9	139.0	--
petroleum	158.3	267.4	303.2	311.6	--
Tourism (holiday arrivals, thousands)	278.9	290.7	273.9	298.1	--

[a] provisional figures
[b] government estimates
[c] government estimates at constant prices
[d] 1975 = 100

Source: Extrapolated from Economic Survey, 1983, pp. 10, 14, 186; Economic Survey, 1982, pp. 9, 13, 39, 178; and Ndegwa Report (1982), p. 80.

personnel argue that because northern borders are insecure, pastoralists on the move are a military problem. It is difficult to determine whether violent cattle raids in which people are killed and cattle stolen are local affairs or incursions from brigands who cross the borders from Somalia, Ethiopia, Uganda, or Sudan. Kenya's pastoralist dilemma is therefore both economic and political.[15]

Energy

Kenya is not an oil-producing country, but it does have a major refinery in Mombasa that produces oil for reexport. Uganda and Rwanda have been the main customers for refined products, Singapore for the oil residuals. Kenya's oil imports in 1979 were $350 million, her exports of refined products $120 million. Because the country itself relies on oil as a major source of commercial energy, however, the entire industrial sector makes demands on the potential reexport supplies. Official estimates are that some 84 percent of commercially used energy is drawn from oil, 16 percent from hydropower, and a fraction from coal.[16]

Hydroelectricity has been a hope, particularly from the new Tana River project, but problems have persisted. Silting and equipment breakdowns have caused innumerable power shortages. During the heavy rains, power can be disrupted by dampness in electrical components and by wind damage to power lines. Line breaks are also caused by monkeys and large birds.

Another dimension of the energy picture is rural nonindustrial usage. Small farmers, herdsmen, and rural artisans rely predominantly on wood and charcoal for fuel, a practice that carries deforestation and other environmental costs. Energy needs in the arid lands are a particular problem, because transportation costs are high and most forms of energy hard to obtain. Charcoal is the common fuel for cooking, kerosene for lighting.

Kenya has made some efforts to curtail its energy consumption through conservation efforts and, on a per capita basis, energy consumption has fallen since 1978. The most widespread change, caused by price differentials, has been to entice drivers from gasoline-powered to diesel-powered vehicles, a savings in cost initially but not in energy consumption. The switch backfired in 1982 and 1983 when diesel fuel was in shorter supply than gasoline.

Transportation

By African standards Kenya has a well-developed road and rail network, a modern deep-water port, and two major international airports at Nairobi and Mombasa. Steady increases occurred between 1976 and 1980 in such transportation categories as road vehicles registered, rail and air shipments, and number of passengers arriving at airports. By contrast, 1981 saw a reduced volume for the railways, airports, vehicle registration, and in the gas pipeline connecting Mombasa with Nairobi. The declines were blamed on the effects of the world recession and on tight foreign-currency controls.[17]

The government operates both the national airline and the railway system, and each is a major industry. Kenya Airways has both a domestic and an international service; the latter links Kenya with neighboring African countries, India, and Europe. In recent years the airline has faced problems of high recurring costs, fuel price escalations, management difficulties, and labor problems.

Railway lines connect Mombasa to Nairobi and the Uganda border, with other lines going to Kisumu, Nanyuki, and Lake Magadi, and to Tanzania through Voi. The Kenya railroad is a major industry. In 1977 its stock included 222 locomotives, 515 passenger coaches, 11,179 freight cars, and 59 railway vehicles. Its major problems concern slow service, an underuse on the Uganda service, and inadequate freight-handling facilities, particularly at smaller stations.

Road systems throughout Kenya are concentrated in the southern portion of the country, running on an axis from Mombasa to Nairobi and the Uganda border. A good rural road network connects the high-population areas, and major feeder roads link the capital with such outlying areas as Wajir and Mandera. Two major international arteries include the Kenya-Ethiopia all-weather road, completed in 1976 to link Nairobi and Addis Ababa, and the construction of an artery linking Nairobi with Juba in southern Sudan.

One of the key problems for the transportation sector is how the government can use the facilities to greatest advantage. Commercial road traffic between Mombasa, Nairobi and Kisumu overburdens the road surface, yet the railroad line that parallels the road is underused. This is partly because commercial truck transportation has been a profitable business for small entrepreneurs. Licenses, sometimes gained by illegal means, have led to an abundance of truckers and rural taxi (*matatu*) operators. Both represent Kenyan enterprise and entrepreneurialism, wherein a great deal of ingenuity goes into keeping the vehicles moving, finding cargoes, opening new routes, and avoiding police checks. Key problems surround the overloading of old, single-rear-axle trucks that then overburden the road surface, and in the case of *matatu* taxis, passenger overloading and high speeds.

Industry and Manufacturing

Since independence, Kenya's industrial sector has seen the fastest growth of any economic sector. It accounts for 15 percent of the GDP and in 1982 employed 141,300 workers in 2241 large, medium, and small firms.[18] The general pattern industry-wide in the decade 1972–1982 has been one of amazing growth and diversity. Leading industries in terms of growth have been cement, flour milling, trucking, raw material processing, and beer and soft drink manufacturing. Only rubber products, furniture, and meat processing among the major industries have recorded downtrends. Other important industries include printing, publishing, chemicals, plastics, and clay and glass processing.

Government investment in the industrial sector includes forty-seven wholly owned companies, a controlling interest in thirty-six, a minority interest in ninety-three, and statutory boards for 147—a total of 323 boards and companies. The range in parastatal operations includes the Central Bank, National Housing Corporation, Kenya Airways, Kenya Meat Commission, Coffee Board of Kenya, Kenya Sugar Authority, Wildlife Fund Trustees, Kenya Cooperative Creameries, Ltd., and the Kenya Farmers Association. Among the 176 companies wholly or partly owned by the government are those involved in insurance, investment, banking, and development and commercial concerns such as milling, sugar, food crop processing, livestock, textiles, rubber, beverages, tourism, mining, and transport.[19]

Although a rapidly growing area in recent years, there are serious problems in the industrial sector. Manufacturing is located in only a few areas: Nairobi, Mombasa, and Thika are the major centers; Nakuru, Eldoret, and Kisumu are secondary. Some 50 percent of the industrial activity is located in Nairobi, 20 percent in Mombasa. The poor spatial distribution limits the wage benefits to the population at large. The main market for Kenya's manufactured foods is within East Africa, curtailed in recent years by the closed Tanzania border and the political turmoil in Uganda. Outside East Africa, sales are small.

For new business ventures, credit is often difficult to establish, export licenses hard to obtain, and contracting conditions slowed by red tape, particularly where the private and public sectors interact. Technical problems in the manufacturing sector mainly concern the lack of spare parts and costly shutdowns because of fluctuations in electrical power.

On an industry-wide basis, Kenya's rapid industrial growth has been based mainly on investments by multinational corporations and the Kenya government in fairly simple, import-substitution industries. This pattern has carried the unfavorable side effect of making the industrial sector increasingly dependent on imported raw materials, components, and spare parts. Production has been capital-intensive and not based very heavily on domestic resources. "Home" industries can be deceptive, as in the "import reproduction" phenomenon, a practice wherein a nearly completed product, whether a truck, baby powder, perfume, or Scotch whiskey, is imported in Kenya in component or bulk form and thereafter assembled. The practice gives a "Built in Kenya" stamp to the product, creates jobs, and adds an impressive array of items to Kenya's trade lists. In fact, there is serious criticism that most of these items are high-priced, elite commodities that do little good in a development sense and use an inordinate amount of foreign currency to acquire the components. Critics suggest that the "Built in Kenya" label is a myth, a method of drawing on local resources and funneling them into the production of luxury items that do not help alleviate poverty. The final judgment is difficult because no one knows, in the aggregate, how much drain really occurs on resources and how much of this drain is offset by the fact that import reproduction does create jobs.

One of the policy problems in the Moi era has been the integration of the industrial and agricultural sectors. The hope is that industry can relate more directly to the needs of farmers. Should import licenses, for example, be awarded for their usefulness to agriculture? Should decisions about industrial development turn on their implications for farming? If so, how can linkages between products and farmers be made more useful, particularly when the government often lacks information about on-the-ground realities?

A major hope is that the manufacturing sector will process more Kenyan agricultural products and be able to export a greater volume of Kenya-made items. Several "ifs," however, cloud the horizon: If Uganda recovers, if Tanzania opens its borders, if trade can be increased to central and southern Africa, and if Saudi Arabia and the Gulf states come farther into Kenya's trade orbit, then the manufacturing outlook is good. Regional trade is a crucial factor.

Trade

Kenya's external trade has expanded dramatically since independence, growing well over six times in value. Coffee, tea, and oil reexports amount to over half the nation's exports. In the first five years of the Moi era, the balance of trade has been unfavorable, although the country has been able to cover its deficits. (See Table 4.) The problem has been attributed to the sagging prices of Kenya's main commodities and to the cost of petroleum products.[20]

In 1982 Kenya export items in terms of value were coffee, petroleum reexports, tea, cement, pineapples, pyrethrum, sisal, hides and skins, soda ash, fluorspar, wattle extract, raw cotton, and meat products. The main imports are crude petroleum, industrial machinery, motor vehicles and chassis, iron and steel, agricultural machinery, chemicals, fertilizers, pharmaceuticals, and paper and paper products.[21]

Officially the Kenya government policy is to improve trade as quickly as possible. The strategy, articulated in the Five Year Development Plan of 1979–1983, calls for a "vigorous campaign of export promotion rather than import substitution," for a more detailed scrutiny and control of imports, and for some tariffs to protect fledgling industries. The strategy to strengthen exports includes an export credit guarantee scheme, the giving of more resources to the Kenya External Trade Authority, establishing export loans, and expanding the Kenya National Trade Authority. There are also incentives for firms to locate outside Nairobi and Mombasa, and thus to engage in greater diversification.[22]

Counterbalancing these initiatives have been the realities of Kenya's external trade. Kenya's markets are limited by the relatively small number of products available for export and the relatively small number of trade partners. Some 85 percent of Kenyan exports go outside East Africa, and imports are almost exclusively from non-African countries. The United Kingdom, West Germany, Japan, and the United States are the main non-African partners. Uganda, Mozambique, Sudan, Rwanda, and Burundi are the main African partners.[23]

A further limitation to trade is the fact that Kenya's industrialization is taking place behind a wall of protection, including tariff quotas, bureaucratic prohibitions, and currency restrictions. The cumulative effect is to create an anti-export bias that makes it more profitable to manufacture and trade on domestic markets rather than to export. How high tariffs should be and what forms of protection should exist is a recurring debate. An economic analyst, S. K. Adjala, puts the issue in perspective:

> With one hand, the Finance Minister calls on local industries to become more competitive against foreign ones. On the other hand, the same Finance Minister imposes high rates of duty on raw materials with which foreign competing industries are not burdened. . . . Import duty on raw materials entering Kenya defeats the whole purpose of import substitution. It puts at risk Kenya's large import-substitution industries set up at a vast cost, much of it in foreign exchange for items such as machinery.[24]

Perhaps the most troubling of Kenya's trade problems is the fact that the export base Kenya relies upon is too narrow for the country's best interests. A "rob Peter to pay Paul" trade situation exists. Items like meat, milk, rice, and wheat are needed for export to gain foreign currency to buy oil and maize. Shortages in these items create unstable political conditions, particularly when the foodstuffs are needed at home.

Tourism

The tourist industry is one of Kenya's economic success stories. Some 350,000 visitors came to Kenya each year between 1972 and 1982, most to enjoy wildlife safaris and the Indian Ocean beaches. While the number of visitors has remained nearly constant in the last decade, tourism earnings went up fourfold, peaking at $113 million in 1982. The boom period in tourism came between 1965 and 1972 when some 40,000 jobs were created for Kenyans (as compared to 95,000 in all manufacturing). By 1981 a total of 22,000 beds were available in Kenya hotels, as compared to fewer than 6000 in 1965.[25]

Of Kenya's 362,000 visitors in 1980, the peak year, some 282,000 were specifically on holiday. They generated some $20 million for the country in foreign exchange. Hotel occupancy in 1980 was at 56.7 percent of capacity nationally, with some luxury hotels ranging up to 95 percent. Seven countries accounted for the majority of visitors in 1980: West Germany (60,600), Britain (40,900), United States (26,300), Switzerland (24,200), Italy (16,700), France (14,600), and Canada (4200). Another 30,600 came from other European countries, and 39,500 from all African states.[26]

Although the long-term potential for tourism is excellent, the industry has its problems. Tourism is a fickle business that can be adversely affected by such events as military unrest or global recession. During periods of recession travelers are less likely to come to Kenya because of their own reduced means, because oil prices have inflated the cost of air tickets, and because costs in Kenya are correspondingly higher for food, liquor, and local transportation and lodging.

Because foreign airlines and travel agents book trips from abroad, Kenya has historically received a relatively small share of the tourist dollar. In trying to realign this imbalance, Kenya's restrictions on visas and charter carriers led to a 15 percent decline in tourism in 1981 and the bankruptcy of a few beach hotels.[27]

There are also social costs of tourism, which thus far Kenya has been willing to pay. Misunderstandings brought about by the obvious differences between poor Kenyans and rich visitors are part of the problem. The demand for luxury food and wines in a nation short of foreign currency is another. Some behavior, whether it is semi-nude Europeans on the beaches offending Muslim elders, or boisterous behavior of tourists in Nairobi hotels, also leads to problems. Nor is the overall cost and benefit picture clear. Should the country import tourist supplies or hoes and tractors? Skeptics suggest that the direct value of foreign tourism to Kenya may not exceed 10 percent of gross receipts.[28] Contrary

Tourist attractions: two of the many species of wildlife in Kenya (photo of male lion by David Keith Jones; female lions and giraffe, UNESCO/Marc Riboud)

to this, in 1983, the Ministry of Tourism estimated that 80 percent of tourist revenues were remitted to Kenya, a figure that is closer to the reality in recent years. Whatever the exact figures, Kenya's official view is total enthusiasm for tourism.

In summary, each of the six main sectors of the Kenyan economy reflects the country's entrepreneurial ethic. In agriculture new research and new plant breeds have improved production, and although there are serious problems of land shortage, there has also been a constant search for solutions, for new plots of land in remote places, and for ways to make the available land produce. In energy, entrepreneurial activity is also seen; by refining imported crude oil for reexport, Kenya has earned important foreign currency. In transportation, small-time entrepreneurs are the backbone of the industry, so aggressively trying to keep their vehicles on the road they are at times a public nuisance. In trade, Kenya has gained a reputation in eastern Africa as a leading marketeer, selling its wares through trade missions, shows, and by direct contact. In tourism, Kenya has adroitly withstood the Tanzania border closing, which curtailed the lucrative Nairobi-Serengeti circuit, and went on to have its best year (1980) despite the handicap. In manufacturing, the capitalistic philosophy has opened the doors to foreign investment.

Through multinational corporations in particular, Kenya has built ties to the West that have long-term economic and political implications.

FOREIGN INVESTMENT
AND MULTINATIONAL CORPORATIONS

President Moi inherited a long tradition of foreign investment in Kenya. During the 1950s Kenya became a regional industrial center, building up a diversified manufacturing and banking infrastructure. Jomo Kenyatta took pains to retain foreign capital and to assure new investors they would be protected. After independence, the Foreign Investment Protection Act of 1964 provided guarantees that capital and profits could be repatriated. The combination of these conditions, with the advantages of Nairobi's communications and climate, has attracted a flow of foreign investment, mainly through multinational corporations (MNCs).[29]

The value of foreign corporate investment in the late 1970s included $500 million from Britain, $200 million from the United States, $60 million from West Germany, and another $100 million from Switzerland, France, India, Italy, and Japan. Nearly 50 percent of the industrial sector is under foreign ownership, the remainder controlled by government parastatal bodies, by Kenyan Asians, and by a few African and European businessmen.[30] The scope of foreign investment includes banking, engineering, food processing, oil refining, tourism, and manufacturing. Manufacturing alone includes auto assembly, chemicals, cigarettes, clothing, metal products, paints, paper, printing, soft drinks, textiles, and tire production. Approximately 350 multinational corporations have operations in Kenya, and another 250 have some kind of sales representation.[31]

In the Moi years three important trends have emerged. First, there has been a leveling off of foreign corporate investment.[32] The reasons include the world recession, the lack of foreign currency, the demise of the East African Community, the weakened export market for Kenyan products, the proliferation of small local firms, and, in the earlier years of the Moi regime, a high corporate tax rate. The coup attempt in 1982 further slowed investor activity.[33] Second, large multinational finance agencies such as the World Bank, the German Development Bank, and the Commonwealth Development Fund have become major sources for new industrial development.[34] Third, the Kenya government has evolved from a minority partner in a few enterprises to a major investor. Holdings include total ownership of companies, partial ownership, and minority partnerships as well as joint ventures. In the latter, local capital, government capital, MNC investment, and investment from multinational lending institutions may be combined in a single operation. Many of the ninety-three firms in which the government has a minority interest follow this pattern.[35]

Kenya's official stance toward foreign investment is to welcome it. Moi periodically appeals to foreign investors to take the "long-term view," to use Kenya as a regional headquarters, to reinvest in Kenya, and to help stimulate local capital.[36] Foreign investment is protected by the Kenya constitution, which stipulates that compulsory compensation must be paid if foreign properties are acquired by the government, and by the Foreign Investment Protection Act of 1964. The Five Year Development Plan (1978–1983) called for foreign investment particularly in needed industries such as steel and heavy machinery, and important investment incentives exist. For the MNCs the incentives include drawbacks of duty, tariffs on goods that compete with Kenya-based MNCs, tax credits for raw materials used in production, and for individual companies the possibility of negotiating special protection mechanisms, particularly if manufacturing is undertaken in new areas of industry.[37]

Despite the incentives, foreign investors point to problems. A "certificate of approved enterprise" is needed to begin operations, Central Bank approval is needed to repatriate profits, and heavy Kenyan taxes and levies must be paid. Regulations and paperwork abound, and pressures to "Kenyanize" have limited the number of expatriate technicians that can be employed. In 1976 the Foreign Investment Protection Act was amended to restructure the repatriation of profits, a move many companies resented as a change of the rules that had been originally agreed upon.[38] Probably the most difficult problem faced by the MNCs and the Moi regime has concerned import license irregularities. "In Kenyatta's time, the customary bribe (called *chai*, or 'tea money') was 2.5 percent of the value of an import-export license, or 5 percent of a government contract. Until steps were taken by Moi in 1982, *chai* requests had doubled and trebled, and filtered down to clerks who demanded it for any effort."[39]

On the other hand, Kenyan officials have a number of complaints against the MNCs. For example, exploitation charges have been leveled at both foreign oil and energy activities. Companies looking for copper, chrome, nickel, and gold have aroused the suspicion of MPs for what has been termed "exploiting and disappearing" with Kenya's minerals. (No major mineral finds have occurred as yet in Kenya, although geologists are hopeful.) International oil companies have also been criticized by Martin Shikuku in Parliament in 1980 for their single-minded profit orientation. He claimed foreign companies were making up to 400 percent profit on their oil import and refinery operations in Mombasa, and he urged the government to bypass them by importing oil directly from the Arabs and buying out the Mombasa refinery.[40]

Other criticisms concern bookkeeping irregularities perpetrated by foreign firms, including over-invoicing of imported raw materials in order to gain greater tax write-offs. Foreign advertising has been criticized as perverting tastes to such things as perfumes and hair tonics, when Kenya needs rudimentary items such as hoes and pumps. A further criticism is that there has been too much indiscriminate investing and too little attention paid to Kenya's development needs, and that there has been little protection for Kenya's own "infant industries" that might flourish without foreign competition.[41]

On balance, the foreign investment picture in Kenya is perceived by the participants as one of mutual benefit.[42] MNCs are making some profits or finding it useful to be based in Nairobi; the government generates tax revenues and finds it useful to have the investment and the technology. In effect, a cabal has been formed between the state and the MNCs. As seen in the next chapter, the equation becomes more complicated when foreign aid donors—British or American or World Bank—join in the investment process.

ECONOMIC OUTLOOK:
THE CONSEQUENCES OF CAPITALISM

Kenya's capitalistic pathway has been a mixed blessing. The country has a long-term trade imbalance, constant problems with world price fluctuations, unemployment at 30 percent of the work force, and little hope that per capita growth will attain the 1963–1978 level in the foreseeable future. The social costs of unfettered entrepreneurialism have been significant in terms of exploitation, corruption, and basic inequities. Some Kenyans have unquestionably profited by the ill-fortune of others.

Conversely, there is also evidence that capitalism has had some positive effects and produced at least a part of the framework for long-term economic success. Today, Kenya ranks twenty-fourth out of fifty-two African states—including oil exporters—in terms of GNP per capita, and on a regional basis it is second-highest among its eight East African neighbors. There has been growth in terms of the numbers of Kenyans who are relatively well-off and growth in the number of those who have accumulated savings, such as small farmers and businessmen. A majority of Kenyans have experienced an improvement in their life-style in the last twenty years, and an estimated 45 percent (the advantaged) have a relatively secure existence.

Looking ahead, there are several reasons why this system will continue. Kenyans are economic survivors, resiliant, enterprising, and ultimately pragmatic. A cushion exists in that some 80 percent of the population pursues a rural, agricultural life-style. New land is being opened with irrigation, new crop varieties are being introduced, and new markets are being developed. There is an important informal economy that offers alternative income, and an "economy of affection" based on kinship and friendship that provides support. There is also mutual support and reciprocity in Kenya, even in the low-income urban slums.

The entrepreneurial ethic is also infectious. It has spread to a great many areas, leading minorities like the pastoral Maasai and others to begin to diversify into a mixture of herding, farming, and small businesses. Women are entering the market economy in greater numbers, and new opportunities are being opened for young people, particularly through the efforts of churches and development agencies. There are a great many Kenyans who work hard and who have improved their way of life. Many urban dwellers are entrepreneurs in their own right. Many

rural folk are diversifying their activities and becoming part-time entrepreneurs.

In the long term, the structural adjustments undertaken by the
Moi government in 1982 and 1983 should be a basis for renewed growth.
Bilateral and multilateral aid will be crucial. In 1983–1984 the scope of
this combined aid included over 500 programs sponsored by thirty-five
different multilateral and bilateral donors, contributing some $450 million.

Finally, Kenya is important to the West and would not be permitted
to slide into economic disarray without strong countermeasures. Kenya
is a symbol of African capitalism and of Western economic values in
Africa, and numerous interests, aside from the thirty-five major aid
donors, are supporting the country. Foreign private investment, multinational corporations, philanthropic organizations, and international
church and missionary groups are only a few. Both in symbolic terms
and because of its geographic position, Kenya and its economic fortunes
are of major interest to many nations in the international arena.

6

The International
Dimension

INTRODUCTION

Kenya's entrepreneurial spirit is reflected in its foreign affairs. Pragmatism, economic self-interest, and a pro-Western, anti-communist bias in trade and aid characterize the Moi era. Aggressive searches for overseas markets go on in Europe, the Middle East, and Indian Ocean states, and President Moi carries the Kenyan message around the world in an energetic, globe-hopping search for aid and new projects. Britain, Germany, France, the United States, China, India, Iraq, and Saudi Arabia are only a few of his recent places of call. Kenyans actively pursue tourist revenues, give preferential treatment to the multinational corporate community, promote Nairobi as a world conference center, and point with pride to the two UN agencies (United Nations Environment Programme—UNEP—and Habitat) and the thirteen other international organizations that have bases there. Kenyan students of all ages compete vigorously for opportunities to study abroad, a trend that began at independence and included a major airlift of students to the United States.

Foreign aid is a crucial element in Kenya's modern development; some 33 percent of all new projects are sponsored by thirty-five nations or international organizations, a situation so complex the country's capacity to absorb the funds is called into question, despite the best efforts of Kenyan entrepreneurs to corner the resources.

Militarily, Britain has been Kenya's "quiet big stick," and the British connection runs deep. Kenya's army is implicitly backed by the British, and most observers believe the United Kingdom would help protect Kenya's interests if invited to do so. Since British commandos assisted Kenya in putting down the army mutiny in 1964, Britain has had a "training" presence in Kenya. All three Kenyan services—army, navy, and GSU—have been organized along British military lines, as was the air force until it was disbanded following the 1982 attempted coup. The U.S. military tie has also grown during the Moi era and represents another pragmatic quid pro quo. U.S. funds, training, and equipment

128

go to Kenya; the country's air bases are available for refueling of U.S. military aircraft; and its deep-water harbor at Mombasa is available for resupply and as a liberty port for the U.S. Navy's Indian Ocean fleet.

Kenya's foreign policy is undefined and open-ended, a "no-policy policy" in terms of ideology that permits maximum flexibility. Few philosophical pronouncements are made, and no theoretical writings have been forthcoming from Kenyan leaders, unlike those leaders of nearby states.

Changes, however, have occurred in how Kenyan leaders view foreign affairs and what initiatives have been taken. From 1963 to 1969 Jomo Kenyatta held the foreign affairs portfolio as part of his presidential duties. In those years Kenyatta's pro-Western stance set the mold and any advocates of change had little influence if they went against the prevailing interests of commerce, trade, or foreign aid. In 1969 the Ministry of Foreign Affairs was handed over to Kenyatta's personal physician and trusted ally, Njoroge Mungai. Under Mungai, foreign relations expanded dramatically, reflecting both Kenya's greater international interests and its greater search for trade partners.

Daniel Moi has been more of a Pan Africanist than Kenyatta, more committed to liberation movements in southern Africa and more inclined to occasionally articulate a philosophy. Moi has said that "love, peace, and unity" apply to Kenya's foreign policy. "This should be the guiding light to all as we face the turbulence of the decade. More than ever before, love for humanity, international peace, and unity among nations is needed to provide the perspective for our actions."[1]

Undoubtedly the most distinctive element in Moi's foreign dealings has been the proliferation of international treaties, trade agreements, and conventions. In 1983 diplomatic consuls or trade representatives were maintained with eighty-one foreign countries, and sixty-nine countries have embassies in Nairobi. Kenya has twenty-four diplomatic missions abroad and takes an active role in the United Nations, the Organization of African Unity (OAU), and the Commonwealth.

AFRICAN RELATIONS

In the early Moi era, Kenya had something of a beleaguered outlook. On every border except that with the Sudan there was hostility, violence, or a divergence in ideology. (See Figure 4.) Relations with Tanzania were cool, as the Nyerere pathway to socialism was at loggerheads with Kenya's brand of capitalism. Violence in Uganda continued well after the fall of Amin and adversely affected Uganda-Kenya relations. To the northwest, relations with Sudan remained friendly, although the common border area was a violent, lawless territory. Throughout the Kenya, Sudan, and Uganda borderlands, drought caused hunger among the resident pastoralists such as the Turkana, inflaming age-old enmities and leading to cattle theft and indiscriminate raiding. Ethiopia, to Kenya's north, remained the most Marxist state in Africa. On the surface, relations between the two nations were amicable, but no one doubted that major

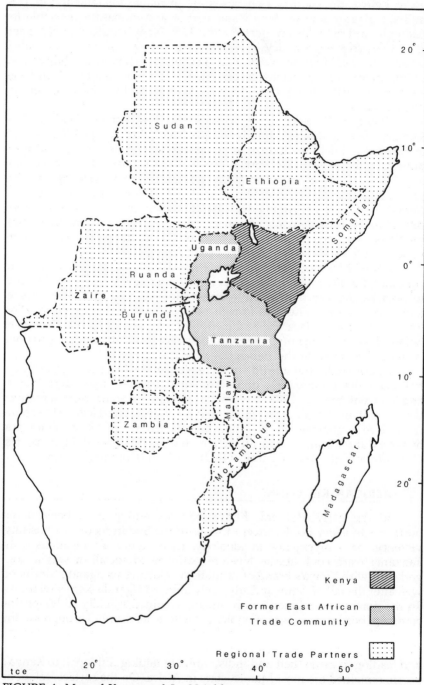

FIGURE 4. Map of Kenya and Its Neighbors

ideological differences existed. Somalia to the northeast was Kenya's nemesis. It is the only country with which Kenya has fought a war, and the only country that has seriously claimed a part of Kenyan territory. The Somali threat, in Kenya's view, is part of the larger picture of regional hostility and potential violence. What are some of the bilateral issues?

Kenya-Tanzania Relations

Kenya's relations with Tanzania have been cool for over a decade. Curiously, Uganda has been a key part of the problem. In 1971 when Idi Amin seized power in Uganda, Tanzania's President Nyerere gave sanctuary to the deposed Ugandan president, Milton Obote, and within a short time refused to meet with Amin. The fracture of Tanzania-Uganda relations had a major impact on Kenya, and although Kenyatta tried to ameliorate the differences and keep the East African Community (Figure 4) together, it proved an impossible task. Tanzania had already shown signs of resenting Kenya's dominant position in the trade community, and this alone probably would have led to a three-way fracture of relations. It was, however, the fact that Kenya allowed arms to be transshipped to landlocked Uganda, and initially kept normal relations with Amin, that angered the Tanzanians. In 1977, due specifically to a series of misunderstandings over debts with their common airline, Tanzania broke economic relations with Kenya and closed the Kenya-Tanzania border. Tanzania partially justified the closure on the basis that the isolation forced local Tanzanian services and industry to develop on its own, avoiding an economic vassal status with Kenya. Presidents Moi and Nyerere met in Lusaka during 1979 and again in 1980, and although their pronouncements were amiable, it was not until late 1983 that the border was re-opened.

Kenya-Uganda Relations

Economic ties have always been important between Kenya and Uganda. Uganda is landlocked, and her major lifeline to the sea is through Kenya. Except for occasional problems, such as the transport of weapons, Kenya has abided by international conventions for landlocked countries. In turn, Kenya uses electrical power from Uganda's Owen Falls Dam on the Nile and is anxious to improve trade relations, so a quid pro quo does exist.

The key factor in the decline of relations with Uganda was the destruction of Uganda's economy under Idi Amin. Kenya's international business, particularly the tourist industry, suffered badly because of the ongoing brutality and violence in Uganda.

Nevertheless, throughout the Tanzania-Uganda war of 1978–1979, Kenya took a "wait and see" attitude that angered Tanzanians. Kenya's attitude reflected uncertainty that a socialist, pro-Tanzanian government in Uganda was in their best interests. The rationale was that Amin, as bad as he was, was a known entity who ideologically did not seriously challenge Kenya. As the governments of Presidents Lule, Binaisa, and finally Obote came to power, political exiles from every camp were found in Nairobi. The continued instability in Uganda, the rise and fall of private armies, and the periodic violence has led Moi to a continuing noninvolvement policy.

A dramatic upturn in relations came in December 1980 when Milton Obote and his Ugandan Peoples' Congress won the general election. As Obote became president, he made it clear that he favored a mixed economy in place of the "move to the left" he had advocated before his fall to Amin. A year later, in January 1981, cooperation between the two states moved a step farther when Presidents Moi and Obote were joined by Zambia's President Kaunda for a one-day conference in which better communications, trade, and anti-smuggling activities were discussed.

The smoothing of Uganda-Kenya relations by Moi is a clear example of Kenya's flexible, pragmatic approach. Once Obote's rise to power was assured, Kenya's policy became conciliatory. Entrepreneurs in Kenya quickly pointed out that the sale of some 70,000 tons of Ugandan coffee that was awaiting shipment would give that country the foreign exchange to buy Kenyan goods. Kenyans agreed to help in the reconstruction of Uganda and to reduce Uganda problems of shipment to the sea; in turn Uganda agreed to a new formula to reschedule its debts to Kenya. The Moi regime's search for new markets and a refurbished trade partner in Uganda lay behind the rapprochement.

Kenya-Ethiopia Relations

Ties with Ethiopia would be stimulated by the entrepreneurial spirit Kenyans apply elsewhere except that there is very little basis of trade and little common economic interest. Diplomatic relations between the two states have been remarkably amiable in both the Kenyatta and Moi eras. Kenyatta had a personal friendship with Haile Selassie based on similar age, Christianity, and common distrust of Islamic Somalia, which had laid claim to portions of both countries. Soon after Kenya's independence, the two states signed a defense treaty and attempted to move closer economically. A major road between Addis Ababa and Nairobi was completed, only to fall into disuse for lack of trade goods.

With the fall of Haile Selassie in 1974, there was a brief hiatus and uncertainty in relations. Kenya voiced disapproval of the palace coup, but true to his realpolitik image, Kenyatta quickly normalized relations with the new military regime of Colonel Mengistu. With the Ethiopian-Somali war of 1977–1978 and the arrival of Cuban-Soviet forces in Ethiopia, capitalist Kenya might have recoiled at the new ideology of its northern neighbor. But Ethiopians privately gave assurances to Kenyans that they were fully in control, and that the Cubans and Soviets were only advisors. Communications remained open when Daniel Moi came to power; he continued the status quo, finding comfort, as did Kenyatta, in Ethiopia's Coptic Christianity and its denunciation of their common adversary, Somalia. Kenya's prime interest is in the strict maintenance of its existing borders, and Ethiopia supports this.

Kenya-Sudan Relations

Between Kenya and the Sudan, relations have been openly convivial during the Moi era. Although their common border is across an arid 200-mile sector of the Lotikip plain, a new road and some trade does pass between the two states. Presidents Numeiry and Moi share a joint concern for peace in the Horn area, both are pro-Western, and both receive major aid from the United States and Europe. Numeiry has openly offered the United States the use of military facilities in the Sudan.

Sudan's problems with its non-Muslim south, particularly in the Equatoria region, occasionally spill into northern Kenya. Periodic refugee arrivals, cholera epidemics, and cattle theft recur in the border region. These problems are played down in deference to the common interests of the two states. Both are moderate politically, both adopt similar stances in the OAU and international bodies, and both have an interest in the import trade link that exists on the Juba-Nairobi-Mombasa axis. It is easier for imports destined for Juba in southern Sudan to use Kenya's port, rather than Port Sudan in the north.

Other ties include a five-year protocol agreement on the sharing of arid-lands water technology, animal husbandry techniques, and other agricultural techniques including sugar processing. A joint committee on telecommunications has been put into place; there are two-way exchanges of press stories. The efforts are directed at bringing the two countries into closer understanding, an appealing idea to both Numeiry and Moi in that they share a common governmental anti-doctrinaire approach and a common alienation from many of their neighbors.[2]

Kenya-Somalia Relations

Tensions with Somalia inherited by Daniel Moi go back at least eighty years, and today are laid unequivocally (by Somalia) on the doorstep of the British colonial office. At the turn of the century Somali peoples were expanding south and west out of their central homeland on the Horn. Claims to territory south of the Juba River were made in what is today Kenya. This area was split by the British-Italian agreement of 1916, ceding a portion of the territory to Italy and keeping a part within Kenya. The agreement was part of the British negotiated settlement to insure Italy's entry as an ally into World War I. Like the arbitrary drawing of the Somali-Ethiopia border by the British after World War II, this earlier colonial decision to draw the Kenya-Somalia border with perhaps 150,000 Somalis within Kenya has haunted all concerned for decades, a "Palestinian question" on the Horn of Africa.

The Somali living in northern Kenya are ethnically, religiously, and linguistically part of Somalia, a remarkably nationalistic and homogeneous country. The Kenya Somali are culturally and racially different from the "green belt" Bantu peoples that predominate in Kenya. Prior to Kenyan independence, Somali leaders in northeastern Kenya lobbied the British to adjust the boundary and include them in Somalia. A

British commission appointed to survey the wishes of the people reported a near-unanimous desire by Somalis to be a part of Somalia, not Kenya. The U.K. colonial office, however, failed to act on these findings and allowed the independence of Kenya to proceed with its northern boundary as it is today.

As noted in Chapter 2, the new flag of Kenya had hardly been raised when the Kenyatta government plunged into a full-blown border war with Somalia. Somali patriots from both sides of the border took easily to guerrilla warfare and often either eluded or vanquished the Kenyan forces. During the fighting the Somali government generally denied supporting the Somali *shifta*, although Mogadishu's radio often broadcast vitriolic encouragement. In 1968 undeclared peace settled over the region.

Part of Kenya's continued unease is the reputation of the Somali as soldiers. Somalis won new luster in the opening months of the Ogaden war in 1977–1978, when their army not only was able to drive 600 miles into Ethiopia, but also was able to effectively resupply its tanks and infantry. A rout of the Ethiopian forces seemed assured before the Soviets interceded. Despite the ultimate Somali defeat, their early tank victories lent mystique to Somali invincibility. When Kenyan officers realized the Somali army was probably ten times larger than Kenya's, then some 120,000 men versus Kenya's 12,000, the uncertainties deepened.

Given the hostilities and violence, one would assume that Kenya's entrepreneurial spirit would be severely curtailed vis-à-vis Somalia. This is not the case. Smuggling on a major scale occurs, particularly in *miraa*, a mildly intoxicating grasslike weed grown near Mt. Kenya and chewed voraciously in Somalia. Foodstuffs, petrol, small manufactured items, and gold move north across the common borders, or around them by sea in small coasters. It is an aggressive, acquisitive, often ingenious illegal trade.[3] Periodically hope is expressed that common economic interests might bring the two states closer. Nothing in this relationship, however, has proceeded with such easy logic. The Kenyans remain suspicious and the Somalis unpredictable and quixotic.

Relations with Other African Nations

Relations with other African states are mainly dictated by trade and commerce. Rwanda and Burundi are major importers of Kenyan refinery products, and Mauritius, Mozambique, Zaire, and Zambia are important regional markets for oil, foodstuffs, and manufactured items.[4] Egypt, Ghana, Algeria, and Réunion are the major trade partners outside eastern Africa.

It is perhaps in relations with South Africa that Kenya's economic and political pragmatism is most evident. Although regularly condemning South Africa's racism, Kenya imports South African foodstuffs, including maize, and allows international flights to and from South Africa to refuel in Nairobi. Kenya defends the refueling by pointing out that it honors international treaties; it also gathers some $10 million a year in landing fees.[5]

RELATIONS OUTSIDE AFRICA

Key relationships in Kenya's broader international spectrum have to do with the Western states—particularly the United Kingdom and the United States—the communist states, and the Middle East. Soon after Moi came to power, the Soviet invasion of Afghanistan and the Iran-U.S. crisis occurred. The confrontations gave Kenya a new strategic importance within the Indian Ocean and Middle East regions and drew Kenyans inexorably into new ties and alliances.

Kenya-U.K. Relations

Britain is Kenya's largest trade partner, the major long-term source of foreign aid, and the main supplier of military arms. Although relations in the Moi era have been close, there have been serious tensions in the past two decades. Kenya clashed officially with Britain over the Unilateral Declaration of Independence in Southern Rhodesia, although not going as far as to break off diplomatic relations. British arms sales to South Africa have also been a bone of contention between the two states, as are levies and taxes British firms pay in Kenya. Since the U.K. is the major source of overseas investment, there are constant negotiations on what the overseas firms will and can do in Kenya. Economic tensions in recent years have centered on fluctuations in prices paid for Kenya's exports, the pricing of oil products controlled partially by oil companies, and how profits in the international tourist industry should be divided.

Kenya-U.S. Relations

Relations between Kenya and the United States are traced diplomatically to 1833 when a U.S. consulate was established on Zanzibar to oversee East African trade. After World War I, U.S. missionaries began to work in Kenya, and more recently, beginning in the mid-1950s, U.S. labor organizations privately began to help Kenyan nationalists. Tom Mboya, the labor organizer and chairman of the Kenya Federation of Labor, was supported by the AFL-CIO. In the same period, 1955, the American Pathfinder Fund started family-planning work in Kenya. Shortly thereafter, U.S. private aid helped organize airlifts for Kenyan students to come to the United States, reaching a peak in 1965 of 1,300 students.

After independence, stress in Kenya-U.S. relations surfaced over U.S. intervention in the Congo, an event that led to a major anti-American demonstration in Nairobi. Later, criticism was voiced of the United States over Vietnam, over U.S.–South African relations, and over the building of a U.S. base on Diego Garcia in the Indian Ocean.

Relations improved in the 1970s. U.S. aid and private investment increased, U.S. teachers, missionaries, and Peace Corps volunteers came in greater numbers to live in Kenya, and the U.S. tourist flow increased to nearly 40,000 a year. In 1979 Moi led a large team of ministers to Washington to discuss with President Carter major expansions in maize and other aid to offset Kenya's food shortage. Military equipment for Kenya, expanded trade, and greater access for U.S. warships to Mombasa harbor and U.S. military aircraft to Nanyuki Air Base in Kenya were part of the agenda. The access agreements were concluded in 1980, permitting only U.S. training and maintenance personnel to be stationed in Kenya. Relations between the two countries remained amiable in the Moi-Reagan era; Kenya was in fact the best friend the United States had in black Africa.

Kenya and the Communist States

While some Kenyan nationalists in the 1950s were establishing friendships in the United States and Britain, a small group of Kenyans led by Oginga Odinga sought assistance from the Soviet Union and, later, China. Historians suggest Odinga was driven to the communist states partly by his rivalry with fellow Luo Tom Mboya, who had rapidly become a close friend of the United States.

Whatever the reason, Odinga by independence in 1963 was the key advocate of close relations with Moscow and Peking. In 1964 he led a mission to both capitals and without cabinet knowledge signed agreements for interest-free loans, technical assistance, and weaponry. The agreements became a cause célèbre. When Soviet arms finally arrived they led to a backfire in Kenya-Soviet relations, partly because the weapons were reported to be of World War I vintage, an insult to Kenya. Because the Soviet arms were also flown to Somalia, which was then hostile to Kenya, the pro-Western Kenyatta had all the evidence he needed to cool Soviet relations and to fetter Odinga. During this period, 1964–1965, China's Zhou Enlai was touring Africa preaching armed revolution, which was seen as anathema to Kenyatta's moderation policies.

Nevertheless, during those turbulent years diplomatic relationships were maintained with China and the Soviet Union, and Kenya continued to receive aid from both, including a major Soviet-built hospital in Odinga's home area. The key problem with the Soviets from Kenyatta's viewpoint, aside from ideology, was the USSR's continued support of Somalia. By the time the Soviet-Somali relationship ended in 1977, both the USSR and China had low profiles in Kenya.

Since 1978 the Moi government has in fact made anti-communism one of its major themes. Speaking on behalf of the president soon after taking office, the vice-president, Mwai Kibaki, stated flatly, "There is no room for communists in Kenya." The president shortly thereafter said publicly at the university graduation ceremonies that it was dangerous to expose students to theories of scientific socialism. The alleged student involvement in the attempted coup of 1982 led to closure of the university, student arrests, and allegations that some lecturers and student agitators had been funded from outside communist sources.

Chinese and Soviet communism are distinguished from one another in Kenya. Relations with China were revived in 1980 when Vice-Premier Ji Penfei visited Nairobi. A month later Moi paid a state visit to China, signing agreements for economic, technical, and cultural cooperation, including the construction of a sports complex near Nairobi and help in developing small industries and new rice technologies, tile, electrical, and biogas projects. In January 1983 Premier Zhao Ziang visited Nairobi in a reciprocal state visit.

Kenya and the Middle East

Kenya's relations with the Middle East and the greater Arab world are important. In 1973 Kenya made a difficult choice in terms of the Arab-Israeli issue. Since independence Kenya had maintained relationships with Israel, both for trade and technical assistance. The pro-Israeli stance was based largely on Kenya's fear of Arab expansionism from Somalia, particularly when evidence of Arab financial support for Somalia's claims was obtained. However, the oil crisis of 1973, coming at a quiet period in Kenya-Somalia relations, changed the equation. Kenya felt obliged to protect its precarious oil imports, and under growing economic pressure from the Arab states broke relations with Israel in late 1973. It was a straightforward quid pro quo within the entrepreneurial spirit, Kenya receiving concessionary oil prices and Arab technical assistance in exchange for an end to the Israeli tie.

Since Moi has come to power the Israeli connection has been informally reopened, particularly in large construction projects, although at the same time Kenyans have made particular efforts to keep Arab aid flowing to Kenya. Moi paid state visits to Saudi Arabia, Abu Dhabi, and Iraq during 1979–1981, mainly in search of oil concessions, aid, and trade. He did win a major breakthrough in Baghdad to supply one-third of Kenya's crude oil, only to see the arrangement collapse in the Iraq-Iran war. The major supplier continued to be Saudi Arabia, supplemented by the smaller Gulf states.

Iran has been the single largest trade partner from the Middle East because of the oil. Other markets are based on processed foods, tinned meat, dairy products, and tourism, including package tours to Kenyan game parks. Overall, the Middle East is the second-largest source of Kenya's imports after the European Economic Community. Saudi Arabia and Iraq have provided major loans to Kenya, as has the Arab Development Bank.

REGIONAL AND INTERNATIONAL ORGANIZATIONS

Since independence Kenya has been a member of five major international organizations: the East African Community, the Organization of African Unity (OAU), the Commonwealth, the European Economic Community, and the United Nations.

Kenya and the East African Community (EAC)

Perhaps the saddest international situation inherited by Daniel Moi when he came to power in 1978 was the abject failure in 1977 of East African economic cooperation. Thrown together by geographic continuity,

Kenya, Tanzania (then Tanganyika and Zanzibar) and Uganda were brought under an administrative umbrella in 1943 known as the East African High Commission. This body had legislative powers to set up and administer common railways, harbors, currency, post and telecommunications, and to carry out a wide variety of services that included tax collection, research in agriculture and industry, and establishing and maintaining an inter-territorial court, a common university, a common market, and later, an airline.[6]

After the independence of Tanzania in 1961, the organization became known as the East African Common Services Organization (EACSO), and when all had attained independence, it became, in 1967, under a treaty that created the East African Community, the East African Common Market (EACM). Although many of the functions in communication, research, and the common university structure continued, dark clouds began to gather over the organization. By 1969 it was obvious that the three countries had embarked on very different ideological pathways. Both Tanzania and Uganda resented Kenya's economic dominance, particularly in the lucrative tourist revenues that found visitors using Nairobi as their main center. Mistrust, coupled with national pride and the desire to develop independent institutions, created constant friction. It was the fall of Obote's government in Uganda in 1971 to Idi Amin's military regime that put further strain on the EAC. Julius Nyerere, appalled and infuriated by Amin, refused to sit at the same meetings with him, and in 1972 a nasty border skirmish between Tanzania and Uganda closed out any possible reconciliation. Kenya and Tanzania carried on a facade of exchanges, but in the main each state went its own way. Total collapse came in 1977. The EAC failure and the Kenya-Tanzania border closure has not only cost Kenya its Tanzanian market and a share of the lucrative Tanzania tourist circuit, but also has blocked Kenya's overland trade connections south to Zambia, Malawi, and Zimbabwe.

One of the major efforts at settlement instigated in 1978 by the World Bank, which is a major creditor, was the appointment of a Swiss arbitrator to give unbiased calculations of the assets and liabilities of the partner states. Dr. Victor Umbricht, noting "obstructive tactics" on the part of Kenya in refusing to give him railway records, concluded that Kenya owed some $200 million for its holdings, Tanzania a small amount, and Uganda nothing—it was due a credit. By 1983 these three states had agreed on the amounts outstanding. The Kenya-Tanzania border re-opened at the end of the year.

Kenya and the Organization of African Unity (OAU)

Kenya is currently an active member of the OAU. Initially Jomo Kenyatta had little interest and little voice in OAU affairs, but with Mungai's appointment as minister of foreign affairs in 1970, this began to change. Rhodesia and South Africa were the two main issues, and Kenya joined most OAU states in criticizing Britain for its inaction. As in the UN, Kenya took a strong stand in the OAU during 1972 on the

South African question, advocating strong sanctions to those who supplied arms to South Africa, and to those who temporized on South Africa's suzerainty over Namibia. Nevertheless, Kenya has occasionally been chided within OAU circles for being a "reactionary" country, meaning essentially too moderate on South African questions. Its pro-Western stance is also occasionally criticized. One Tanzanian spokesman suggested that "non-alignment" to Kenyans meant "non-aligned between the E.E.C., the World Bank, the U.K. and the U.S.A." Such comments have been muted since Zimbabwe became independent and since Kenya served as the site of the OAU meetings in June 1981. Moi served as president of the OAU in 1981–1982, and in fact was forced to carry on the post into 1982–1983 due to the OAU's problems of meeting in Libya and thereby making Colonel Qaddafi the next president.

Kenya and the Commonwealth

Membership in the Commonwealth is another important relationship that Kenya uses for fostering economic cooperation with other Commonwealth nations such as Nigeria, India, Britain, Canada, Australia, and others. Kenya has also used the Commonwealth to press for peaceful change in South Africa.

Economic development monies and military equipment and training funds are occasionally funneled through Commonwealth sources, particularly in Kenya's case from Britain and Canada. Grants from the Commonwealth Development Fund for coffee and tea development as well as major undertakings in land and settlement projects are a part of the Commonwealth benefits.

Kenya and the European Economic Community

This trading bloc, including Britain and West Germany, is a major outlet for Kenyan exports. EEC loans are also important to Kenya; in 1978, for example $60 million was provided.[7] Kenya was a signatory of the Lomé Treaty, which made the country part of the EEC circle and made it eligible for preferential trade as well as large-scale aid and financial assistance through the European Development Fund. Such projects have included an arid lands integrated development project in Machakos—a $26 million investment over four years—as well as transport and road programs that provide links to nearby states.[8]

Kenya in the United Nations

In UN proceedings Kenya is usually pro-Western but may vote with the African bloc on symbolic Third World issues. Kenya opposed the United States and Britain on Rhodesian issues and has been increasingly harsh about South Africa, taking a stance that advocates violence for the liberation cause. Kenya has, however, stopped short of outright condemnation of allies of South Africa and has had a friendship with Malawi, contrasted to the usual disdain southern African states have had for Malawi.

Kenya embraced the Nuclear Test Ban Treaty of 1963 and the Non-Proliferation Treaty as important in keeping the Indian Ocean free of East-West tensions. The "zone of peace" proposals of India and Sri Lanka, which opposed Western and Soviet bases in the Indian Ocean, were also vigorously embraced. In another area of UN activity, Kenya is the headquarters of two UN agencies, the United Nations Environment Programme (UNEP) and the United Nations Center for Human Settlements (Habitat).[9]

THE AID BRIGADE

Foreign aid in a country like Kenya is enormously complicated. It involves development aid, military aid, food and housing aid, grants, loans, occasional credits, concessions, new projects, old projects, bilateral funding (between Kenya and one other country) and multilateral funding (between Kenya and an international organization such as the World Bank).[10]

UNDP (United Nations Development Program) calculated in January 1978 that the total aid to Kenya in the previous year amounted to $459 million in direct grants and $993 million in loans.[11] The figure can be misleading because it represents the total commitment on the books during that year, which may have begun several years earlier. For a twelve-month period in 1978, officials of USAID (United States Agency for International Development) estimated total disbursements of grants and loans from all sources to Kenya to be in the $350 million range. In 1983, 517 projects were under way, sponsored by thirty-five donors and valued at approximately $450 million.[12]

Major bilateral aid comes from Britain, West Germany, the United States, Sweden, the Netherlands, and to a lesser degree France, Canada, Australia, Denmark, Norway, Italy, and Japan. Other aid is through multilateral assistance, particularly the World Bank, UNDP, FAO (Food and Agriculture Organization), UNICEF (United Nations International Childrens Emergency Fund), WHO (World Health Organization), the European Development Fund, and the Arab Development Bank. The breakdown of aid at the beginning of the Moi era reflected a strong pro-Western bias: 61 percent of Kenya's loans came from the West, 32 percent from the World Bank, some 4 percent from the East, and 2.5 percent from the Middle East and other African states.[13] Since independence, three main phases of foreign aid to Kenya have been discernible.

Phase I. 1963–1970

The first phase was dominated by two major aid programs that were a part of the transition to independence: the land transfer program, wherein European settlers were paid for their farms, and second the land reform program that redistributed farmland through registration, adjudication, and the transfer of ownership. British aid funded the Kenya government to carry out the programs. A total of £56 million was spent in the period 1962–1970. In 1964, 80 percent of all aid to Kenya was from Britain. By 1972 British aid had dropped to 25 percent, and by 1979 to 13 percent.

Phase II. 1970–1978

Proliferation of aid during this eight-year period was the key characteristic of a trend that began in the late 1960s. Between 1970 and 1974, some twelve bilateral donors and fourteen multilateral agencies contributed to Kenya to the extent that the total contribution ranked seventh in aid given to sub-Saharan countries. Part of the proliferation of aid was a flow of funds to the East African Community and to quasi-regional organizations such as the East African University. Most of this funding ceased when the East African Community broke up in 1977. During the 1970–1978 period the World Bank became Kenya's leading donor, providing some 25 percent of the total aid. The United Kingdom remained second, and the United States was third. West Germany and the Netherlands steadily increased their input. During this period nearly two-thirds of all grants and loans were in agricultural development, water development, and road expansion.

Phase III. 1978–1983

This five-year period has been the period of "crisis aid," when tensions in Uganda, Somalia, Ethiopia, and the Indian Ocean area led Western states to invest heavily in Kenya, particularly in military aid. The United States during this period increased its commitments (not actual financial obligations) to $119 million for 1982 and $144 million for 1983. This was a substantial portion—11 percent and 16 percent—of the total U.S. assistance proposed for all of Africa by the U.S. Congress. During the same period a major upsurge in multilateral aid occurred, partly to offset the impact of the world recession on Kenya's declining economy. Since 1980 the World Bank has provided 35.8 percent of all donor assistance to Kenya. The European Economic Community, through both grants and loans, has accounted for 8.6 percent of all donors, and the International Monetary Fund some 6.8 percent. Other multilateral contributors include the European Investment Bank, the African Development Bank, OPEC (Organization of Petroleum Exporting Countries); Commonwealth Development Corporation, African Development Fund, UNDP, and others.

The explosive rise in recent U.S. aid provides an interesting example of how the fortunes of an aid-recipient can change. U.S. aid began in 1951 when the United States and the United Kingdom signed a general agreement for technical cooperation in colonial Kenya. U.S. assistance effectively began in 1953. In the first twenty-eight years, 1953–1980, the total economic assistance was $344.4 million and the total military assistance $109.5 million, including loans and grants. At the end of thirty years, 1953–1982, the totals were $461.9 million for economic assistance and $189.2 million for military assistance. The assistance was provided in fourteen funding categories (Table 5).

TABLE 5
U.S. Economic and Military Assistance to Kenya, 1953-1984,
in Obligations and Projected Obligations ($ millions)

		1953-1980	1981	1982	Total Obligations 1953-1982	1983 (est.)	1984 (est.)	Obligations & Projections 1953-1984
ECONOMIC ASSISTANCE	Total	344.4	50.7	66.8	461.9	129.0	96.5	687.4
loans		135.4	23.8	19.6	178.8	66.5	25.0	270.3
grants		209.0	26.9	47.2	283.1	62.5	71.5	417.1
AID and predecessor agency	Total	196.6	20.3	38.9	255.8	59.2	80.0	395.0
loans		88.4	7.8	4.6	100.8	8.0	20.0	128.8
grants		108.2	12.5	34.3	155.0	51.2	60.0	266.2
Food for Peace	Total	61.1	23.4	18.0	102.5	18.0	8.0	128.5
PL 480 Title I loans		29.9	16.0	15.0	60.9	15.0	5.0	80.9
PL 480 Title II grants		31.2	7.4	3.0	41.6	3.0	3.0	47.6
Other economic assistance	Total	32.8	3.1	1.7	37.6	2.4	2.6	42.6
Peace Corps grants		32.8	3.1	1.7	37.6	2.4	2.6	42.6
Centrally & Regionally funded[a]	Total	36.8	3.9	8.2	48.9	8.4	5.9	63.2
loans		--	--	--	--	2.5	--	2.5
grants		36.8	3.9	8.2	48.9	5.9	5.9	60.7
Housing guarantees	Total	17.1	--	--	17.1	41.0	--	58.1
loans		17.1	--	--	17.1	41.0	--	58.1
MILITARY ASSISTANCE	Total	109.5	26.5	53.2	189.2	56.0	(NA)	245.2
loans		107.0	6.0	22.0	135.0	17.0	(NA)	152.0
grants		2.5	0.5	11.2	14.2	19.0	(NA)	33.2
grants for construction[b]		--	20.0	20.0	40.0	20.0	(NA)	60.0

[a] Includes projects for which USAID had actual dollar amounts and projects for which USAID information permitted reasonable estimates of dollar amounts applicable to Kenya.

[b] Total of $60 million in military construction is a firm figure. Individual years are estimates.

(NA) = not available.

Source: U.S. Overseas Loans and Grants and Assistance from International Organizations. Obligations and Loan Authorizations July 1, 1954-September 30, 1981, Fiscal Year 1984 Congressional Presentations, USAID/Kenya (January 31, 1983).

During 1981 the USAID mission to Kenya identified five priority issues they hoped to address: population growth, rural production and employment, energy issues, the problem of the high recurrent costs of services such as health and water, and the need for trained manpower. With the Reagan administration came a new focus on aid: to help develop the private sector in the hope that local capitalism will assume a larger burden of development.

Behind the broad priorities are endless calculations and an enormous bureaucratic effort on the part of both the United States and Kenya. The USAID mission takes a project approach, which includes a design and planning phase; thereafter the project usually is put out for bid and implemented by U.S. technicians working with Kenyans. The 1980 program, for example, included 40,000 tons of wheat, a fertilizer program, an ongoing project on range development, expansion of Edgerton (agricultural) College, the promotion of livestock and small farm credit systems, and the support of an extension-training institute in the Coast Province. Funds were also used for road building and graveling, for food storage facilities, for support for a population research institute, for development of community water supplies, and for renewable energy and health programs. Support also went to several voluntary organizations.[14]

In order to continue to carry out such projects, the USAID mission in Kenya employs a technical and administrative staff of twenty-five individuals from the United States and more than fifty Kenyans as a support staff. Overall, the Kenya mission is one of the largest in Africa, although in terms of dollar commitment it shared a high priority in 1983 with the Sudan, Somalia, and Zimbabwe. A major USAID regional office is also located in Kenya that services many countries in East Africa and southern Africa.

Looking at foreign aid from Kenya's viewpoint, aid monies accounted for about one-third of new development projects in 1980–1981, as compared with over two-thirds of new projects in neighboring Tanzania. (The figure for Tanzania approached 100 percent in 1982–1983.) Most of the USAID funds go through Kenya's various ministries; the top five ministries in this respect in 1981–1982 were the Ministry of Transport and Communications (K£ 58 million), Agriculture (K£ 31.8 million), Water Development (K£ 20.6 million), Finance (K£ 20 million), and Environment and Natural Resources (K£ 15.7 million).[15]

As in most Third World countries, problems in the Kenyan foreign aid programs abound. Many projects get highly politicized, and perhaps understandably in capitalist Kenya, the bigger the resource, the bigger the intrigue. Other projects become bogged down in the red tape of both the donor and recipient bureaucracies. Monies are often given without the involvement or consensus of the grass-roots communities they are intended to serve, and the heralded "trickle-down" theory in fact rarely works well. Three basic problems are: Kenya's ability to absorb the aid that is given, problems of duplication between aid donors, and problems of cultural conflict between expatriots and Kenyans.

First, when the absorption capacity of a country like Kenya is overtaxed, waste and dissipation occur. There are limits to the amount of money a bureaucracy can effectively use, and although most officials understand this, there is a built-in drive to keep processing funds. It is not that money is scarce, but managerial help, secretarial help, time, space, transportation, and tools in the right place at the right time are scarce. Overflows of money can also disrupt ongoing operations. Enthusiastic new demands to "expand and improve" can in fact cause operations to grind to a halt.

Second, duplication and overlap of effort between donor agencies occurs, mainly due to inadequate reporting and incomplete information about the 500 or more projects underway at any one time. Although the UNDP has developed a "Compendium on Development Assistance" covering fifteen multilateral and eighteen bilateral donors working in Kenya as of the beginning of 1980, it is an incomplete report. Some donor governments do not fully report their "aid," some report it as a static figure, some as ongoing commitment; programming practices differ in terms of disbursement and in terms of fiscal years used in accounting practices. Some UN agencies operate under worldwide budget restraints that do not permit their commitments to equal their actual disbursements. Most countries do not. Political events between bilateral donors and the host country change; funds are offered, withdrawn, reoffered, and delivered according to the political issues of the moment. At any given time a "major" project may totally skew the aid picture. Germany, for example, in 1981 was ranked first in bilateral aid to Kenya on the basis of its large projects begun in the 1960s that alone contributed over $50 million in 1981. The UNDP compendium measures commitments in effect at the end of the year, an assessment that includes projects that may have been in operation for several years; this situation too, distorts the total aid picture.

Discounted loans, foreign obligations, concessions, fluctuations in Kenya's currencies and those of donor countries also complicate the picture. The crowning difficulty is that even if every donor were 100 percent accurate in its reporting, some officers in the Kenya government would not want the total aid picture to be known. Duplication and overlapping are inevitable, but for some with the entrepreneurial spirit, very lucrative.

Third, the entrepreneurial Kenya spirit creates other, human problems in the foreign aid arena, starting with the fact that "outsiders" are coming to help "insiders." The chance for social and economic misunderstanding is great. Most aid projects have both technical and cultural needs, the latter requiring deeper and more reliable understandings on the part of donors—more "old African hands" and fewer "two-year technicians." The situation creates a basic social impasse. To do an operational job, technical expertise is required, and the easy way is to bring in operational "experts," essentially to do the job for Kenya. Yet many of these people are broadly ignorant of Kenyan society and language. If their technical competency or their ability to relate professionally is not extremely high they may in fact contribute negatively rather than positively. The cost can be enormous. One UN estimate in 1981 was that a senior technical person would cost $120,000 per year—half in salary and half in support of per diem costs, overseas education for children, maintaining a Land Rover, and so on. The salary figure alone is six times as high as that of a senior Kenyan official.

A further problem is the cumulative effect of a small army of foreign aid officials from thirty-three agencies arriving in Kenya. Fulfilling their needs for housing, food, recreation, and dependent education may simply overtax the society. The housing market is adversely affected for wealthy and middle-income Kenyans, duty-free privileges are abused, rich-poor differences become apparent, petty crime and security problems proliferate around the expatriate compounds, and clannishness within expatriate groups evolves. The basic lament is that little social integration with Kenyan society occurs. Few expatriates on two-year assignments learn about the people and the country well enough to interact effectively, although in fairness this is partly due to the Kenyans' choice and to the cool social atmosphere of Nairobi. There is a low level of social exchange, even between Kenyans of different ethnic groups.[16]

On balance, the social costs must be examined against the positive effects of the aid that does flow into Kenya. Despite the waste and occasional blunders, there is little doubt that in the minds of Kenyan leaders the long-term benefits of aid outweigh the short-term problems. Their argument is a pragmatic example of the Kenya spirit: Until a "new international economic order" is in place that gives Kenya economic self-reliance, some half-way house is needed. Foreign aid is providing at least a part of the shelter.[17]

KENYA AND THE WORLD

In terms of the larger realpolitik of the day, it is the ongoing tension in the Indian Ocean and the Middle East that concerns Kenyan leadership the most. Because of its strategic location, Kenya is drawn into the larger East-West contest. Events like the Soviet invasion of Afghanistan, the Iran-U.S. hostage crisis, and the Iran-Iraq war, all occurring in Moi's early years in office, have had unsettling effects in Kenya. Kenyan diplomats fear that such larger power struggles will draw Kenya into military problems, no matter how nonaligned it claims to be.

Oil is behind much of the tension, and oil-rich Saudi Arabia is a key regional focus. In Kenya the main concern is that when Soviets' home oil supplies run low, supposedly in the early 1990s, tension will rise. With Ethiopia and South Yemen (PDRY—Peoples' Democratic Republic of Yemen) firmly in the Soviet camp, the argument is that Moscow will have easy access from Africa across the Red Sea to try to secure Saudi Arabian oil, a situation that would lead to a major regional, if not world, crisis.

Oil and the Indian Ocean crisis atmosphere have led to a few new patterns in Kenya's foreign relations. First, there is an expressed exasperation at how other nations relate to Kenya. A recurring theme is that Kenyan interests are not well understood in the West, that the short-term diplomats who populate the embassies and aid missions are politically and culturally ill informed about Kenya. Those of the West who have in-depth understanding of Kenya, mainly scholars and missionaries, rarely have a voice in policy issues. The plea is for greater appreciation of the internal dynamics and complexities of Kenya, a more African-centric, Kenya-centric policy.

Second, today an open admission is made that ties with Britain and the United States are the cornerstone of Kenya's contemporary foreign affairs. The British connection is reinforced by Commonwealth links that give Kenya easy relations with a broad pool of countries. What is new is the open admittance that the British-Kenya connection is strong. President Moi's first state visit after assuming power was to Britain, a symbolic as well as a practical gesture. Similarly, ties with the United States are well known to include crucial food aid, military aid, and friendly advocacy in World Bank circles. The steady flow of U.S. business people, Peace Corps volunteers, and tourists has reinforced the tie.

Third, a pattern of more open debate exists on these ties. The links with Britain and the United States have cost the Moi government criticism from within, particularly just before and after the 1982 coup attempt. Kenyan dissidents point to the increased U.S. military aid as a destabilizing factor. They suggest that too much money flowed to the military, causing it to expand rapidly and to become an unstable element in the society. Further, they charge that Kenya is drifting toward a totally dependent "client" relationship with the West, particularly with the United States and Britain, an unfortunate connection that has traded Kenya's strategic geography for help in aid, trade, food and oil.

A fourth discernible pattern is a defense of the close links with all states in the West on a "what's good for Kenya" basis. The central argument here is that Kenya's pragmatic, low-key, anti-communist foreign policies have been good for business. There is an assumption that entrepreneurialism, the search for markets, the promotion of tourism, and the welcoming of multinational corporations should go hand-in-hand with Kenya's foreign relations. The argument, in fact, defends the reality. Kenya has used the United Nations, for example, as a platform from which to argue its economic case, particularly in stabilizing world prices of Kenyan products and in pressing for its share of UN development monies. On this score it can be seen as one of the most successful countries in Africa.

Finally, the recession of 1980–1983, the tensions in the Indian Ocean, and Kenya's internal military upheaval have had a sobering impact on foreign relations. Kenyans fully realize they are both politically and economically isolated from their immediate neighbors. These realities

have led to Moi's globe-trotting search for aid, to the wooing of the Arabs, to the scramble for new contracts, even to the drift toward client status with the West. In effect, Kenya's reaction to international tensions is to seek new aid, trade, and entrepreneurial ties. The pursuit of foreign relations, even in difficult times, is a part of the quest for prosperity.

Conclusion

What has the Kenya ethic wrought? What will determine whether the quest for prosperity within this entrepreneurial system goes on? A rough balance sheet shows that the system has led to some economic growth, to a regionally high income per capita, to international investment, to an abundance of foreign aid, to new technology, to expansive business practices, and to an important informal economy. A small elite has prospered, and perhaps 60 percent of the population have attained a life-style that is relatively secure in terms of basic human needs.

At the same time the costs have been high. Class distinctions based on wealth and political power have emerged. An elite controls much of the society and there is widespread inequity not only in wealth but also in terms of education, employment, health, and social welfare. Rural women and ethnic minority groups have not yet had equal opportunities. Corrupt, unfair practices have proliferated in both business and government, partly because of the open economic system. The wooing of foreign aid has outstripped Kenya's ability to absorb new funds and at the same time has put Kenya in the position of at least partial dependency. Abject poverty has continued to be the lot of perhaps 20 percent of the population, although this is not unique to Kenya or to its economic approach.

Elite dominance has been the realpolitik of independent Kenya. As a group the governing elite are "descendants" of the European power block. They control much of Kenya's agricultural economy and are partners with foreign investors in the control of the industrial sector. It is also true that some of this governing elite periodically control dissent through the manipulation of Parliament, through control of protest groups, through pressure on the press, through the shaping of public opinion, and through the control of the resources that are allocated to keep the patronage system in place. That the elite system emerged hand-in-hand with the entrepreneurial ethic is understandable if one keeps in mind it is based on a patron-client structure. Less understandable is the lack of resentment against the elite. With notable exceptions in 1975 and 1982, the system has not been seriously challenged. This is

148

due in part to the fact that the elite are a small, urban-based class in a rural country, in part to the fact that the masses have seen the elite as people to be emulated, not chastised. In fact, farmers, rather than resenting the elite, have tended to look on them as examples of what can be attained. Much of the wealth has been amassed in a single generation, and there is hope that one's children can do as well. Many of the wealthy use their money to support relatives and political followers. Many of the large estates owned by the elite are managed by others who have come to view the arrangement as a job, not a symbol of class distinction. There is no doubt that the distinctions exist; there is doubt, however, even after the demonstrations and looting in August 1982, that there are deep-felt class cleavages that will inevitably lead to confrontation. In the past, at least, this has not been the reality of Kenya.

A crucial question in the country's third decade concerns Kenya's capacity to change. Its capacity to be open and flexible has been severely tested in recent years, and the country has vacillated between periods of tranquillity and upheaval. The tides have risen and fallen on the basis of internal Kikuyu tensions, upcoming elections, and the assassinations of Mboya and Kariuki—cresting with student upheavals and the military uprising. In effect, the rules change periodically in Kenya, the system becoming expansive or defensive as the regime in power reacts to the events.

Crucial questions surround Kenya's capacity to feed its citizens, to slow population growth, to provide employment for school graduates, to gain greater equity in income, and to remain self-reliant in world politics. A central question for the economy is its capacity to grow. A question for the entire system surrounds Kenya's capacity to remain politically stable.

Stability, at the core, depends on whether or not the elite can garner enough resources—money, jobs, contracts, and the like—to keep Kenya's patronage system operating. Looking ahead, three factors are important. The first concerns the availability of resources when lean economic times occur in the private sector. Some necessary resources might be claimed from the government, but this process is slow unless corruption is involved. Informal economic activity generates some wealth for a few elite to dispense, but on a small scale. Greater hope lies in channeling foreign-aid monies into the patronage system, but this practice borders on illegality and is against donors' wishes.

A second factor that will affect stability is Kenya's capacity to stem corrupt practices in both public and private sectors. The fundamental issue is how the leaders can prevent corruption from undermining confidence in government. This is not an easy task, because Kenyans themselves are ambivalent about some of the illegalities. Some of the governing elite are involved in corrupt practices and many have made their fortunes in such ventures as commodity smuggling and currency violations. Among ordinary citizens, small-time smuggling is usually seen as a form of adventure. Nevertheless, the system is endangered and stability undermined when the bureaucracy cannot stop forms of illegal exploitation. When "big men" take the law unto themselves, bypassing regulations, giving and taking bribes, and pilfering public coffers, there are outcries. When the elite directly victimize farmers and the working poor in land grabs or other exploitations, their activities call into question the government's ability to protect its ordinary citizens.

A third factor in the stability equation concerns the ability of the elite to share the resources. In hard times flexibility on this score disappears, and no one can be certain Kenyan leaders have the capacity to keep the system open. The alternative is greater dissatisfaction, greater dissent, and the formation of harder class lines than exist today. As anger and despair rise, the issues become polarized along simplified "have" and "have-not" lines.[1]

Given these problems of future stability, the intriguing question is how and why Kenya's entrepreneurialism has worked relatively well in the past. One answer is that most citizens have found some economic reward despite the inequities. Another is that Kenya, as a rural agricultural society, provides a cushion of support for urban, entrepreneurial activity. It has been the small-scale entrepreneurs in both rural and urban settings who have been the bedrock of the system. Large-scale entrepreneurs are important, but it is the ordinary farmers and businessmen, operating from communities where family and communal values prevail, who have sustained the system.

What are the possibilities for the future? Because of its capitalistic history, Kenya's entrepreneurial ethic has a broad base of support in the structure of the society and will survive as long as the present philosophy of government is maintained. The national leadership may change, and given the cyclical, occasionally violent nature of Kenyan politics, a change in leadership could occur at any time. The entrepreneurial approach, however, is more durable than the individuals in power. Many institutions operating today are established as private enterprises, and the government's involvement with the private sector through parastatal organizations is on the wane. Even more important, the elite, the middle class, and many of the working poor want the system to continue.

If Kenyan leaders are not able to control dissent from the military, the university, the Parliament, or a major ethnic group such as the Luo, then at least two other possibilities exist. The country could drift into factional disputes which in turn could lead to a greater military role in government. This could be a bureaucratic-military coalition, a veiled military rule with a symbolic civilian president and civilian figureheads, or a straightforward military form of government. In either case, the economic philosophy, after a hand-wave at greater equity, could remain conservative. A second possibility would involve a change that leads to greater equity and a greater sharing of the national resources. This change could come about by the election of younger, more liberal members of Parliament, by changes in the government's economic philosophy based on international monetary pressures, or by changes in the viewpoints of key government leaders.

Whatever the form of government, many of Kenya's basic problems will remain. The country is short of resources and poor in minerals— a disjointed, ethnically divided land that can be buffeted by global factors totally beyond its control. The eastern Africa region is not politically stable, and Middle East tensions inexorably draw Kenya into East-West politics. A danger exists that these tensions could push Kenya further into a client relationship with the West, a situation in which increased foreign aid simply makes self-reliance impossible and internal reform unlikely. However, Kenya's basic entrepreneurial ethic would reject complete client status, if for no other reason than it inhibits the country's aggressive and adventurous economic way of life. The system has survived in part because Kenyans have skills that allow for the rise and fall of economic fortune, and in part because a majority of the population are pragmatic, adaptive individuals who believe their system, despite all its drawbacks, carries greater advantages for them than do those of the less open, more centralized African regimes. Rather than accept overseas dominance, the Kenyan reaction would be to accept foreign aid but turn it quickly to their own advantage. Historically this has been Kenya's way of dealing with most foreigners who have come bearing gifts. In Kenya, pragmatism has always gone hand in hand with the quest for prosperity.

Notes

INTRODUCTION

1. For detailed geographic descriptions of Kenya see Francis F. Ojany and Reuben B. Ogendo, *Kenya: A Study in Physical and Human Geography* (Nairobi: Longman, 1973); Simeon H. Ominde, *Land and Population Movements in Kenya* (London: Heinemann, 1968); Alan Best and Harm J. de Blij, *African Survey* (New York: Wiley, 1979), Chapter 25; and G. M. Hickman and W.H.G. Dickins, *The Land and Peoples of East Africa* (London: Longman, 1960).

CHAPTER 1. THE COLONIAL LEGACY

1. See Laurel Phillipson and David Phillipson, *East Africa's Prehistoric Past* (Nairobi: Longman, 1978); Sonia Cole, *The Prehistory of East Africa* (New York: Mentor, 1963); and Richard Leakey and Roger Lewin, *People of the Lake: Mankind and Its Beginnings* (New York: Avon, 1979).

2. For a discussion of the early trade between Kikuyu and Maasai see Peter Marris and Anthony Somerset, *African Businessmen: A Study of Entrepreneurship and Development in Kenya* (London: Routledge and Kegan Paul, 1971), pp. 34–42. Also see Roland Oliver, "The East African Interior," in Roland Oliver, ed., *The Cambridge History of Africa*, Vol. 3 (Cambridge: Cambridge University Press, 1977).

3. The Portuguese may also have brought millet and cereal crops to Kenya through their southern African enclaves—crops that had come to Africa earlier across the Indian Ocean from the Indo-Polynesian migration. See George P. Murdock, *Africa: Its Peoples and Their Cultural History* (New York: McGraw-Hill, 1959), pp. 21–24.

4. Western commercial interests in the Sultan's domain began in 1833 when the United States established the First Commercial Treaty with the Sultan of Zanzibar; a U.S. Consul arrived in 1837; commercial representatives from Britain came in 1839, from France in 1844, and from the Hanseatic Republic in 1859. See also Richard D. Wolff, *The Economics of Colonialism: Britain and Kenya 1870–1930* (New Haven, Conn.: Yale University Press, 1974), p. 32, footnotes 155–156; Kenneth Ingham, *A History of East Africa* (New York: Praeger, 1962), Chapters 1–3; and Thomas Spear, *Kenya's Past: An Introduction to Historical Method in Africa* (London: Longman, 1981), Chapter 5.

5. Wolff, *Economics of Colonialism*, p. 36. Other factors influenced the early expansion of commercialism. Markets in East Africa were often located on borders between different ecological zones (coastal belts and dry interior, open grassland and forest, at the base of large hills or mountains), at borders between ethnic groups (as between Kikuyu and Maasai), or on interregional trade routes that provided travelers with food and shelter. Kenya's constantly changing ecology, varied ethnic makeup and crisscrossing trade routes made the region particularly conducive to the development of commercialism. See P. L.

Wickins, *An Economic History of Africa from the Earliest Times to Partition* (Oxford: Oxford University Press, 1981), p. 118.

6. Britain's move into East Africa was far more complicated than this summary suggests. Kenya's geographic position on the Indian Ocean, the strategic resupply port of Mombasa, the location near Zanzibar, the moral anti-slavery considerations, and other Indian Ocean interests also combined to put London's sights on Kenya. The region had been important strategically to the movement to stamp out slavery and to bring Christian enlightenment. The challenge of this mission over Islam was for the hearts and minds of Africans in the interior; the mission became a compelling cause for hundreds of missionaries who followed David Livingstone. In short, Kenya was geographically strategic and a religious challenge. When the fertile lands and commercial potential of the territory became known, the final enticements were in place.

7. See Arthur Hazlewood, *The Economy of Kenya: The Kenyatta Era* (London: Oxford University Press, 1979), for further economic rationale behind the railroad. There is an extensive literature on the railroad. See Charles Miller, *The Lunatic Express* (New York: Macmillan, 1971), for an excellent overview and bibliography.

8. See Wolff, *Economics of Colonialism*, pp. 31–32, for further discussion of the early Asian economic presence in East Africa.

9. See Jeremy Murray-Brown, *Kenyatta* (London: George Allen and Unwin, 1972), pp. 21–32, for a background sketch of the coming of the white man to central Kenya.

10. Pacification of central Kenya came more easily than it did further west. Two major military expeditions were necessary to suppress the Nandi on the western slopes of the Rift Valley—one expedition in 1895, another in 1900. The technical superiority the British possessed in firearms, particularly in the Maxim gun, a predecessor to the machine gun, ovecame even the most valorous Nandi assaults. Resistance continued sporadically until 1912.

In northern Kenya, intermittent hostilities continued even longer, and periodic expeditions were necessary to bring rule to the "northern frontier," as Kenya's desert lands came to be called. Somali, Boran, Rendille, and other ethnic groups remained recalcitrant and nearly ungovernable throughout the colonial period.

11. See Best and de Blij, *African Survey*, pp. 434–451.

12. For discussion on the settler's view of *Empire* and their differences of opinion on expanding the British Empire, including the Marxist critique, see Wolff, *Economics of Colonialism*, p. 1, and his footnote 3, p. 151.

13. As early as 1902, when a deliberate settlement policy was launched, land had become the preoccupation of Europeans. Even earlier, in 1899, Britain had decided that "wastelands and other unoccupied land and that occupied by savage tribes" came under Crown control and therefore could be dispersed as the Crown saw fit. In 1902 the Protectorate administration received from London the right to both lease and sell land in parcels between 160 and 640 acres. Each lease was for 99 years, until changed. Other key legislative and land developments in this period, listed chronologically, were:

- 1902–1903: Township ordinance, hut tax. Departments of forestry, medicine, and agriculture established. Judiciary established. Colonial Office takes over. Crown Land Ordinance provides for sale or lease of 160–640-acre farms to Europeans for 99 years.
- 1904–1905: Colonial Office takes over East African Protectorate from Foreign Office. First executive council set up. Land treaty with the Maasai moves them from the Rift Valley to southern grazing grounds extending to Tanganyika border, leaving them also Laikipia and parts of Kinangop.
- 1907: First legislative council organized.
- 1911–1912: Headmen given extended powers in local government. Northern and southern Maasai agree to join in a consolidated land reserve "south of the railway line," including a large part of the western Mau escarpment, an area Maasai had seldom penetrated.
- 1915: Crown Land Ordinance of 1915 establishes African Reserves and gives Europeans 999-year leases.

14. The Allied forces in particular were a polyglot group. African soldiers and the Carrier Corps came from a dozen Kenyan tribes, but with large numbers of Nandi and Kamba; the Europeans were British Kenyans and other whites living in Kenya, a South African force that arrived by sea, and a Belgian force. In addition, a large contingent of Asian troops from India, mostly officered by British, completed the Allied contingent. The German forces were made up largely of African regulars, Carrier Corps and support troops, and German officers and non-commissioned officers who had either been in the German administration or pressed into the army from the ranks of German settlers.

15. The campaign surged over a vast area of Tanganyika, Mozambique, and Zambia. The armies, trailed by an array of camp followers, moved like two giant millipedes. The German ranks included soldiers and porters, wives with babies, cooks, mechanics, carpenters, tent riggers, and camp workers, the followers at times outnumbering the combatants. Porters were necessary for both armies since such roads as existed were so bad as to preclude mechanical transport. Animal power was reduced to insignificance by the tsetse fly and the consequent sleeping sickness, one report suggesting the average life of a team of oxen when they left the cool highlands in Kenya was three days.

16. See Vincent Harlow, E. M. Chilver, and Alison Smith, *History of East Africa* (Oxford: Clarendon Press, 1965), Vol. 2, p. 156, and Leonard Mosley, *Duel for Kilimanjaro* (London: Weidenfeld and Nicolson, 1963), pp. 234–235.

17. See Zoe Marsh and G. W. Kingsnorth, *An Introduction to the History of East Africa* (Cambridge: Cambridge University Press, 1961), p. 186. Those who continued to farm for the war effort faced serious labor shortages, and even when food could be harvested, the lack of market transport led to rot and spoilage. In fact, there was little transportation, whether by truck or rail car, available for anything but the war. Available transport was seriously over-committed and under-maintained.

18. Marsh and Kingsnorth, *Introduction to the History of East Africa*, p. 187.

19. Ibid.

20. Wolff, *Economics of Colonialism*, pp. 119–120.

21. Ibid., p. 126. Wolff reports that between 1921 and 1931 the Kikuyu population increased 1.5 percent, while the squatters' population increased 6.2 percent. The squatter population on European farms in the early 1930s has been estimated at 110,000.

22. Lord Hailey, *An African Survey* (London: Oxford University Press, revised 1956), p. 750.

23. Although there were hard times between 1919 and 1922 and in the world recession of 1929–1935, the years 1923–1929 were a growth period for both agriculture and Kenya's small industrial sector. Corporate expansion until the late 1920s had been insignificant. Most of the thirty-three firms that had been legally registered failed in their first nine years of operation. None had included African entrepreneurs. The corporate pattern was to organize an interlocking directorship made up mostly of the same men and their families. Evert Grogan and Lord Delamere, their wives, and extended families contracted many ventures. Although Africans were excluded from company formation in these years, Asians were not, and some capital for new enterprises flowed into Kenya from India. As corporate expansion increased, however, it was overseas capital from Britain that contributed substantially.

24. Wolff, *Economics of Colonialism*, p. 145.

25. Ibid., p. 146, pp. 132–133, and pp. 144–146. See also C. C. Wrigley, "Kenya," in Harlow, Chilver, and Smith, *History of East Africa*, pp. 204–264.

26. For example, a Japanese matchstick factory was dismantled because it threatened British manufacturers, and local sisal twine manufacturing was curtailed. Another natural manufacturing endeavor would have been cotton cloth. In 1925 Kenya imported 24 million square yards of cotton goods, despite repeated Asian attempts to set up textile mills to use East African cotton, first planted under missionary initiatives in 1904. See Nicola Swainson, *The Development of Corporate Capitalism in Kenya, 1918–1977* (London: Heinemann, 1980), p. 27. See also E. A. Brett, *Colonialism and Underdevelopment in East Africa: The Politics of Economic Change, 1919–1939* (New York: Nok Publishers, 1973).

27. Ingham, *History of East Africa*, pp. 279–281.

28. Murray-Brown, *Kenyatta*, Chapters 9 and 10. During this time Kenyatta studied anthropology at the University of London and in 1938 published a book, *Facing Mt.*

Kenya, about the Kikuyu people. It was the first anthropological text written by an African. He remained in England during World War II.

29. Best and de Blij, *African Survey,* p. 439.

30. George Bennett, "Settlers and Politics in Kenya," in Harlow, Chilver, and Smith, *History of East Africa,* p. 330. See also George Bennett, *Kenya, A Political History: The Colonial Period* (London: Oxford, 1963).

31. See Colonial Office, "Historical Survey of the Origins and Growth of Mau-Mau," Corfield Report, Cmnd. 1030 (London: Her Majesty's Stationery Office, 1960), p. 316; see also Carl G. Rosberg, Jr., and John Nottingham, *The Myth of "Mau Mau": Nationalism in Kenya* (New York: Praeger, 1966), pp. 303, 279–319; and Ingham, *History of East Africa,* pp. 407–410.

32. For further details on settler politics of the 1950s, see Rosberg and Nottingham, *Myth of "Mau Mau,"* pp. 277–319; M.P.K. Sorrenson, *Land Reform in the Kikuyu Country: A Study in Government Policy* (Nairobi: Oxford University Press, 1967), pp. 236–252; Elspeth Huxley, *The New Earth: An Experiment in Colonialism* (London: Chatto and Windus, 1960); Elspeth Huxley and Margery Perham, *Race and Politics in Kenya* (London: Faber and Faber, 1955), revised edition; and Gavin N. Kitching, *Class and Economic Change in Kenya: The Making of an African Petite Bourgeoisie, 1905–1970* (New Haven, Conn.: Yale University Press, 1980), pp. 159–324.

33. Marris and Somerset, *African Businessmen,* p. 46.

34. Swainson, *Development of Corporate Capitalism,* p. 115; Hazlewood, p. 7. Hazlewood reports that in 1960, with 61,000 Europeans and 169,000 Asians in Kenya, "Eighty percent of the value of the marketed produce of agriculture came from the European-owned farms and estates; fifty-five percent of the total wage bill accrued to non-Africans, though they amounted to only ten percent of the labor force. Profits from manufacturing and trade were received almost entirely by non-African individuals or companies. . . . Africans receive money income from wages and from the sale of agricultural produce, and it is this sale of produce which constituted virtually the whole of the monetary output of the African-owned economy. . . no more than three to four percent of the gross domestic product in 1960."

35. Marris and Somerset, *African Businessmen,* p. 12.

36. Ibid., p. 48; Swainson, *Development of Corporate Capitalism,* p. 181.

37. The main political activity in 1962 was the drafting of yet another constitution that would allow the transfer of power from a colonial government to an African internal self-government that would control all ministries except military and external affairs. The key constitutional debate centered around how the new government should be structured: a regional form, which the KADU minority favored, or a centralized form, which KANU favored. The regional approach won in London, due mainly to pressure from the Colonial Office. For an excellent analysis of the transition period see Gary Wasserman, *The Politics of Decolonization: Kenya Europeans and the Land Issue, 1960–1965* (Cambridge: Cambridge University Press, 1976).

38. Wolff, *Economics of Colonialism,* p. 143.

39. Frank Holmquist, personal communication, March 15, 1983.

CHAPTER 2. INDEPENDENCE: THE KENYATTA ERA

1. Henry Bienen, *Kenya: The Politics of Participation and Control* (Princeton, N.J.: Princeton University Press, 1974), p. 74.

2. Irving Kaplan, et al., *Area Handbook for Kenya* (Washington, D.C.: American University, 1976), pp. 45–46. Also see Jeremy Murray-Brown, *Kenyatta* (London: George Allen and Unwin, 1972).

3. M. Tamarkin, "The Roots of Political Stability in Kenya," *African Affairs* 77 (July 1978), p. 308.

4. The Independence Constitution that brought Kenya to statehood is a massively detailed 200-page document that seemingly covered every facet of political life. Some of the original key features were: a parliamentary system of two houses, a Senate and a House of Representatives; allegiance to the Queen of England; a Prime Minister overseeing

a cabinet, which was to be drawn from those elected to Parliament; a Bill of Rights carrying explicit protection for human rights and particular guarantees in the area of property rights; an independent, watchdog judiciary; and a built-in amendment process that made the system exceptionally difficult to change. Kenya's unique Bill of Rights, designated in thirteen sections of the constitution, provides protection in the area of civil liberties, procedural rights, and due process; guarantees freedom of thought and religion, freedom of expression and of assembly, and the freedom to organize, including labor unions; protects against unlawful entry or arbitrary search; guarantees a fair and prompt trial; forbids discrimination in terms of color, creed, race, tribe, or place of origin; and protects property rights, although in the national interest the government may expropriate private property with prompt payment of compensation.

5. Death of a president constitutionally calls for an interim period in which the vice-president becomes acting president. An election must be held within three months, the new president taking office the day after the election.

6. Government service is a coveted career that is sought after by school graduates. Since government is the predominant employer in Kenya, civil service jobs are very competitive and generally stratified by educational attainment. In 1969 some 77,000 civil servants were employed (95 percent Kenyan, 5 percent expatriate). By 1980 the number had risen to 214,800 in the central government, with another 257,000 in the larger public sector (local government, parastatal, etc.). See Republic of Kenya, *Economic Survey, 1981* (Nairobi: Government Printer, 1981), p. 55. Officers are divided into classes, starting at the top with "Administrative Officer"; the second echelon is designated "Executive Officer," which includes both professional and technical positions. Pay scales may be higher for individuals in the executive class than in the administrative class; transfers rarely occur to Administrative Officer status because many Executive Officers are doctors, engineers, or technicians.

7. Each provincial headquarters is headed by a provincial commissioner who in turn has between three and seven districts beneath him, each headed by a district commissioner. The "DC" is the representative of government to the people in each of Kenya's forty districts. He has an administrative staff at his headquarters, plus several senior assistants (district officers) who are assigned responsibilities over smaller geographic areas called divisions. Beneath divisions in the lower echelons of the central administration within the districts are locations and sublocations, administered by chiefs and subchiefs. These titles are administrative titles carried over from the colonial years when the British actually appointed and paid "chiefs" as local administrators and magistrates. Very few ethnic groups in Kenya, unlike in Tanzania and Uganda, had traditional chiefs. Today most of the "chiefs" chosen to serve are educated members of the civil service. Their locations overlap in some cases the geographic areas covered by local government authorities.

8. See Nicola Swainson, *The Development of Corporate Capitalism in Kenya, 1918–1977* (London: Heinemann, 1980), p. 183. See also G. Lamb, *Peasant Politics, Conflict and Development in Muranga* (Sussex: Julian Friedman, 1974), p. 25.

9. The act restructured the legal system and became the source of Kenya's various laws. It also established the formal court system at four levels: a Court of Appeals for East Africa, to review cases from Uganda, Tanzania, and Kenya; a High Court of Kenya that had original jurisdiction and appellate responsibility; the Resident Magistrates Courts, and the District Magistrates Courts. In addition, African Customary Law continues to be recognized for most civil matters such as marriage and inheritance disputes. Islamic law also may be invoked on civil issues, if not in conflict with the statutory laws. See Kaplan, *Area Handbook for Kenya,* pp. 199–202.

10. Frank Holmquist, public lecture, Dartmouth College, August 10, 1982. See also Frank Holmquist, "Defending Peasant Political Space in Independent Africa," *Canadian Journal of African Studies* 14, No. 1 (1980), pp. 157–167, and "Class Structure, Peasant Participation and Rural Self-Help," in Joel D. Barkan with John Okumu, eds., *Politics and Public Policy in Kenya and Tanzania* (New York: Praeger, 1979), pp. 130–153. See also P. Mbithi and B. Rasmussen, *Self Reliance in Kenya: The Case of Harambee* (Uppsala: Scandinavian Institute of African Studies, 1977).

11. Njuguna Ng'ethe, *Harambee and Development Participation in Kenya* (Ottawa: Carlton University, 1979), Chapter 4, unpublished Ph.D. thesis.

12. Tamarkin, "Roots of Political Stability," pp. 303–305.

13. No press members or other observers were allowed at the execution. See David Goldsworthy, *Tom Mboya: The Man Kenya Wanted to Forget* (Nairobi and London: Heinemann, 1982), pp. 279–289; see also Norman N. Miller, "Assassination and Political Unity: Kenya," *American Universities Field Staff Report* 8 (5) (Hanover, New Hampshire, 1969).

14. Emmet B. Evans, Jr., "Sources of Socio-Political Instability in An African State: The Case of Kenya's Educated Unemployed," *African Studies Review* 20, No. 1 (April 1977), p. 39. See also Stanley Meisler, "Tribal Politics Harass Kenya," *Foreign Affairs* 49 (October 1970), pp. 111–121.

15. Offices analyzed included the presidency, cabinet, assistant ministers, permanent secretaries, deputy permanent secretaries, provincial commissioners, district commissioners, and others. See John R. Nellis, *The Ethnic Composition of Leading Kenyan Government Positions* (Uppsala: Scandinavian Institute of African Studies, 1974), pp. 14–15.

16. The Kenya constitution provides citizenship to anyone born in Kenya after independence, to anyone born in Kenya before independence if one parent was Kenya-born, and to anyone married to a Kenya citizen who registers for citizenship. A final category covers those adults who have resided in the country for five years. This category became more restricted in 1965, individuals having to meet tests of language, character, and intention of permanent residence.

17. The role of the British forces was never publicized. Over the years they were small units on training rotation from the U.K., usually kept inconspicuously out of the capital, but widely believed to be available to the civil government if called upon.

18. Alan Best and Harm J. de Blij, *African Survey* (New York: Wiley, 1979), pp. 442–444. See also John W. Harbeson, *Nation Building in Kenya: The Role of Land Reform* (Evanston, Ill.: Northwestern University Press, 1973), and Gary Wasserman, *The Politics of Decolonization: Kenya Europeans and the Land Issue, 1960–1965* (Cambridge: Cambridge University Press, 1976), Chapters 2 and 3.

19. Colin Leys, "Development Strategy in Kenya Since 1971," *Canadian Journal of African Studies* 13, Nos. 1–2 (1979), p. 299.

20. Ibid., p. 311.

21. Kaplan, *Area Handbook for Kenya*, pp. 304–307.

22. Gavin N. Kitching, *Class and Economic Change in Kenya: The Making of an African Petite Bourgeoisie, 1905–1970* (New Haven, Conn.: Yale University Press, 1980), p. 325. See also Hans Ruthenberg, *African Agricultural Production Development Policy in Kenya, 1952–1965* (Berlin: Springer-Verlag, 1966).

23. *Sunday Times* (London), "Kenya on the Brink," August 12, 17, and 23, 1975.

24. Arthur Hazlewood, *The Economy of Kenya: The Kenyatta Era* (London: Oxford University Press, 1979), pp. 24–28. See also Republic of Kenya, *Economic Survey, 1979* (Nairobi: Government Printer, 1979).

25. Recommendations specifically focused on government spending in the rural areas; on the need for greater labor-intensive investment to provide jobs; the need to manufacture foods for low income consumers; the need to develop these goods for export markets rather than internal consumption; the need to develop small farm production capacities through further land redistribution, extension, and pricing; the need to reassess and help the "informal" small-scale sector in lieu of large-scale capital-intensive enterprises; and the need to develop small labor-intensive production. See International Labour Office, *Employment, Incomes, and Equality: A Strategy for Increasing Productive Employment in Kenya* (Geneva: ILO, 1972), "Summary of Recommendations," pp. 9–30. See also Leys, "Development Strategy in Kenya Since 1971," pp. 305–306.

26. Republic of Kenya, Sessional Paper No. 10, 1973, on employment—the government response. See also Leys, "Development Strategy in Kenya Since 1971," pp. 309–311; Swainson, *Development of Corporate Capitalism*, p. 184; and Dharam Ghai, Martin Godfrey, and Franklyn Lisk, *Planning of Basic Needs in Kenya* (Geneva: ILO, 1979), pp. 155–161, an annex entitled "Implementation of the 1972 ILO Mission Recommendations up to August 1978." See also Njuguna Ng'ethe, "Income Distribution in Kenya: The Politics of Mystification," in J.F.R. Rweyemamu, *Industrialization and Income Distribution in Africa*, (London: Zed Press, 1980). A subsequent expert group under World Bank

sponsorship provided a "what happened" view on the recommendations. See Hollis Chenery et al., *Redistribution With Growth* (London: Oxford University Press, 1974).

27. Ng'ethe, "Income Distribution in Kenya," pp. 1–5.

28. E. Crawford and E. Thorbecke, "Employment, Income Distribution, Poverty Alleviation and Basic Needs in Kenya" (Report of an ILO Consulting Mission, Cornell University, 1978), published in Ghai, Godfrey, and Lisk, *Planning of Basic Needs in Kenya*, p. 19.

29. Hazlewood, *Economy of Kenya*, p. 13.

30. Steven W. Langdon, *Multinational Corporations in the Political Economy of Kenya* (London: Macmillan, 1981), pp. 31–32. See also Raphael Kaplinsky, ed., *Readings on the Multinational Corporations in Kenya* (Nairobi: Oxford University Press, 1978). For case studies of multinational firms in Kenya, see Swainson, *Development of Corporate Capitalism*, pp. 250–284, and Hazlewood, *Economy of Kenya*, pp. 59–65.

For a broader view of MNCs in the Third World, see Joseph La Palombara, *Multinational Corporations and Developing Countries* (New York: The Conference Board, 1979), and V. N. Balasubramanyam, *Multinational Enterprises and the Third World* (London: Ditchlong, 1980).

31. Langdon, *Multinational Corporations in Kenya*, pp. 34 and 194. The trends have been to decrease foreign ownership as the government increased its participation in the firms. Hazlewood estimated roughly a 60–40 split in value added in manufacturing by international versus local firms in the years prior to 1972 (Hazlewood, *Economy of Kenya*, p. 59).

32. Swainson, *Development of Corporate Capitalism*, p. 235.

33. Guy Arnold, *Modern Kenya* (London: Longman, 1981), p. 117.

34. The Kenyatta period saw major changes in the employment picture. Between 1964 and 1977 agricultural employment dropped from 51 percent to 39 percent of those employed in the private sector. Manufacturing increased from 13 percent to 18 percent, construction from 2 percent to 6 percent, and other services from 17 percent to 22 percent. Trade and transport remained the same at around 15 percent. The total private employment in the same period rose from 292,400 to 526,500, compared to total public-sector employment that rose from 182,000 to 376,400 (Hazlewood, *Economy of Kenya*, p. 22).

35. Sources of material on corruption in the Kenyatta period include the *Sunday Times* (London), August 12, 17, and 25, 1975; Tamarkin, pp. 303–307; Goran Hyden, Robert Jackson, and John Okumu, *Development Administration: The Kenyan Experience* (Nairobi: Oxford University Press, 1970), pp. 31–37, 60; Arnold, *Modern Kenya*, pp. 79–85; Esmond B. Martin and Chryssee Martin, *Cargoes of the East* (London: Hamish Hamilton, 1978); and Norman N. Miller, "The Indian Ocean: Traditional Trade on a Smuggler's Sea," *American Universities Field Staff Report* 7 (Hanover, New Hampshire, 1980). For broader interpretations see Joseph Nye, "Corruption and Political Development: A Cost Benefit Analysis," *American Political Science Review* 16 (1967), pp. 417–427; and R. Wraith and E. Simpkins, *Corruption in Developing Countries* (New York: Norton, 1963).

36. See Kenneth King, *The African Artisan: Education and the Informal Sector in Kenya* (London: Heinemann, 1979), pp. 48–65; see also ILO Report, Chapter 13; Republic of Kenya, *Economic Survey, 1977* (Nairobi: Government Printer, 1977), p. 41; and Hazlewood, *Economy of Kenya*, pp. 4, 21, 25, 41, and 86.

37. Tamarkin, *Roots of Political Stability*, p. 304; the *Sunday Nation* (Nairobi), September 10, 1977.

CHAPTER 3. MODERN SOCIETY

1. Kenya had had eight census enumerations since 1911. The first four, in 1911, 1921, 1926, and 1931, tallied Europeans and did not include Africans. The 1948 census, which did include Africans, estimated the population at 5.4 million. The 1969 census reported 10.7 million, the 1979 census some 15.3 million. The last census was the most extensive in terms of preparation and control. See *The Kenya Population Census, 1979*, Vol. I (Nairobi: Central Bureau of Statistics). See also Simeon H. Ominde, *Land and Population Movements in Kenya* (London: Heinemann, 1968), Chapter 6; Norman N. Miller,

"Population Review 1970: Kenya" and "Politics of Population," *American Universities Field Staff Reports 9*, Nos. 1 and 2 (1970); UNICEF, *Country Profile: Kenya 1981* (Nairobi: UNICEF East Africa Regional Office, 1981); Frank Mott and Susan Mott, "Kenya's Record Population Growth: A Dilemma of Development," *Population Bulletin* (Washington, D.C.: Population Reference Bureau, October 1980); and *Kenya Fertility Survey, 1978*, Vols. 1 and 2 (Nairobi: Central Bureau of Statistics, 1980). See also Rashid Faruguee, "Fertility and Its Trends in Kenya," *Rural Africana* 13 (Fall 1982), pp. 25–48.

2. Mott and Mott, "Kenya's Record Population Growth," p. 4.

3. Ibid., pp. 31, 34.

4. UNICEF, *Country Profile: Kenya 1981*, pp. 2–3. See also the Kenya government's 1969 census, *The National Demographic Survey* (1977), and *Kenya Fertility Survey* (1978).

5. UNICEF, *Country Profile: Kenya 1981*, pp. 3–5.

6. Republic of Kenya, *Economic Survey, 1981* (Nairobi: Government Printer, 1981), p. 34.

7. Miller, "Population Review 1970," p. 4.

8. Mott and Mott, "Kenya's Record Population Growth," pp. 9 and 28.

9. Ibid.

10. "The Implications of Kenya's High Rate of Population Growth," *Social Perspectives* 4 (1), Central Bureau of Statistics, Ministry of Economic Planning and Development, Government of Kenya, Nairobi, November 1979, pp. 5 and 6.

11. "Acceptors" rose in the first years of the program, 1969–1975, but so, too, did the number of women who later rejected family-planning techniques. See Irving Kaplan et al., *Area Handbook for Kenya* (Washington, D.C.: American University, 1976), p. 83, and Miller, "Population Review 1970," pp. 17–19. See also *Kenya Fertility Survey, 1978*, and *Wall Street Journal*, April 11, 1983, p. 1.

12. UNICEF, *Country Profile: Kenya 1981*, pp. 3–4.

13. See G. P. Murdock, *Africa, Its Peoples and Their Cultural History* (New York: McGraw-Hill, 1959), Chapters 35, 38, 39, 44, and 45; and John D. Kesby, *The Cultural Regions of East Africa* (London: Academic Press, 1977), Chapters 1–5.

14. Kenya Central Bureau of Statistics, 1979 Census (unofficial breakdown). For details of ethnic group size, see Kaplan, *Area Handbook for Kenya*, pp. 86–87, and Miller, "Population Review 1970," p. 4.

15. This discussion of stratification is designed only as an introduction to the subsequent treatment of poverty, equity, and economic class.

16. Kaplan, *Area Handbook for Kenya*, p. 114.

17. Private conversation, anonymity requested, United Kenya Club, December 28, 1981.

18. Republic of Kenya, *Economic Survey, 1982* (Nairobi: Government Printer, 1982), p. 45. For percentage distribution of rural households by income group see Leonard Berry, *Eastern Africa Country Profiles: Kenya* (Worcester, Mass.: Program for International Development, Clark University, 1980), p. 118.

19. Three percent of the population were not tabulated. See Berry, *Eastern Africa Country Profiles: Kenya*, p. 108, based on William House and Tony Killick, "Social Justice and Development Policy for Kenya's Rural Economy," Rural Employment Policy Research Program, n.d., pp. 6–7.

20. Estimates based on author's field work in Kenya, 1960–1984. See also Berry, *Eastern Africa Country Profiles: Kenya*, pp. 108, 109–120, and Kenya Government, *The Integrated Rural Survey, 1974–75* (Nairobi: Central Bureau of Statistics, 1977), pp. 8–10.

21. See Arthur Hazlewood, *The Economy of Kenya: The Kenyatta Era* (London: Oxford University Press, 1979), pp. 197–204; also see E. Crawford and E. Thorbecke, "Employment, Income Distribution, Poverty Alleviation and Basic Needs in Kenya" (Report of an ILO Consulting Mission, Cornell University, 1978); see also D. J. Casley and T. Marchant, "Smallholder Marketing in Kenya." (Food and Agriculture Organization, FAO Marketing Development Project, 1979).

22. Berry, *Eastern Africa Country Profiles: Kenya*, pp. 230–231.

23. See Marc H. Ross, "Political Alienation, Participation and Ethnicity in the Nairobi Urban Area," in John N. Paden, *Values, Identities and National Integration* (Evanston,

Ill.: Northwestern University Press, 1980), pp. 173–181, and Herbert H. Werlin, *Governing an African City: A Study of Nairobi* (New York: Africana Publishing, 1974).

24. See UNICEF, *Country Profile: Kenya 1981*, pp. 1–3; *Economic Survey, 1982*, p. 222. Minority census figures are unofficial releases from the Kenya Bureau of Statistics, Nairobi.

25. See P. R. Moock, "The Efficiency of Women as Farm Managers," *American Journal of Agricultural Economics* 58, No. 5 (1974), pp. 831–835; A. O. Pala, "Women's Access to Land and Their Role in Agriculture and Secession Making on the Farm: Experiences of the Juluo of Kenya" (Nairobi: Institute of Development Studies, 1978), Paper 263; and Jennifer Berger et al., "Women's Groups in Rural Development" (Nairobi: Program for Better Family Living, 1974), Report No. 15.

26. *Economic Survey, 1982*, pp. 206–213; UNICEF, *Country Profile: Kenya 1981*, p. 19.

27. See Norman N. Miller, "Education for What?" *Ekistics* 43, No. 259 (June 1977), pp. 342–345.

28. See David Court and Dharam P. Ghai, eds., *Education, Society and Development: New Perspectives from Kenya* (Nairobi: Oxford University Press, 1974); K. Prewitt, "Education and Social Equality in Kenya," in ibid., pp. 199–216. See also James R. Sheffield, *Education in Kenya: An Historical Study* (New York: Columbia University Teachers College Press, 1973). For national comparisons see David Court, "The Education System as a Response to Inequality in Tanzania and Kenya," *Journal of Modern African Studies* 14, No. 4 (1976), pp. 661–690.

29. Kaplan, *Area Handbook for Kenya*, pp. 152–165.

30. UNICEF, *Country Profile: Kenya 1981*, p. 20; *Economic Survey, 1981*, p. 204.

31. The disease profile of the country includes parasitic and nonparasitic diseases, often caused by water-borne, insect-borne, and excreta-borne pathogens. Malaria is Kenya's leading malady, thought to be hyperendemic at altitudes below 5000 feet. Some forms are resistant to antimalarial drugs. Upper respiratory infections, including pneumonia, are the greatest cause of hospitalization. Venereal diseases are the most difficult to treat today because of the constant movement of many of those affected, such as soldiers, drivers, and migratory workers. Diarrheal diseases and intestinal disorders are the leading cause of illness in children. Schistosomiasis, transmitted by snails living in fresh water, affects people near lake shores and irrigation projects. It has resisted control measures. Leprosy, which is found mostly in the west and along the coast, affected an estimated 100,000 people in the mid-1970s. Leading causes of death among young children are measles, gastroenteritis, colitis, kwashiorkor, tetanus, scabies, and whooping cough. Nomadic peoples are susceptible to trachoma and other eye problems; filariasis, found along the coast, is transmitted by the bite of an infected black fly, mosquito, or mangrove fly. Infected sand flies can transmit visceral leishmaniasis, a serious problem in some northern areas. Sleeping sickness, which was considerably reduced by a vigorous control program in the 1970s, shows signs of spreading again as tsetse flies are beginning to multiply. Large-scale government efforts are underway to control tuberculosis, a serious urban problem. Dysentery and parasitic infections are common in many rural areas. Other problems found less frequently include poliomyelitis, brucellosis, and hemorrhagic conjuctivitis. See "A Working Paper on Health Services Development in Kenya: Issues, Analysis and Recommendations" (Washington, D.C.: Family Health Institute, 1978), pp. 9–11 and 29–32. See also "Health Sector Assessment for Kenya" (Nairobi: USAID/Kenya, 1978); L. C. Vogel et al., eds., *Health and Disease in Kenya* (Nairobi: East African Literature Bureau, 1974); *Economic Survey, 1981*, pp. 207–208; and *Economic Survey, 1982*, pp. 8, 213–217.

32. *Economic Survey, 1981*, p. 207. Totals include 216 hospitals, 241 health centers, and 1087 centers and dispensaries. Kenya in 1980 had 27,691 hospital beds—an average of 174 per 100,000 population.

33. Ibid. Other medical personnel included 1618 clinical officers (3 yrs. special training), 6692 registered nurses, and 5691 enrolled nurses.

34. Norman N. Miller, "Traditional Medicine in East Africa," *American Universities Field Staff Report* 22 (1980).

35. B. E. Kipkorir, "Towards a Cultural Policy for Kenya: Some Views," University of Nairobi, Institute of African Studies (mimeo), No. 131, 1980, p. 34; and *The Organization of African Unity Charter* (Addis Ababa, Ethiopia: OAU, 1976), pp. 2–3.

36. See Ngugi wa Thiong'o, *Detained: A Writer's Prison Diary* (London: Heinemann, 1981). See also Kivuto Ndeti, *Cultural Policy in Kenya* (Paris: UNESCO Press, 1975).

37. Kaplan, *Area Handbook for Kenya*, p. 114.

38. Barrett assesses 6,000 breakaway churches and revival movements in Africa, several dozen of them in Kenya. See David Barrett, *Schism and Renewal in Africa* (London: Oxford University Press, 1968). See also Thomas Hodgkin, "Prophets and Priests," in *Nationalism in Colonial Africa* (New York: New York University Press, 1957); John S. Mbiti, *African Religions and Philosophy* (London: Heinemann, 1969); and Kaplan, *Area Handbook for Kenya*, pp. 114–119.

CHAPTER 4. MODERN POLITICS: THE MOI ERA

1. Kenyatta died unexpectedly on August 23, 1978, at the presidential home in Mombasa on Kenya's coast. Within hours Daniel arap Moi, the vice-president, was sworn in as the three-month interim president. A plot, allegedly to assassinate Moi and others and to deliver power to the Kiambu-based Kikuyu group, fizzled when caught in its formative stage by President Kenyatta's sudden demise. See Joseph Karimi and Philip Ochieng, *The Kenyatta Succession* (Nairobi: Transafrica Book Distributors, 1980).

2. In the election the Moi government attained a clear mandate. Seven of Kenyatta's ministers and fifteen assistant ministers lost their seats and Moi had the luxury of forming a new cabinet from a broad popular base.

3. See John Dickie and Alan Rake, *Who's Who in Africa* (London: African Buyer and Trader, 1973), p. 203.

4. Kenya took on a new religious atmosphere after Moi's ascendency. Hymns and church music filled the radio waves, meetings were opened by prayer, MPs handed out Bibles (or received them if their constituents suspected them of being less than Christian or less than sober).

5. Guy Arnold, *Modern Kenya* (London: Longman, 1981), p. 32.

6. See the *Standard* (Nairobi), December 22, 1981, and Republic of Kenya, *Economic Survey, 1981* (Nairobi: Government Printer, 1981), pp. 1 and 13.

7. For the analysis of the Moi period I have drawn on Arnold, *Modern Kenya*, pp. 78–79. For political corruption see ibid., pp. 84–85, and Colin Legum, ed., *Africa Contemporary Record: Annual Survey and Documents, 1980-1981* (New York: Africana Publishing, 1981), pp. B230–238. For cabinet changes, see Arnold, *Modern Kenya*, pp. 87–88, and Legum, *Africa Contemporary Record*, p. 215; for cabinet structure in the Kenyatta period see Irving Kaplan et al., *Area Handbook for Kenya* (Washington, D.C.: American University Press, 1976), p. 204. For economic developments see Arnold, *Modern Kenya*, pp. 25–28. On the curtailing of tribal unions, the restaffing of the cabinet, and changes in the armed forces see Legum, *Africa Contemporary Record*, pp. 215–223. For tribal unions, political upheavals, and economic policies see Arnold, *Modern Kenya*, pp. 32 and 91.

8. For events prior to the uprising see the *Financial Times* (London), February 26, 1982, the *Economist* (London), March 20, 1982, and *African News* (Durham, N.C.), June 14, 1982, pp. 6–7.

9. For events following the August uprising see *African News*, August 30, 1982, p. 12, and October 18, 1982, p. 19. See also the *New York Times*, September 1, 12, 16, 23, and 24, 1982.

10. See Smith Hempstone, *Globe Democrat* (St. Louis), August 20, 1982.

11. See *Africa Now* (London), September 1982, pp. 14–19.

12. Although Daniel Moi has made attempts to overcome the distance and isolation that affects Kenyan politics, the basic spatiality or political geography of Kenya has remained the same for two decades. It is a center-to-periphery political process. Nairobi is the hub from which everything radiates. It is the seat of power, the railhead and national epicenter. Beyond Nairobi the political map fragments into a mosaic. There is a middle zone that encompasses some forty political and administrative districts, each with an urban center. These political centers are usually market towns; they are central places for the exchange of resources, for political information, for decisions of who gets what, when, and how. Beyond these lesser centers are over 6000 tiny political communities—

neighborhoods that typically cluster around an established market, or near a school, church, dispensary, or subchief's office. These neighborhoods are the home areas of perhaps two-thirds of Kenya's population, each a mini-political enclave, often unrelated and unattached to the central system except through a few local leaders. For further discussion of Kenyan political characteristics see Arnold, *Modern Kenya*, pp. 78–92; for comparisons with Tanzania see Rodger Yeager, *Tanzania: An African Experiment* (Boulder, Colo.: Westview Press, 1982), pp. 59–78.

13. The three main military bodies, apart from the police and paramilitary Government Service Unit, have been the army, the air force, and the navy. Kenya's army is commanded by a major-general. Four infantry battalions are each supported by small mortar and anti-tank units. In addition there is a support battalion that includes an elite paratrooper unit and a transport battalion. The army is built around light weaponry. The chief firepower lies in mortars and recoilless rifles, with heavy artillery on order. A major tactical element is the "Flying Troops," who can be moved quickly by air transport to be deployed from remote air strips or as paratroopers. The Kenya Air Force, established in 1964 and disbanded after the 1982 coup attempt, was made up of three branches: a technical wing, an administrative wing, and a flying wing—the latter divided into a strike squadron, an air support squadron, and a transport squadron. Until 1975, when Kenya purchased six U.S. jets, the air force had been equipped largely with British aircraft and trained by British or Canadian personnel. Kenya's navy is charged with coastal patrols, distress assistance, anti-smuggling surveillance and inspections, and general coastal security. Navy personnel are estimated at 800 men. The force headquarters in Mombasa harbor has four patrol vessels in the 103 foot-to-123 foot class. See Kaplan, *Area Handbook for Kenya*, pp. 399–422, and Legum, *Africa Contemporary Record*, pp. 216–217.

14. Since independence two main newspaper groups have competed in Kenya. The *Standard*, whose beginnings go back to 1899 in Mombasa, currently publishes the *Standard* and a Swahili weekly, *Baraza*. The Nation group, which came to Kenya in 1959, publishes the *Daily Nation*, the *Sunday Nation*, and in Swahili, *Taifa Leo* and *Taifa Kenya*, the latter a weekly. Since 1973 U.S.-trained writer/publisher, Hilary Ngweno, has brought out a number of publications including a humor magazine, *Joe*, and the *Weekly Review*. Five weeklies, eighteen monthlies, and twelve other quarterlies or semi-annual publications are also published. See Kaplan, *Area Handbook for Kenya*, pp. 182–183.

15. For further discussion of the political role of the university see Kaplan, *Area Handbook for Kenya*, pp. 156–166; see also writings of David Court, Dharam Ghai, Kenneth Prewitt, and G. S. Fields in David Court and Dharam P. Ghai, eds., *Education, Society, and Development: New Perspectives from Kenya* (Nairobi: Oxford University Press, 1974).

16. The state of capitalism in Kenya is a central theme in a great deal of literature. The contemporary debate surrounds discussion of class, the existence of a "middle peasantry" or an "emerging bourgeoisie," and inequity issues. See Crawford Young, *Ideology and Development in Africa* (New Haven, Conn.: Yale University Press, 1982) for a review of ideological developments in Africa (pp. 1–21) and for a historic recap of Kenya's pathway as an African capitalist state, pp. 203–219; see also Goran Hyden, *Beyond Ujamaa in Tanzania: Underdevelopment and an Uncaptured Peasantry* (Berkeley: University of California Press, 1980).

17. For literature representing Marxist and socialist perspectives see Gavin N. Kitching, *Class and Economic Change in Kenya: The Making of an African Petite Bourgeoisie, 1905-1970* (New Haven, Conn.: Yale University Press, 1980); Nicola Swainson, *The Development of Corporate Capitalism in Kenya, 1918-1977* (London: Heinemann, 1980); and *Review of African Political Economy* 8 (1977), pp. 90–98. The latter dedicated an entire issue to Kenya under the title "Kenya: The Agrarian Question," No. 20 (1981), with articles by P. Angang' Nyong'o, D. Mukaru Ng'anga, Apollo L. Njonjo, S.B.O. Gutto, Michael C. Cowen, Michael Chege, and John Mulaa. See also Colin Leys, *Underdevelopment in Kenya* (London: Heinemann, 1975).

18. For literature representing liberal and conservative perspectives see Arthur Hazlewood, *The Economy of Kenya: The Kenyatta Era* (London: Oxford University Press, 1979). See also the writings by John Harbeson, Henry Bienen, Peter Marris, and Anthony Somerset in Peter Morris and Anthony Somerset, *African Businessmen: A Study of Entrepreneurship and Development in Kenya* (London: Routledge and Kegan Paul, 1971). See

also "Kenya African National Union, the KANU Manifesto for Independence Social Democracy and Stability" (Nairobi, 1960), and Cherry J. Gertzel, Maurice Goldschmidt, and Donald Rothchild, eds., *Government and Politics in Kenya* (Nairobi: East African Publishing House, 1969).

19. See Raphael Kaplinsky, ed., *Readings on the Multinational Corporations in Kenya* (Nairobi: Oxford University Press, 1978); and S. Langdon and M. Godfrey, "Partners In Underdevelopment: The Transnationalization Thesis in a Kenyan Context," *Journal of Commonwealth and Comparative Politics* (March 1976), pp. 42–63.

20. See John Carlsen, *Economics and Social Transformation in Rural Kenya* (Uppsala: Scandinavian Institute of African Studies, 1980); Per Kongstad and Mette Monsted, *Family Labour and Trade in Western Kenya* (Uppsala: Scandinavian Institute of African Studies, 1980); and Torben Bager, *Marketing Cooperatives and Peasants in Kenya* (Uppsala: Scandinavian Institute of African Studies, 1980).

21. Hyden, *Beyond Ujamaa in Tanzania*, p. 190.

22. M. Tamarkin, "The Roots of Political Stability in Kenya," *African Affairs* 77 (July 1978), pp. 300–301. See also Emmet B. Evans, Jr., "Sources of Socio-Political Instability in an African State: The Case of Kenya's Educated Unemployed," *African Studies Review* 20, No. 1 (April 1977), pp. 37–54.

23. Tamarkin, "Roots of Political Stability," p. 300.

CHAPTER 5. MODERN ECONOMIC REALITIES

1. Republic of Kenya, *Economic Survey, 1972, 1975, 1978, 1981, 1982* (Nairobi: Government Printer, 1972, 1975, 1978, 1982). See also Arthur Hazlewood, *The Economy of Kenya: The Kenyatta Era* (London: Oxford University Press, 1979), Chapter 3.

2. World Bank, *World Development Report, 1981* (New York: Oxford University Press, 1981), p. 74.

3. See *Kenya Development Plan, 1979–1983* (Nairobi: Government Printer, 1979), Parts I, II.

4. Republic of Kenya, "Development Prospects and Policies," Sessional Paper No. 4 (Nairobi: Government Printer, 1982), p. 5.

5. Philip Ndegwa, chairman, "Working Party on Government Expenditures: Report and Recommendations of the Working Party" (Ndegwa Report) (Nairobi: Government Printer, 1982), p. 80.

6. The prestigious *Institutional Investor*, which provides international credit ratings, reported that in mid-1982 Kenya's rating dropped from seventh to ninth in Africa, still ranking ahead of all black African countries except Nigeria, Ivory Coast, Gabon, and Cameroon. Kenya's global rank was 71 out of 107 nations evaluated. Uganda was last. See *Institutional Investor* (New York), September 1982, p. 304.

7. Ndegwa Report, p. 15. The chronic financial and balance-of-payments problems were also the subject of the government's Sessional Paper No. 4 of 1982 (see Note 4).

8. This sector analysis touches only a part of the Kenya economy. For details on Kenya's money, banking, and financial structure and on public finance, including public debt, see Republic of Kenya, *Economic Survey, 1982*, Chapters 5 and 6. See also *Economic Survey, 1983*, the same chapters. For monetary and fiscal policies see Sessional Paper No. 4 of 1982, pp. 27–33.

9. World Bank, *World Development Report, 1981*, p. 75; Guy Arnold, *Modern Kenya* (London: Longman, 1981), p. 47; *Economic Survey, 1982*, pp. 100–137.

10. *Economic Survey, 1982*, pp. 102–103.

11. Ibid., p. 100; see also pp. 4–5 and 100–124. It is important to note, however, that agricultural performance cannot be judged by marketing board and government statistics alone. Many small farmers bypass the marketing boards or sell illegally on the open market, resulting in sizably lower official statistics than the actual total economic activity. It should be emphasized that maize is the most important food crop, raised on 40 percent of all cultivated land and providing the diet staple for both rural and urban Kenyans. Although sales of surplus maize serve as a supplemental income for some farmers, the majority of farmers are not self-sufficient in maize.

12. Republic of Kenya, "National Food Policy," Sessional Paper No. 4, 1981 (Nairobi: Government Printer, 1981), p. 8.

13. Norman N. Miller, "Journey in a Forgotten Land," Parts 1 and 2, *American Universities Field Staff Report*, 1974.

14. Administratively, the government's problems range across a wide spectrum: disease control, eradication of the tsetse fly (anti-sleeping sickness measures), adjudication of rangeland, registration of land titles, provision of credit, improvement of stock breeding techniques, and improvement of holding grounds, water pans, dams, pumps, and boreholes.

15. Much of this section draws on Norman Miller, "Journey in a Forgotten Land"; Irving Kaplan et al., *Area Handbook for Kenya* (Washington, D.C.: American University Press, 1976), pp. 320–322 and 373; *Economic Survey, 1981*, Chapter 8, and *1982*, pp. 117–121; L. W. Cone and J. F. Lipscomb, *The History of Kenya Agriculture* (Nairobi: University of Africa, 1972), Chapter 16. See also Harold Schneider, *Livestock and Equality in East Africa: The Economic Basis for Social Structure* (Bloomington: Indiana University Press, 1979), Chapter 4.

16. During 1980, 75 percent of Kenya's petroleum consumption was accounted for by retail pumps: for road transport (476,700 tons), for commercial and industrial uses (431,500 tons), and for nongovernment uses (352,400 tons). Other categories included power generation (151,500 tons), government use (172,600 tons), nongovernment marine use (134,500 tons), rail transport (70,000 tons), and agriculture (69,000 tons). The total of 1,671,000 tons included a balance item of 87,700 tons. See *Economic Survey, 1981*, p. 145.

17. *Economic Survey, 1982*, p. 191.

18. See L. Berry, *East Africa Country Profiles: Kenya* (Worcester: Clark University Program for International Development, 1980), p. 42. The figure of 141,300 compares to 106,400 in 1972, when the average number of employees per firm was 63; the first 100 largest firms average 371 employees per firm. These estimates do not include very small-scale entrepreneurs. In 1975 some 3340 of these firms were registered with the government. Most were workshops of 8–10 people. At least twice that many "informal" workshops existed, employing one or two artisans plus a few helpers.

19. Ndegwa Report, p. 92.

20. Considering all factors (imports and exports from East Africa, outside East Africa, commercial and government) over a five-year period, the trade balance in millions of Kenya shillings has been: 1978: −265.4; 1979: −207.4; 1980: −444.4; 1981: −423.5. See *Economic Survey, 1981*, p. 90, and *1982*, p. 83 (1981 figures provisional).

21. *Economic Survey, 1981*, pp. 95 and 99, and *1982*, p. 89.

22. See *Country Report: Kenya* (London: Barclay's Bank Group Economics Department, March 5, 1980).

23. *Economic Survey, 1981*, pp. 100 and 102.

24. S. K. Adjala, the *Standard* (Nairobi), April 29, 1981.

25. The *Standard* (Nairobi), February 12, 1981 and January 23, 1983.

26. *Economic Survey, 1981*, p. 178.

27. See Allan Frank, "The Market's Discipline," *Forbes*, November 22, 1982, pp. 102–106, and the *Standard* (Nairobi), February 12, 1981 and January 23, 1983.

28. Berry, *East Africa Country Profiles: Kenya*, p. 54.

29. MNCs have been cited in previous chapters with the implied understanding that readers know in general what these internationally-dealing corporations are. Specifically, an MNC is a firm that has direct investment in more than one country, owning and controlling income-generating assets such as factories, plantations, and mines. See Colin Kirkpatrick and Frederick Nixon, "Transnational Corporations and Economic Development," *Journal of Modern African Studies* 19, No. 3 (1981), p. 369. For further information on MNCs in Kenya see Hazlewood, *Economy of Kenya*, pp. 12, 59–64, 75–85, 119–121, 131–133; Swainson, Chapters 2, 4, 6, and 7; S. Langdon and M. Godfrey, "Partners in Underdevelopment: The Transnationalization Thesis in a Kenyan Context," *Journal of Commonwealth and Comparative Politics*, March 1976; and Raphael Kaplinsky, ed., *Readings on the Multinational Corporations in Kenya* (Nairobi: Oxford University Press, 1978). I am also indebted to Wendy Oatis for permission to draw on material cited in her unpublished

research paper, "In Support of Multinational Corporations" (Kenya), Environmental Studies Seminar, Dartmouth College, 1982.

30. Arnold, *Modern Kenya*, p. 69.

31. The major British firms include Leyland, Shell B.P., Unilever, Lonrho, Portland Cement, and Brooke Bond. U.S. firms include Exxon, General Motors, Union Carbide, Pfizer, Firestone, Citibank, and Xerox. Others are, from Japan, Kenya Toray Mills, Ataka (engineering, African Radio assembly); from West Germany, Hoechst Drug, Siemens (engineering), Hobby Hotels; from India, Pan African Paper Mills, Raymond Woolen Mills, Aga Khan's Diamond Trust (real estate); from Holland, Twentsche Overseas Trading; and from Denmark, DCK (fruit and flowers export). See Hazlewood, *Economy of Kenya*, pp. 59 and 69, and Swainson, *Development of Corporate Capitalism*, pp. 236–249.

32. The leveling off occurred from a high of some 60 percent of value added in manufacturing between 1967 and 1972; see ILO Report, Table 73, and Hazlewood, *Economy of Kenya*, p. 59.

33. Coca Cola, Pepsi Cola, and part of the Union Carbide operations, for example, departed from Kenya in the 1978–1983 period.

34. Swainson, *Development of Corporate Capitalism*, p. 233.

35. Ndegwa Report, pp. 93–101.

36. Arnold, *Modern Kenya*, p. 68.

37. For further discussions on the regulations affecting foreign investment in Kenya see ibid., pp. 23–26, 30, 40–41, and Hazlewood, *Economy of Kenya*, pp. 76–77 and 131–133.

38. Hazlewood, *Economy of Kenya*, pp. 79–80; W. Oatis, "In Support of Multinational Corporations," Environmental Studies Seminar, Dartmouth College, 1982 (unpublished), p. 14.

39. Frank, "The Market's Discipline," p. 102.

40. The *Standard* (Nairobi), January 25, 1983; Colin Legum, ed., *African Contemporary Record: Annual Survey and Documents, 1980–1981* (New York: Africana Publishing, 1981), p. B233.

41. Other problems involve technical transfers that carry unanticipated social problems such as pollution. The charge is that MNCs engage in precious little long-term planning concerning the ecological impact of much of the technology. See Berry, *East Africa Country Profiles: Kenya*, pp. 30–31, and Hazlewood, *Economy of Kenya*, pp. 82–85 and 156.

42. The World Bank suggests that Kenya has a clear need to attract foreign capital. "Although some of the past investments in Kenya have not really benefited the country, she will continue to need a steady flow of private investment both to supply the capital and to provide entrepreneurial ability and technical knowhow. The issue we see is not whether foreign investment is desirable, but rather whether Kenya can continue to attract foreign private investment more efficiently for the benefit of the country." See World Bank, *World Development Report, 1981*, p. 43.

CHAPTER 6. THE INTERNATIONAL DIMENSION

1. The *Standard* (Nairobi), January 1, 1980, p. 7.

2. Sudan-Kenya relations were temporarily strained during the Kenyatta succession intrigue of 1978. When the president died unexpectedly, the alleged "Ngoroko" coup plot misfired, and one of its principals, Police Commander Mungai, fled from his Nakuru base across the Sudanese border to take asylum first in Sudan and then in the U.K. Although Mungai eventually came home to an "all is forgiven" reception, the complicity of at least some Sudanese caused consternation in Kenya.

3. Norman N. Miller, "The Other Somalia: Illicit Trade and the Hidden Economy," Part 1, *American Universities Field Staff Report* 29 (Hanover, New Hampshire, 1981), and "The Indian Ocean: Traditional Trade on a Smuggler's Sea," *American Universities Field Staff Report* 7 (Hanover, New Hampshire, 1980).

4. See "Trade with African Countries 1977–1981," Republic of Kenya, *Economic Survey, 1982* (Nairobi: Government Printer, 1982), p. 95.

5. Colin Legum, ed., *African Contemporary Record: Annual Survey and Documents, 1980–1981* (New York: Africana Publishing, 1981), pp. B224–225.

6. For greater detail on East African attempts at regional integration see Rodger Yeager, *Tanzania: An African Experiment* (Boulder, Colo.: Westview Press, 1982), pp. 97–104. See also Anthony J. Hughes, *East Africa: The Search for Unity* (London: Penguin Books, 1963), pp. 213–264.

7. Guy Arnold, *Modern Kenya* (London: Longman, 1981), pp. 29 and 41.

8. Ibid., p. 59.

9. See Norman N. Miller, "The United Nations Environment Programme," and Norman N. Miller and James F. Hornig, "Habitat: The New UN Initiative in Human Settlements," *American Universities Field Staff Reports* (Hanover, New Hampshire, 1979 and 1981).

10. Aid here is discussed as bilateral and multilateral funding between governments and international organizations. It should be noted that aid also flows to Kenya through nongovernmental organizations such as missionary programs, private foundations like the Ford and Rockefeller foundations, and dozens of specifically targeted trusts and foundations such as the African Wildlife Foundation and the Leaky Foundation.

11. Arthur Hazlewood, *The Economy of Kenya: The Kenyatta Era* (London: Oxford University Press, 1979), p. 122.

12. From USAID officers, Nairobi, March 1983; see also Republic of Kenya, *Development Estimates for the Year 1981–1982* (Nairobi: Government Printer, 1981), p. 88.

13. Arnold, *Modern Kenya*, p. 40.

14. United States Agency for International Development, "Current Aid Programs and Assistance Strategy," USAID, Kenya, June 1981, p. 1 (mimeo).

15. Republic of Kenya, *Development Estimates for the Year 1981–1982*, p. 88.

16. Some of the cultural ineptness that characterized foreign aid personnel in the 1960s and 1970s may be changing. USAID employees, for example, tend currently to be former Peace Corps volunteers or individuals with graduate degrees and broad experience in the developing world.

17. For further reading on the aid process see Gerald Holtham and Arthur Hazlewood, *Aid and Inequality in Kenya: British Development Assistance to Kenya* (London: Croom Helm, 1975); James C. Scott, "Patron-Client Politics and Political Change in South East Asia," *American Political Science Review* 66 (March 1972), pp. 91–113; and R. D. McKinlay and R. Little, "The U.S. Aid Relationship: A Test of the Recipient Need and Donor Interest Models," *Political Studies* 27 (June 1979), pp. 236–250.

CONCLUSION

1. Emmet B. Evans, Jr., "Sources of Socio-Political Instability in an African State: The Case of Kenya's Educated Unemployed," *African Studies Review* 20, No. 1 (April 1977), p. 38.

Selected Bibliography

BIBLIOGRAPHIES ON KENYA

Howell, John B. *Kenya: Subject Guide to Official Publications.* Washington, D.C.: Library of Congress, 1978.
Killick, Tony. *The Economies of East Africa.* Boston: G. K. Hall and Company, 1976.
Webster, John B., with Shirin G. F. Kassam, Robert S. Peckham, and Barbara A. Skapa. *A Bibliography on Kenya.* Syracuse, N.Y.: Program of Eastern African Studies, Syracuse University, 1967.

HISTORY

Barnett, Donald L., and Njama Karari. *Mau Mau from Within.* New York: Praeger, 1966.
Bennett, George. *Kenya, A Political History: The Colonial Period.* London: Oxford University Press, 1963.
Brett, E. A. *Colonialism and Underdevelopment in East Africa: The Politics of Economic Change, 1919–39.* New York: Nok Publishers, 1973.
Clark, Desmond J. *The Prehistory of Africa.* Baltimore: Penguin Books, 1963.
Cone, L. W., and J. F. Lipscomb. *The History of Kenya Agriculture.* Nairobi: University Press of Africa, 1972.
Freeman-Grenville, G.S.P. *The East African Coast: Select Documents From the First to the Earlier Nineteenth Century.* Oxford: Clarendon Press, 1962.
Huxley, Elspeth. *White Man's Country: Lord Delamere and the Making of Kenya,* Vols. 1 and 2. London: Macmillan, 1935.
Miller, Charles. *The Lunatic Express.* New York: Macmillan, 1971.
Mungeam, G. H. *British Rule in Kenya, 1895–1912.* London: Oxford University Press, 1966.
Muriuki, Godfrey. *A History of the Kikuyu, 1500–1900.* Nairobi: Oxford University Press, 1974.
Ogot, Bethwell A. *Historical Dictionary of Kenya.* Metuchen, N.J. and London: Scarecrow Press, 1981.
Oliver, Roland, and Gervase Mathew. *History of East Africa,* Vols. 1, 2, and 3. Oxford: Clarendon Press, 1963, 1965, 1976.
Prinze, A.H.J. *The Swahili-Speaking Peoples of Zanzibar and the East African Coast: Arabs, Shirazi and Swahili* (Ethnographic Survey of Africa Series. Daryll Forde, ed., "East Central Africa," Pt. 12), London: International African Institute, 1961.
Sorrenson, M.P.K. *Origins of European Settlement in Kenya.* Nairobi and London: Oxford University Press, 1968.
Spear, Thomas. *Kenya's Past: An Introduction to Historical Method in Africa.* London: Longman, 1981.
Tignor, R. L. *The Colonial Transformation of Kenya.* Princeton, N.J.: Princeton University Press, 1976.

Wickins, P. L. *An Economic History of Africa from the Earliest Times to Partition.* Oxford: Oxford University Press, 1981.
Wolff, Richard D. *The Economics of Colonialism: Britain and Kenya, 1870–1930.* New Haven: Yale University Press, 1974.
Zwanenburg, Roger van. *The Agricultural History of Kenya to 1939.* Nairobi: East African Publishing House, 1972.

SOCIETY AND CULTURE

Cameron, John. *The Development of Education in East Africa.* New York: Columbia University Teachers College Press, 1970.
Clifford, W. *An Introduction for African Criminology.* Nairobi: Oxford University Press, 1974.
Court, David, and Dharam P. Ghai, eds. *Education, Society and Development: New Perspectives From Kenya.* Nairobi: Oxford University Press, 1974.
De Blij, Harm J. *Mombasa: An African City.* Evanston, Ill.: Northwestern University Press, 1968.
Evans, Emmet B., Jr. "Education, Unemployment, and Crime in Kenya." *Journal of Modern African Studies* (London) 13, No. 1 (March 1975), pp. 55–66.
_____. "Sources of Socio-Political Instability in an African State: The Case of Kenya's Educated Unemployed," *African Studies Review* 20, No. 1 (April, 1977), pp. 37–52.
Fedders, Andrew, and Cynthia Salvadori. *Peoples and Cultures of Kenya.* Nairobi: Transafrica Book Distributors, and London: Rex Collings in association with the Kenya Tourist Development Corp., 1979.
Hickman, G. M., and W.H.G. Dickins. *The Lands and Peoples of East Africa.* London: Longman, 1960.
Kaplan, Irving, et al. *Area Handbook for Kenya.* Washington, D.C.: American University, 1976.
Kenya (Survey of Kenya). *National Atlas of Kenya.* 3rd ed. Nairobi: Survey of Kenya, 1970.
Kenyatta, Jomo. *Facing Mount Kenya.* London: Secker and Warburg, 1938.
Kercher, Leonard C. *The Kenya Penal System: Past, Present and Prospect.* Washington, D.C.: University Press of America, 1981.
Kesby, John D. *The Cultural Regions of East Africa.* London: Academic Press, 1977.
King, Kenneth. *The African Artisan: Education and the Informal Sector in Kenya.* London: Heinemann, 1979.
Legum, Colin, ed. *Africa Contemporary Record: Annual Survey and Documents, 1980–1981.* New York: Africana Publishing, 1981.
Miller, Norman N. "Journey in a Forgotten Land." (Part 1: Food and Drought in the Ethiopia-Kenya Border Lands.) *American Universities Field Staff Report*, Northeast Africa Series 9 (4). Hanover, New Hampshire: AUFS, December 1974, pp. 1–24.
_____. "The Politics of Population." *American Universities Field Staff Report*, East Africa Series 9 (1). Hanover, New Hampshire: AUFS, December 1970.
_____. "Population Review 1970: Kenya." *American Universities Field Staff Report*, East Africa Series 9 (1). Hanover, New Hampshire: AUFS, December 1970.
Morgan, W.T.W., ed. *East Africa: Its People and Resources.* 2nd ed. Nairobi: Oxford University Press, 1972.
Murray, Jocelyn, ed. *Cultural Atlas of Africa.* New York: Facts On File Publications, 1981.
Mutiso, G.C.M. "Technical Education and Change in Kenya," *East Africa Journal* (Nairobi) 7 (No. 8, August 1971), pp. 28–39.
Ndeti, Kinuto. *Cultural Policy in Kenya.* Paris: UNESCO Press, 1975.
Ogendo, R. G. *Industrial Geography of Kenya.* Nairobi: East African Publishing House, 1970.
Ojany, Francis F., and Reuben B. Ogendo. *Kenya: A Study in Physical and Human Geography.* Nairobi: Longman, 1973.
Ominde, Simeon H. *Studies in East African Geography and Development.* Berkeley: University of California Press, 1971.
_____. *Land and Population Movements in Kenya.* London: Heinemann, 1968.

Pratt, D. J., P. J. Greenway, and M. D. Gwynne. "Classification of East African Rangeland," *Journal of Applied Ecology* (Oxford) 3 (1966), pp. 369–382.

Seidman, Robert B. *A Source Book of the Criminal Law of Africa.* Law in Africa, No. 21. London: Sweet and Maxwell, 1966.

Sheffield, James R., ed. *Education, Employment and Rural Development.* Proceedings of a conference at Kericho, Kenya, September 1966. Nairobi: East African Publishing House, 1967.

Soja, Edward W. *The Geography of Modernization in Kenya: A Spatial Analysis of Social, Economic and Political Change.* Syracuse, N.Y.: Syracuse University Press, 1968.

Sorrenson, M.P.K. *Land Reform in the Kikuyu Country: A Study in Government Policy.* Nairobi: Oxford University Press, 1967.

Stichter, Sharon. *Migrant Labour in Kenya: Capitalism and African Response 1895–1975.* Harlow, Essex: Longman, 1982.

Thiong'o, Ngugi wa. *Detained: A Writer's Prison Diary.* Nairobi: Heinemann, 1981.

Vogel, L. C., A. S. Muller, R. S. Odingo, Z. Onyango, and A. De Geus, eds. *Health and Disease in Kenya.* Nairobi: East African Literature Bureau, 1974.

Whiteley, W. H., ed. *Language in Kenya.* Nairobi: Oxford University Press, 1974.

Wipper, Audrey. *Rural Rebels: A Study of Two Protest Movements in Kenya.* Nairobi: Oxford University Press, 1977.

Young, Crawford. *Ideology and Development in Africa.* New Haven: Yale University Press, 1982.

POLITICS AND GOVERNMENT

Arnold, Guy. *Kenyatta and the Politics of Kenya.* London: J. M. Dent & Sons, 1974.

Barkan, Joel D. "Further Reassessment of 'Conventional Wisdom': Political Knowledge and Voting Behavior in Rural Kenya," *American Political Science Review* 70, No. 2 (June 1976), pp. 452–456.

————, ed. *Politics and Public Policy in Kenya and Tanzania.* Rev. ed. New York: Praeger, 1982.

Bienen, Henry. *Kenya: The Politics of Participation and Control.* Princeton, N.J.: Princeton University Press, 1974.

————. "The Military and Society in East Africa: Thinking Again About Praetorianism," *Comparative Politics* 6 (1974), pp. 489–518.

Burke, Fred G. "Political Evolution in Kenya," in Stanley Diamond and Fred G. Burke, eds., *The Transformation of East Africa: Studies in Political Anthropology.* New York: Basic Books, 1966.

Clayton, Anthony, and Donald C. Savage. *Government and Labour in Kenya, 1895–1963.* London: Frank Cass, 1974.

Court, David, and Kenneth Prewitt. "Nation as Region in Kenya: A Note on Political Learning," *British Journal of Political Science* (London) 4, No. 1 (January 1974), pp. 109–114.

Gertzel, Cherry J. *The Politics of Independent Kenya, 1963–68.* Evanston, Ill.: Northwestern University Press, 1970.

Gertzel, Cherry J., Maurice Goldschmidt, and Donald Rothchild, eds., *Government and Politics in Kenya.* Nairobi: East African Publishing House, 1969.

Godfrey, E. M., and G.C.M. Mutiso. "Political Economy of Self-Help: Kenya's 'Harambee' Institutes of Technology," *Canadian Journal of African Studies* (Ottawa) 8, No. 1 (1974), pp. 109–133.

Goldsworthy, David. *Tom Mboya: The Man Kenya Wanted to Forget.* Nairobi: Heinemann, 1982.

Hyden, Goran. *Beyond Ujamaa in Tanzania: Underdevelopment and an Uncaptured Peasantry.* Berkeley: University of California Press, 1980.

Hyden, Goran, Robert Jackson, and John Okumu, eds. *Development Administration: The Kenyan Experience.* Nairobi: Oxford University Press, 1970.

————. "Local Government Reform in Kenya," *East Africa Journal* (Nairobi) 7 (No. 4, April 1970), pp. 19–24.

Jackson, Tudor. *The Law of Kenya: An Introduction.* New York: Rowman and Littlefield, 1971.

Kagombe, Maina. "The Impact of Foreign Governments on Kenya's Domestic Policies," *Pan-African Journal* 3, No. 2 (Spring 1970), pp. 50–65.

Karimi, Joseph, and Philip Ochieng. *The Kenyatta Succession.* Nairobi: Transafrica Book Distributors, 1980.

Lamb. G. *Peasant Politics, Conflict and Development in Muranga.* Sussex: Julian Friedman, 1974.

Leonard, D. K. *Rural Administration in Kenya.* Nairobi: East African Literature Bureau, 1973.

Leys, Colin. "The Post-Colonial State," *Review of African Political Economy* 5 (1976).

———. *Politics in Kenya: The Development of Peasant Society.* Nairobi: Institute of Development Studies, 1970.

———. *Underdevelopment in Kenya: The Political Economy of Neo-Colonialism, 1964–1971.* Berkeley: University of California Press, 1974, and London: Heinemann, 1975.

Mboya, Tom. *The Challenge of Nationhood.* New York: Heinemann, 1970.

Murray-Brown, Jeremy. *Kenyatta.* London: George Allen and Unwin, 1972.

Mutiso, G. *Kenya: Policies, Policy and Society.* Nairobi: East African Literature Bureau, 1975.

Nellis, John R. *The Ethnic Composition of Leading Kenyan Government Positions.* Scandinavian Institute of African Studies. Research Report No. 24. Uppsala: SIAS, 1974.

———. "Expatriates in the Government of Kenya," *Journal of Commonwealth Political Studies* (London) 11, No. 3 (November 1973), pp. 251–264.

Nyangira, Nicholas. *Relative Modernization and Public Resource Allocation in Kenya.* Nairobi: East African Literature Bureau, 1975.

Odinga, Oginga. *Not Yet Uhuru: An Autobiography.* New York: Hill and Wang, 1967.

Rosberg, Carl G., Jr., and John Nottingham. *The Myth of "Mau Mau": Nationalism in Kenya.* New York: Praeger, 1966.

Rothchild, Donald S. *Racial Bargaining in Independent Kenya.* London: Oxford University Press, 1976.

Spencer, John. *James Beauttah: Freedom Fighter.* Nairobi: Stellacope, 1983.

Tamarkin, M. "The Roots of Political Stability in Kenya," *African Affairs* 77 (July 1978).

Wasserman, Gary. *The Politics of Decolonization: Kenya Europeans and the Land Issue, 1960–1965.* Cambridge: Cambridge University Press, 1976.

Werlin, Herbert H. *Governing an African City: A Study of Nairobi.* New York: Africana Publishing, 1974.

Yeager, Rodger. *Tanzania: An African Experiment.* Boulder, Colo.: Westview Press, 1982.

ECONOMICS AND DEVELOPMENT

Allen, Christopher, and Kenneth King, eds. *Development Trends in Kenya.* Edinburgh: Centre of African Studies, University of Edinburgh, 1973.

Bhatia, Rattan J., and Saul L. Rothman. "Introducing the Extended Fund Facility: The Kenya Case," *Finance and Development* 12, No. 4 (December 1975), p. 38.

Brett, E. A. *Colonialism and Underdevelopment in East Africa: The Politics of Economic Change 1919–1939.* New York: Nok Publishers, 1973.

Cowen, M. P. "Capital and Peasant Households," in Scott MacWilliam and M. P. Cowen, eds., *Essays on Capital and Class in Kenya.* London: Longman, 1976.

Fearn, H. *An African Economy: A Study of the Economic Development of the Nyanza Province of Kenya, 1903–1953.* London: Oxford University Press, 1961.

Freeman, Donald B. "Development Strategies in Dual Economies: A Kenyan Example," *African Studies Review* 18 (2), p. 17.

Godfrey, M., and S. Langdon. "Partners in Underdevelopment: The Transnationalization Thesis in a Kenya Context." *Journal of Commonwealth and Comparative Politics* 14, No. 1 (1976), pp. 42–63.

Harbeson, John W. *Nation Building in Kenya: The Role of Land Reform.* Evanston, Ill.: Northwestern University Press, 1973.

Hazlewood, Arthur. *The Economy of Kenya: The Kenyatta Era*. London: Oxford University Press, 1979.

———. *Rail and Road in East Africa*. Oxford: Basil Blackwell, 1964.

———. *Economic Integration: The East African Experience*. London: Heinemann, 1975.

Helleiner, G. J. "Agricultural Development Plans in Kenya and Tanzania, 1969–1974," *Rural Africana* 13 (Winter 1971), pp. 36–42.

Henley, John S. "Employment Relations and Economic Development: The Kenya Experience," *Journal of Modern African Studies* 11 No. 4 (1973), p. 559.

Heyer, Judith, J. K. Maitha, and W. M. Senga, eds. *Agricultural Development in Kenya: An Economic Assessment*. Nairobi: Oxford University Press, 1976.

Holtham, Gerald, and Arthur Hazlewood. *Aid and Inequality in Kenya: British Development Assistance to Kenya*. London: Croom Helm, 1975.

International Bank for Reconstruction and Development. *The Economic Development of Kenya*. Baltimore: Johns Hopkins University Press, 1963.

International Labour Office. *Employment, Incomes, and Equality: A Strategy for Increasing Productive Employment in Kenya*. Geneva: ILO, 1972.

Kaplinsky, Raphael, ed. *Readings on the Multinational Corporations in Kenya*. Nairobi: Oxford University Press, 1978.

Kitching, Gavin N. *Class and Economic Change in Kenya: The Making of an African Petite Bourgeoisie, 1905–1970*. New Haven: Yale University Press, 1980.

Kongstad, Per, and Mette Monsted. *Family Labour and Trade in Western Kenya*. Uppsala: Scandinavian Institute of African Studies, 1980.

Langdon, S., and M. Godfrey. "Partners in Underdevelopment: The Transnationalization Thesis in a Kenyan Context," *Journal of Commonwealth and Comparative Politics*, March 1976.

Marris, Peter, and Anthony Somerset. *African Businessmen: A Study of Entrepreneurship and Development in Kenya*. London: Routledge and Kegan Paul, 1971.

National Christian Council of Kenya. *Who Controls Industry in Kenya?: Report of a Working Party*. Nairobi: East African Publishing House, 1968.

Ruthenberg, Hans. *African Agricultural Production Development Policy in Kenya, 1952–1965*. Berlin: Springer, 1966.

Schneider, Harold. *Livestock and Equality in East Africa: The Economic Basis for Social Structure*. Bloomington: Indiana University Press, 1979.

Swainson, Nicola. *The Development of Corporate Capitalism in Kenya, 1918–1977*. London: Heinemann, 1980.

———. "The Rise of a Kenyan Bourgeoisie," *Review of African Political Economy* 8 (1977).

———. "State and Economy in Post-Colonial Kenya," *Canadian Journal of African Studies*, Winter 1978.

Thomas, P. A., ed. *Private Enterprise and the East African Company*. Dar-es-Salaam: Tanzania Publishing House, 1969.

World Bank. *Kenya: Into the Second Decade*. Baltimore and London: Johns Hopkins University Press, 1975.

Index